T0210832

Social Media

Social media platforms have captured the attention and imagination of many millions of people, enabling their users to develop and display their creativity, to empathize with others, and to find connection, communication and communion. But they are also surveillance systems through which those users become complicit in their own commercial exploitation. In this accessible book, Graham Meikle explores the tensions between these two aspects of social media.

From Facebook and Twitter to Reddit and YouTube, Meikle examines social media as industries and as central sites for understanding the cultural politics of everyday life. Building on the new forms of communication and citizenship brought about by these platforms, he analyses the meanings of sharing and privacy, internet memes, remix cultures and citizen journalism. Throughout, *Social Media* engages with questions of visibility, performance, platforms and users, and demonstrates how networked digital media are adopted and adapted in an environment built around the convergence of personal and public communication.

Graham Meikle is Professor of Communication and Digital Media at the University of Westminster, UK.

Social Media

Communication, Sharing and Visibility

Graham Meikle

Routledge
Taylor & Francis Group

NEW YORK AND LONDON

First published 2016
by Routledge
711 Third Avenue, New York, NY 10017

and by Routledge
2 Park Square, Milton Park, Abingdon, Oxon OX14 4RN

Routledge is an imprint of the Taylor & Francis Group, an informa business

© 2016 Graham Meikle

British Library Cataloguing in Publication Data
A catalogue record for this book is available from the British Library

Library of Congress Cataloging in Publication Data
Meikle, Graham, 1965-
Social media : communication, sharing and visibility / Graham Meikle. --
1 Edition.
pages cm
Includes bibliographical references and index.
ISBN 978-0-415-71223-1 (hardback) -- ISBN 978-0-415-71224-8
(pbk.) -- ISBN 978-1-315-88417-2 (ebook) 1. Social media. 2. Online
social networks. 3. Citizen journalism. 4. Social media--Moral and
ethical aspects. I. Title.
HM742.M457 2016
302.23'1--dc23
2015030076

ISBN: 978-0-415-71223-1 (hbk)
ISBN: 978-0-415-71224-8 (pbk)
ISBN: 978-1-315-88417-2 (ebk)

Typeset in Sabon
by Taylor & Francis Books

Contents

Acknowledgments

One of the best bits of writing a book is being able to thank in public the people who've helped. Thanks to Erica Wetter, Simon Jacobs and everyone at Routledge. Thanks also, often for many things over some years, to Stuart Allan, Chris Atton, Steve Collins, Victoria Esteves, David Gauntlett, Matthew Hibberd and Marie O'Brien. Special thanks, as ever, to Sherman Young, who took the time to read the whole manuscript and make some valuable suggestions. And thanks for everything else and more, to Fin, Rosie and Lola, with love.

Parts of Chapter 3 have appeared in V. Esteves and G. Meikle (2015) '"LOOK @ THIS FUKKEN DOGE": Internet Memes and Remix Cultures' in C. Atton (ed.) *The Routledge Companion to Alternative and Community Media*, London: Routledge.

Parts of Chapter 4 have appeared in (2014) 'Citizen Journalism, Sharing, and the Ethics of Visibility' in E. Thorsen and S. Allan (eds) *Citizen Journalism: Global Perspectives, Volume 2*, New York: Peter Lang.

Parts of Chapter 6 have appeared in (2015) 'Distributed Citizenship' in P. Weibel (ed.) *Global Activism: Art and Conflict in the 21st Century*, Karlsruhe: ZKM | Center for Art and Media and Cambridge, MA: MIT Press; and in (2014) 'Social Media, Visibility and Activism: The "Kony 2012" Campaign' in M. Ratto and M. Boler (eds) *DIY Citizenship: Critical Making and Social Media*, Cambridge, MA: MIT Press.

Introduction

In 2014, a well-known frozen-food company introduced a new product called Mashtags. These are frozen mashed-potato chunks, shaped like common images from our daily online lives – email @ symbols, #hashtags and two different kinds of smiley :-) faces. So our daily diet can now include not just typing these social media icons, but also eating them, as they displace the alphabet-shaped potatoes that have themselves gone the way of the dinosaur-shaped potato. Mashtags are one index of just how quickly and deeply social media have taken root in our everyday lives. The social media repertoire of friending and following, of liking and tagging and commenting and sharing, has become second nature in a few short years.

The size and reach of the largest networks, many of which are still only a few years old, can still astonish, as can the speed with which they have embedded themselves in daily life. The early mythology of Facebook had become a major Hollywood film within six years of the firm's creation, with *The Social Network* winning Oscars before the actual social network had yet gone public on the stock exchange. As I write this, Facebook is eleven years old and can claim one in every five people on earth as a regular user. YouTube is ten, and boasts that 300 hours of video are uploaded to its site every minute. Twitter hashtags now appear on screen throughout the TV news, and as prompts to viewer action in reality shows, current affairs debates, live sport broadcasts and even the weather forecast.

The contours of the contemporary social media environment were drawn in a short period in the middle of the first decade of the twenty-first century. The opening act was the purchase of MySpace in 2005 for US$580 million by Rupert Murdoch's News Corporation. Murdoch's takeover put social networks into the headlines, and signalled that they could be a mainstream proposition. In July 2006, Twitter launched. In September, Facebook dropped its membership restrictions and opened up to anyone over 13 who wanted to join. And in October, Google bought YouTube for US$1.65 billion, leading *Time* magazine to pronounce that *you* were the person of the year. In January 2007, Apple announced its first iPhone, going on to introduce its App Store the following year. In this short period we can see the convergence of established media companies, software services, user-generated content platforms, social networks and new communications devices built around ubiquitous connection. These emerging social media services helped drive demand for smartphones, and smartphones helped network effects to kick in for the successful social media services. Social media apps are consistently popular and help platforms to consolidate and expand their number of users and keep them using their service. The top five free iPhone apps listed in the UK App Store at the time of writing in July 2015 are WhatsApp, Messenger, Facebook, YouTube and Instagram – of these five, only YouTube is not owned by Facebook.

Such rapid change, of course, brings fresh anxieties – anxieties that we can see being worked out in popular culture. Social media have quickly come to animate the plots of dystopian novels, films and television programmes; these mirror the utopian fictions of the mission statements and press releases of the social media firms themselves, to which we'll return in Chapter 2. For example, anxiety about the authenticity of those with whom we may communicate in online networks has prompted the cautionary *Catfish* documentary feature film and its spinoff TV series. The original documentary unravels the relationships of its protagonist Nev, as his online friend Megan is gradually revealed to be a fantasy construct of multiple fake profiles and accounts maintained by someone else entirely. Inevitably, for a film about fakery, *Catfish* itself prompted some viewers to question its own authenticity, suspicious that the documentary about trolls was itself a troll documentary. A different kind of anxiety about authenticity informs the heart-breaking drama 'Be Right Back', an episode of Charlie Brooker's TV series *Black Mirror*, in which the dead can be recreated through software that analyses and mimics their lifetime archive of public profiles and postings, offering their loved ones a posthumous presence with whom they can chat online, as though we are reducible to the sum of our likes and shares and tags.

Fictional dystopias of social media explore, above all, questions of visibility, privacy and surveillance, even if they struggle to match the non-fictional dystopia revealed by Edward Snowden (to be discussed in more detail in Chapter 5). In Dave Eggers's novel *The Circle*, a fictional corporation with a heavy resemblance to Google has remade the web with a unified payment and password system called *TruYou* that has brought all online anonymity to an end: 'Your devices knew who you were, and your one identity – the *TruYou*, unbendable and unmaskable – was the person paying, signing up, responding, viewing and reviewing, seeing and being seen' (Eggers 2014: 21). This inescapable ID makes the characters in the book ever more visible, ever more exposed, as the marketing advantages of *TruYou* feed an ideology of forced transparency. By late in the book, millions of people have 'gone transparent', pledging to share every last moment, however intimate, with their online networks through wearable cameras. In Eggers's novel, social media are depicted as the point of intersection between the words *Orwellian, Maoist* and *corporate*, with a pivotal speech by one character (Eggers 2014: 303) identifying the ideology of his corporation in the slogans:

SECRETS ARE LIES
SHARING IS CARING
PRIVACY IS THEFT

The irony in Eggers's novel works because it connects with anxieties about social media that we see in the non-fictional storytelling of the news. Journalists are now quick to scrutinize new developments in the products of Google or Facebook or Apple for risks to users' privacy. Such anxieties about the direction of the internet have their own pre-histories. At the beginning of the twenty-first century, in a book called *Future Active*, I described two different possible directions for the internet. At one end, was what I called Version 1.0. This described an internet that would be shaped by the values that had underpinned and directed its early development – open architecture, distributed control, a grassroots democratization of popular and political cultures. Version 1.0 would be an open, participatory media space. At the other end, and before anyone had started to talk about Web 2.0, was what I called Version 2.0 of the internet. This described an internet that would be shaped by the values of the corporate interests that had begun to commercialize it in the 1990s – closed architecture, centralized control, a corporate commodification of popular and political cultures. Version 2.0 would be a closed, proprietary media space. Which version, I asked in that book, would be the internet that we would get in the future? Now, that future is already here (*if just not very evenly distributed yet*, as the novelist William Gibson says). And it's clear that we got both versions together.

The contemporary platforms that we call *social media* enable anyone to develop and display their creativity, to empathize with others and to find connection, communication and communion. But the platforms we call *social media* are also surveillance systems through which users become complicit in their own commercial exploitation. The platforms we call *social media* are those through which any user, in principle: can say or make things; can share the things that they and others have said and made; and can make all of this saying, making and sharing visible to others. But the price of all this is that the user becomes visible to unimagined others and unforeseen audiences, including those providing the service. The cost of this creativity, sharing and visibility is that the user loses control over what is done with their personal information, loses control over the new contexts into which others may share it, and loses control over to whom the social media firms might sell it.

But wait. This phrase *social media* – aren't *all* media social? This is a common objection to the term (see Papacharissi 2015 for an important example). So yes, all media are social. But not all media are social media. It is, of course, obvious and true to observe that all media are social, insofar as all media are used for communication, for education, for governance, for advertising, for information (and misinformation). All media are social in that all media are bound up in the ways that we organize ourselves and each other. But such *social uses of media* are not the same thing as *social media*. This term means something specific, and refers to a particular set of developments in the internet in the first part of the twenty-first century. It does not just refer in general to all contemporary media or to everything on today's internet.

To speak of social media is to speak of a particular set of technological affordances, a particular set of business models and corporate practices, a particular set of organizations, and a particular set of cultural habits, practices and expectations. In this book, *social media* describes a specific set of internet-based, networked communication platforms. These use a business model of a database built by its own users. And they enable the convergence of public and personal communication. This definition includes Facebook and Twitter, Reddit and Tumblr, Pinterest and Instagram, Blogger and YouTube, among others.

Social media have enabled new kinds of connection between new kinds of users. They make possible networked communication, organization and mobilization between new kinds of publics, from the Arab Spring to #blacklivesmatter, from #BringBackOurGirls to #jesuischarlie. And for each individual user, they allow moments of everyday affirmation, as one clicks *like* on one's contacts' posts, and shares the meanings that one has made from the day. Gertrude Stein, who saw most things quicker than other people, almost seems to anticipate this dimension of social media, with the undeniable pleasures of its networked likes and shares, in this passage from her 1925 novel *The Making of Americans*:

> There are many that I know and they know it. They are all of them repeating and I hear it. I love it and I tell it. I love it and now I will

write it. This is now a history of my love of it. I hear it and I love it
and I write it. They repeat it. They live it and I see it and I hear it.
They live it and I hear it and I see it and I love it and now and
always I will write it. (Stein 1990: 264–5)

But alongside these very real pleasures, social media also allow limitless
trolling, and accompanying controversies about cultural boundary lines
and speaking rights (Phillips 2015). And they allow dark new strains of
mob-shaming and persecution, as individuals find to their cost that they
have transgressed the codes of their unseen and perhaps unimagined
audiences (Ronson 2015). The social media environment of *like* and
share is also the environment of involuntary porn and slut-shaming, of
#GamerGate and the #Fappening, in which young women in particular
can find themselves not just sharing, but being shared; not just choosing
to make themselves visible, but being cruelly exposed.

Social media make all of these things possible because of the ways that
they combine public and personal communication. Before the rise of
social media, we were used to thinking of communication as *either* personal *or* public. But now these converge. Social media are those that
bring together personal communication and public media. You + the
tube = YouTube. Before the web, *public* communication was the stuff
that we used to think of *as* media – newspapers and magazines, TV and
radio, recorded music, cinema and videogames; and books, books too,
even though they were always somehow excluded as an object of
research in the study of media, with longer established fields claiming
books as their own turf (something that no doubt contributed to the
rather low-grade image of media studies as somehow not quite intellectual enough for its many critics). Public communication was something
done *for* its publics, rather than *by* them. It was a one-way media
environment in which, as the late James Carey had it: 'Some get to speak
and some to listen, some to write and some to read, some to film and
some to view' (Carey 1989: 87).

Personal communication, in contrast, was the stuff that we did for
ourselves, and with people whom we more or less knew directly. Personal
communication wasn't really meant for broadcast or publication – phone
calls and emails, text messages and letters, online chat and postcards.
We didn't use to really think of much of this as *media* at all. Media were
the systems, the organizations and institutions, and the technologies that
brought us the content that had been made for public consumption.
Whereas the kinds of personal communication that we did with our
friends and lovers, our families and colleagues, were not *media*. They
were just between ourselves.

Social media bring together these two ways of thinking about communication. Social media are platforms that combine what we used to think of as *public* with what we used to think of as *personal* communication. Both now take place in the same frame. Both public and personal happen within the same interaction. Public messages – news stories, music videos, advertisements, stand-up comedy routines, political speeches, film trailers – are copied and circulated, repositioned and recontextualized every day by hundreds of millions of users of Facebook and Twitter, Google and YouTube, Instagram and Pinterest. Public media become personalized, as each of these messages is embedded within a new context, as part of an individual user's performance of online identity. And those same users make their personal comments and opinions and emotions, their prejudices and beliefs, their secrets and virtues, visible to others. Personal communication takes on a public aspect.

This convergence of the public and the personal is part of a larger cultural pattern that Graeme Turner (2010) has labelled 'the demotic turn'. Turner points to the pervasiveness of the ordinary and the non-professional across the media landscape of the twenty-first century (Britain's most popular TV show is amateurs baking cakes in a tent), and the ways in which this fuels new commercial strategies and business models. Reality TV, for example, manufactures an annual cast of micro-celebrities from non-professionals, as singing contests not only reveal the machinery by which amateurs are manufactured into stars, but also draw the audience into this process, using their weekly votes to determine the eventual product they can be sold at the end of the season. UK broadcaster Channel 4 has generated a lucrative international format in *Gogglebox*, whose viewers watch on screen other actual viewers watching other television programmes in their own homes; the interactions and mild idiosyncrasies of those filmed in this vicarious TV viewing are sufficiently compelling for the show to rate very well against other shows that *Gogglebox*'s viewers would otherwise have to watch for themselves. Talkback radio provokes and aggregates the responses of its own audience to provide the raw material for daily witch-hunts and demagoguery. And the news invites participation from its users, who can extend the depth, breadth or duration of coverage of a story (Bruns 2011), and who can bear witness in new ways (Allan 2013). Networked mobile devices enable a new kind of non-professional journalistic authority to be derived from being present as a bystander or participant at the scene of an event in real-time. Here comes everybody, as James Joyce put it.

Social media are very much part of this cultural turn towards the demotic, the everyday, the non-professional and the personal, and they are very much part of its drive towards new kinds of business model.

From one perspective, all of this can be seen as a democratization of public culture (Hartley 2009, 2012) – a sharing around of the licence to speak, a recognition of different kinds of claims on our attention, an enabling of diversity among voices. All of this is real, true and valuable. But from another perspective, it can also be seen as a kind of unpaid digital labour (Terranova 2000, Scholz 2013) – a new kind of exploitation, as users do all the work of building the database that YouTube or Facebook gets to sell to advertisers. It has become a cliché to observe that if you don't have to pay to use an online service, then you are its product rather than its customer – but that doesn't make that observation any less true.

The internet of free stuff, moreover – in which we get free services in exchange for just allowing access to our address books, personal messages, photo albums, daily movements, tastes, preferences, opinions, emotions, relationships and secrets – is not without other kinds of cost. 'For most users', Geert Lovink points out, 'the Internet is not free; they pay considerable money for hardware and cables, external drives, connectivity, software and upgrades, design features, and subscriptions' (Lovink 2008: xxv). To this we can add the different kinds of costs and forms of exploitation borne by those engaged in the manufacture of our devices. Richard Maxwell and Toby Miller offer a sobering catalogue of such costs in their book *Greening the Media*. The metals and minerals used in the manufacture of those electronic devices are mined in contexts that may include child and adult slave labour; in the case of the Democratic Republic of Congo, a primary source of one key metal, 90% of the mining industry is reportedly run by mercenaries who use violence and rape to control their workers. Assembling the devices from these raw materials is outsourced to plants in Asia. Workers for Foxconn in China who manufacture the best known devices of Apple, among others, have reportedly been poisoned by unsafe manufacturing practices in working conditions governed by military-style discipline, and some have been driven to clusters of suicides (Qiu 2012, Ross 2013, Fuchs 2014a). Then there are also the environmental costs of the disposal and destruction of the many tens of millions of computers and phones that we render obsolete each year (Maxwell & Miller 2012). Free stuff always has its costs.

This book is about how people in developed, mostly English-speaking countries use social media. It is not a book about how people *do not* use social media, including those who cannot because they fall on the wrong side of a digital divide. The International Telecommunication Union (ITU) reports in its 2015 statistics that 3.2 billion people are now online, including two billion in developing countries; but this leaves four billion people who are not online, the vast majority in developing countries. In developed countries, 80% of households have access to the internet, but only 34% have access in developing countries (ITU 2015). Universal access is likely to remain elusive even in developed countries. In the UK, communications regulator Ofcom reports that 15% of adults do not have household access to the internet, and that the majority of those have no intention of getting it (Ofcom 2015a: 352). Moreover, such divergent access to communications infrastructure is only one kind of digital divide – other kinds of inequality also figure, including those built around age, gender, class, disability and literacy. In writing about how people who do have internet access use social media, I do not mean to suggest that these digital divides don't matter – they do. But they are beyond the scope of this book.

Six of the top twenty most visited web domains in the world are based in China (Fuchs 2015a). At the time of writing, three of the world's biggest social media brands are from China – QQ, Qzone and WeChat – giving their parent firm Tencent one of the world's largest shares of active social media users. Other Chinese platforms such as Sina Weibo also command hundreds of millions of active users. The global designs of a Facebook or a Google confront the obstacle of these enormous indigenous networks, before they even get to the linguistic and political hurdles (on the contemporary Chinese media environment and its contexts, see Hjorth & Arnold 2013, Hjorth & Khoo 2015, Rawnsley & Rawnsley 2015). But in this book, I do not discuss these Chinese platforms because, as a non-Chinese speaker, the difficulties of analysing in this way how these Chinese social media are used and why they matter are insuperable. This is because my approach is inductive rather than deductive, by which I mean that I try to draw concepts, definitions and analysis from looking at the social media platforms, their uses and users themselves, rather than deducing my analysis from pre-existing, off-the-shelf concepts. If we want to understand what social media are, rather than slot them into our existing frameworks, then this is, I think, the way to go.

Chapter 1 defines social media. Any system of communication has technological, economic, social and cultural dimensions. So to define social media, this chapter sets them in the context of the ongoing development of the internet. Social media are a convergence of three key developments in online cultures in the first decade of the twenty-first century: the user-generated content of Web 2.0 platforms such as YouTube; the personal connection databases of networking services such as LinkedIn; and the always-on mobile connectivity and communication made possible by smartphones and other mobile devices. Social media bring together *public media* and *personal communication*, and the key words to understanding such media are *network, database* and *platform*.

Chapter 2 discusses social media as a particular kind of media industry – the sharing industry. A service like Facebook has to constantly prompt its users to add fresh information to its database – new status updates, new friend connections, new pages to like, new groups to join, new photos to share, new comments to post. *What's on your mind?* asks Facebook every time we log in, in a prompt to add more data. This is because that database is what it draws upon in attracting advertisers. Facebook, like other social media firms, uses the complex word *share* to describe both its business model and what its users do on Facebook. This chapter examines how Facebook represents itself to different kinds of publics, and why the language of *sharing* matters.

Chapter 3 explores a particular genre of media texts that is intrinsic to the social media environment – internet memes. Each of these starts as an in-joke within an online community, which means that internet memes can often seem bewildering or daft to those not in on the joke. But often these are not only adopted or shared, but are also adapted or remixed into new contexts, bringing new people into the joke as it's moved across different networks, both online and offline. So internet memes are an important index of how people communicate ideas on social media.

Chapter 4 turns to a quite different system of media texts – the news. News is a collaborative process of making and sharing meanings from events. The news is now made in a media environment characterized by the convergence of computing, communications and content. This chapter explores forms of news designed for this social media environment. It focuses on the convergence of *computing* (data journalism, newsgames, listicles), *communications* (the importance of news in real-time) and *content* (who gets to create it and what they get to do with it). It discusses platforms such as BuzzFeed, Twitter and Reddit, and considers the limits of citizen journalism.

Chapter 5, 'TMI' (Too Much Information), looks at the relationships between social media and visibility. The usual way of talking about these is in terms of privacy, and asking whether social media pose threats to that. This is, of course, a very important question (with a very simple answer – *yes*). But it limits its own scope too much. Privacy is too limiting a frame through which to look at social media. Not everything we share on social media is intended to be private in the first place. That's why we shared it. So rather than privacy, this chapter focuses on questions of visibility – to whom are we made visible, and how can we know? It discusses the now ubiquitous cultural form of the *selfie*, a form that illustrates the convergence of smartphone, social networking and user-generated content in the simplest possible image. Selfies, like internet memes, are made for sharing. Each is a presentation of self, a statement of identity. Privacy isn't the right word with which to approach images taken for deliberate public display, because it invokes a crude binary of private/not private. The motivations of users in sharing images and the potential consequences for those being shared are more complex than that. So this chapter also looks at the darker aspects of online visibility, from the brutal outing of involuntary porn to the systematic, pervasive and indiscriminate government surveillance of internet users revealed by Edward Snowden.

Chapter 6 argues for the need to rethink our relationships with social media firms and other users in terms of *citizenship*. It discusses a range of movements and political alternatives, from Occupy Wall Street to the Bitcoin crypto-currency, and argues that these show the contours of an emerging form of *distributed* citizenship. This term describes the development of creative political relations with other people within networks. It describes a kind of citizenship that isn't restricted to a particular geographical space but is instead defined by shared meanings, by collaborative creativity and by creative political action within and through networked digital media.

The concluding chapter draws the book's various threads together in an argument about the importance of bringing social media into debates about media literacy, and media literacy into debates about social media (the concluding sections of earlier chapters are kept quite brief, the better to bring them together in this final chapter). Taken as a whole, the book addresses the major social media platforms and their specific affordances and uses. It examines social media as industries and as central sites for understanding the cultural politics of everyday life. It engages with questions of technologies and texts, of audiences and users, and of how networked digital media are adopted and adapted in an environment built around the convergence of personal and public communication.

Chapter 1

What Are Social Media?

For a time, I thought Facebook was trolling me. It began to recommend to me lots of *people you may know* who were dead philosophers or media theorists – Michel Foucault, Walter Benjamin, Neil Postman, Jacques Lacan, Pierre Bourdieu, Marshall McLuhan and others. I asked my Facebook friends, many of whom are in the same line of work, whether they were seeing them too. But no, was the consensus. Just me. So I turned it into a small game. Each time another dead thinker appeared as a recommended Facebook friend, I would take a screenshot of this and share it on my Timeline with a caption referencing their work and making a joke about how it might connect to Facebook. So Walter Benjamin – the work of friendship in the age of mechanical reproduction. Marshall McLuhan – the Zuckerberg Galaxy. And so on.

The first to appear was Jean-Jacques Rousseau, so I shared a screenshot of this +1 *Add Friend* image with a caption modifying Rousseau's famous line from *The Social Contract* of 1762 ('Man is born free, and everywhere he is in chains', Rousseau 1987: 141) to read instead 'Man is born free, and everywhere he is on Facebook'. The response, like the joke itself, was unremarkable. About fifteen of my friends clicked the *like* button, mostly other academics, mixed in with a couple of former students, while two other people also shared it with their own networks. One of my friends, a professor from Canada with whom I've interacted very often on Facebook for more than six years but have never met, added a comment and we began a conversation, on-screen below the Rousseau image:

ANDREW: Graham, did you coin the phrase, 'Man is born free, and everywhere he is on Facebook'?

ME: I did, Andrew, although Rousseau had done most of the work on it before I got there.

ANDREW: heheh. Is it OK if I use/cite this wonderful rhetorical coinage in a piece I am writing?

ME: Absolutely :-)

ANDREW: Great. I am going to take a screen shot of it, so your name will
appear. Is that OK?

[continues ...]

This exchange went on for a dozen more lines, some of which drew
other responses and *likes* from other people, before, as happens, we all
suddenly got bored at the same time and moved on to something else.
What was this? What was going on in this small, brief (and, to be
clear, utterly unimportant) moment on Facebook? In this chapter, I'll
argue that it offers an example that helps us to define what social media
actually are, and how they are different from other kinds of media. In
this example – just one of billions of interactions that take place through
that network every day – we can see the main elements that define social
media and how they can be understood. So let's take that tiny flake of
online interaction, entirely familiar and unremarkable in its contours to
anyone who uses something like Facebook, and following John Fiske's
(1990) advice about communication, let's take it to pieces instead of
taking it for granted.

First, it was a moment of networked communication that began with
a media image. Facebook is, after all, a media company. But it was an
image created by me, the user, not by the media company. Facebook,
like other social media firms, is a media company that does not itself
actually create any media. This is something that sets those companies
apart from media firms that developed in the twentieth century in order
to make and distribute images and stories and ideas – the BBC, say, or
Disney – all of the things that we now describe with the unlovely word
content. Instead, Facebook provides a *platform* for its users to do this
themselves.

Second, it was a moment of communication prompted by Facebook's
database, by every previous interaction and connection I had made on its
network, and by its algorithms suggesting that I might have some connection with the late Jean-Jacques Rousseau. This database is the engine
of Facebook. It's the engine of that company's daily operations and
expansion, determining how it shows certain material and certain interactions to certain users, based on what it takes to be their desires, and
recording how those users respond, in the attempt to get them to use
Facebook more. And this database is also the engine of its business
model. The business of social media is in selling information derived
from its database to advertisers and marketers (Elmer 2002). The business models of social media platforms are built around a particular
conception of the database, in a way that was identified as characteristic

of Web 2.0 early in the twenty-first century (O'Reilly 2005, 2006, Hinton & Hjorth 2013). That business model is to sell uses of their database of users' personal information to other businesses, and to have the users build that database by using the service. Every time a user posts a video, likes a photo, searches for a product or sends a message to a friend, this interaction becomes a new part of the database and adds to its value for the company.

Third, it was a moment of communication that drew together a number of members of my personal *network* on Facebook. Like every other Facebook user's personal network, mine is not a homogenous group, and most of them would not have a clue who most of the others are (and nor would they be likely to think about it). In fact, of course, they're not a group at all, and it would be really surprising if they imagined they were. Instead, each is an individual at the centre of their own unique Facebook network, and each also becomes implicated in lots of different networks, some centred around different individuals, each time they interact on Facebook. Each is part of multiple networks, coming together in different configurations for different interactions on Facebook – and everywhere else in their lives as well (Rainie & Wellman 2012). Social media tools allow users to participate in communication networks and to establish their own networks of relationships, connections, friends or colleagues with whom they can interact through these services. Such communication can flow in multiple directions between multiple combinations of people, although it may be misleading to use the phrase *many-to-many* communication, as the numbers involved in a given communicative event may be quite small.

And fourth, it was a moment of communication that brought together aspects of the *public* and the *personal*. When I took my screenshot and posted it on my Timeline, I wasn't trying to communicate with anyone in particular – just with *any* of my Facebook network who might be interested or amused. Of course, like everyone else, there are some people with whom I enjoy interacting on Facebook more than others, and I'm sometimes disappointed if those favourite people don't respond to particular things I post. But for the most part, I share things without a specific person in mind, and I note this here because I think it is characteristic of social media. In the case of my Rousseau screenshot, I was only sharing it with a few hundred people, but I wasn't sharing it with any one of them especially. This has certain things in common with the broadcast model of communication, through which messages are sent with the implied address of 'To whom it may concern' (Peters 1999: 206). Now, a few hundred people on Facebook is certainly a long way from the audience for, say, *Game of Thrones*. But it shares with that show a certain mode of address: a certain *this is for you, if you want it* quality (Thompson 1995, Scannell 2000). In this sense, it is *public* communication.

But it's also *personal* communication, because the interaction included not just the sharing of the image with whoever might want it, but also the one-to-one conversation that took place beneath that image. Before social media, Andrew and I would have had our exchange of messages through some one-to-one medium – email or text messaging or on the phone – and this would have been quite separate from the media image that prompted the exchange. But with social media, the *public* message and the *personal* communication take place in the same space. More than this, they are both visible to others within that networked moment.

Social media are those that allow people: to say or make things; to share those things with others; and to have that saying, making or sharing made visible to still others. Tagging, friending, liking and the personal curation of media material into playlists or channels, or into media streams like Facebook's news feed, are all common activities whose significance is not only that users can and do share them, but that these actions are made visible to others. Any of my other Facebook friends could have seen that exchange; indeed, Facebook may have sent a notification to some of them to alert them that it existed. It's most likely, of course, that pretty much no one paid any real attention to that particular conversation; but in principle, the personal interaction between Andrew and me was visible to others, some of them unimagined. And this too is characteristic of social media communication.

Defining Social Media

To understand social media we first need to consider how they can be defined. And like any important term in the field of media, culture or communication, the meaning of *social media* is contested. Christian Fuchs collates a useful collection of contending definitions from the academic literature which emphasize certain recurring concepts including sharing, collaboration, and opportunities for users to both create their own media material and to publish it in networked spaces (Fuchs 2014b: 35–7). But these definitions overlap, compete and at times contradict each other. One reason for this is that the term emerged first as a marketing slogan, rather than as a concept. This sets a challenge for researchers to retrospectively repurpose a slogan as an analytical concept that can explain emerging and fast-moving communicative practices and expectations in the media environment. The earliest use of the term recorded by the *Oxford English Dictionary* dates from June 2004, when it was used to brand a business and technology conference in California called 'The Business of Social Media'. The conference announcement, archived at the Internet Archive's 'Wayback Machine' (http://archive.org), opens by using the phrase *social media* to connect a list of then-novel internet developments to the promise of commercial opportunities:

> *Blogs ... social networks ... RSS readers ... syndication ...* the tools of social media are creating powerful new business opportunities, but to take advantage, technologists, professionals and investors need to understand this new, fast-emerging technology and the unique language it uses.

So like the contemporaneous term *Web 2.0*, with which it has considerable overlap, the term *social media* was coined as a marketing tool. This in itself tells us something about how we should respond to the more excitable claims about its potential to empower users. We could probably pursue examples of usage of the two words *social* and *media* together going back into the 1990s, but these would describe different kinds of phenomena to those we use the term for today. The web address socialmedia.com was registered in 1999 (Bercovici 2010), although the archived copies of that site maintained by the Wayback Machine suggest that it was nothing more than a holding-spot for years. In the same way that *Web 2.0* was an obvious term because the *2.0* label was well established in the computing sector and offered a clear pitch to investors that there were new kinds of web firm starting up in the wake of the dot.com bust, so *social media* was an obvious coinage to describe the various emerging internet phenomena of the day, including blogs, RSS feeds, aggregators, emerging platforms for user-generated content and profile-based networking services like LinkedIn and Friendster. Again like *Web 2.0*, the term *social media* began as an attempt to describe certain common features of emerging web-based media and technology platforms and their business models. Some of the practices which the term was devised to describe no longer attract the attention that they once did (RSS readers, for example), and while *social media* is now generally taken to refer to profile-based platforms such as Facebook, LinkedIn and Instagram, the term draws attention to broader shifts in everyday communicative practices and expectations in the media environment.

The label *social media* is so powerful and so ubiquitous that it's worth underlining here that not all contemporary internet phenomena are social media. Otherwise we would not need the term at all, and could just say *internet* instead. So Wikipedia, for example, is not social media. Wikipedia is obviously a user-generated content project, and in some senses may be the most important of those (as in, for example, its rejection of advertising, which makes it one of the most powerful examples of the possibilities of a non-commercial, public service internet). But Wikipedia lacks the dimension of personal communication that is so central to social media. A user can create an account to gain editing privileges on Wikipedia, but there is no provision to connect these accounts into networks of friends or contacts, or for other dimensions of networking beyond discussions of editing details with other editors. A Wikipedia account should not be confused with a profile, in the senses that that term is understood by users of Facebook or Twitter. And the convergence of public media with *personal* communication is actively dissuaded on Wikipedia, which demands instead that its contributors adhere to a 'Neutral Point of View' in everything they contribute – no opinions, no assertions, no original research, no judgmental language, no personal perspectives.

Not all smartphone apps are social media either, however important manipulating digital sweeties in *Candy Crush* may be to contemporary online life. And nor is a service like Uber social media. At the time of writing, Uber, which allows people looking for taxis to connect with non-professional drivers nearby, is often touted as something of a flagship for the *sharing economy* (see Benkler 2012). But while *sharing* is a pivotal word for social media, as we'll discuss in more detail in Chapter 2, not everything that is tagged with this buzzword is about social media. Uber relies on a database and it's certainly networked, and it's at its most useful as a phone app, but it lacks any dimension of either personal or public communication.

So, let's pull all of this together into a definition – one that tries to acknowledge the whole complex of technological, economic, industrial, social and cultural developments that are caught up in the term 'social media'. So social media are *networked database platforms that combine public with personal communication*. Each of the key words in this definition points to a different aspect of these complex phenomena, and each highlights broader shifts in everyday communicative practices and expectations in the media environment.

To focus on the word *networked* is to focus on the technological systems, and on the ideas about social organization that they embody and express. Technologies do not determine how we organize ourselves and each other – rather, they embody ideas about how we should do this. The ideas come first. But the ways in which those technologies are then both adopted and adapted once in use can open up new possibilities. 'The street finds its own uses for things', as William Gibson put it (Gibson 1986: 215), but so too do governments and corporations.

To focus on the words *database* and *platform* is to focus on the business models, and on the ways in which firms try to exploit the possibilities of networked digital media. The foundational development here is the convergence of content, computing and communications – a selfie, for instance, which is an image (content) that's created with and viewed upon computerized devices, and distributed through telecommunications systems. As all forms of media are now digital, these can be experienced on any kind of computer-enabled device. The expansion of networked communications makes it possible for users to not only *experience* digital media, but also to create and circulate media for themselves. In doing this, they also create and circulate information *about* themselves, and databases of such information then become valuable commercial resources. Social media offer us platforms for communication, but we should always be conscious that they make commercial use of not just that information that we choose to communicate, but also of that which we communicate without realizing.

And to focus on the words *public and personal communication* is to focus on the cultural aspects of social media. Social media are a formation made possible by the convergence of what people do together on social network sites, with how we use user-generated content platforms of the kind described by the label Web 2.0, and with the uses we find for mobile devices such as smartphones, tablets and laptops that enable ubiquitous connection at all times. The media environment of the twentieth century was one built around large numbers of people listening to stories told by smaller numbers of people. This environment still persists, of course – the public communication systems of TV or cinema are not going to disappear completely, and nor are important textual systems such as the news. But these are all changing as new uses are found for such systems in a networked digital environment. One central use is that networked individuals can now make and circulate their own meanings. The public space of the media industries and the personal space of the individual response can now occupy the same space – social media. The following sections explore how these key words – *networked, database, platform, public* and *personal communication* – can be brought together to help us understand social media.

Networked

In 1968, networked computing was still experimental. It would not be until the following year that the first connections would be made on what would become the ARPANET, the precursor network of all those that are brought together today as the internet (Leiner *et al.* 2000). Two leading figures from the agency behind that network – the Pentagon's Defense Advanced Research Projects Agency, or DARPA – were J.C.R. Licklider and Bob Taylor. In 1968, Licklider and Taylor wrote a paper that foresaw that the computer would not just be used for processing information but for communicating with other people. This is such a taken-for-granted feature of everyday life in the twenty-first century that it's easy to miss how very visionary it was in the days before the development of the personal computer. Licklider and Taylor predicted that online communication would lead to the development of new kinds of community: 'communities not of common location, but of *common interest*' (Licklider & Taylor 1999: 108, original emphasis). And they predicted the emergence of a cluster of software programs that would be within the network, not on an individual machine (an anticipation of the cloud), and that would operate as a kind of intelligent agent for its user. Here are some of the things that they predicted this system would do for its users:

> take notes (or refrain from taking notes) on what you do, what you read, what you buy and where you buy it. It will know who your friends are, your mere acquaintances. It will know your value structure, who is prestigious in your eyes, for whom you will do what with what priority, and who can have access to which of your personal files. (p. 109)

Almost 50 years later, this sounds rather like a description of Facebook's algorithms, although Facebook *never* refrains from taking notes about what its users do: it even saves the abandoned drafts of messages and comments that its users start to write but decide not to post, and records how long they spend looking at material that they decide not to comment on or *like*.

The development of the internet from the ARPANET towards what we now call social media, is in part a story of *connections* – it's a story of new ways of connecting ideas and information, and a story of new ways of connecting computers into networks. It's also in part a story of *communication*, and a story of the ways that people communicate through networked digital media to form *communities* of many different kinds. And it's also in part a story of *commerce*, in which the pre-web internet, whose developers and users were largely one and the same, gives way to a commercial media space in which developers transform their users into their product.

Licklider and Taylor's vision of communication was different from many of the other most important concepts that were to shape the internet. Vannevar Bush's *memex*, Ted Nelson's *hypertext* and Tim Berners-Lee's *World Wide Web* were all pivotal moments in theorizing how *information* and *ideas* could be connected in new ways. But Licklider and Taylor saw how *people* could be connected in new ways.

> life will be happier for the on-line individual because the people with whom one interacts most strongly will be selected more by commonality of interests and goals than by accidents of proximity ... communication will be more effective and productive, and therefore more enjoyable. (Licklider & Taylor 1999: 110)

'All watched over by machines of loving grace', as Richard Brautigan had put it in a poem of 1967 (Brautigan 1967) – indeed, the counterculture of which Brautigan was such a distinctive voice would go on to find important expression and legacies in the development of the internet (Castells 2001). So ideas of personal communication and the formation of online community were present in internet cultures from the very beginning. *Community* would go on to become one of the central tropes through which the early internet was to be understood (Rheingold 1993). But communities of common interest are only one aspect of how people use social media. These are better understood not as communities but as networks.

A central analysis of the concept of the *network* is that of Manuel Castells, in his *Information Age* trilogy of the late 1990s. Castells describes a world in which the rapid and pervasive development of information technology, the shifting alignments of both capitalist and statist systems, and the rise of new social movements interact in a society for which *network* is the key term. Networks, he argues, of 'production, power, and experience' (Castells 1998: 350). Castells's emphasis on network as both metaphor and concrete description is shared in different ways by figures such as Latour (2005) who argues for an understanding of social life characterized by shifting patterns of networked association. Lee Rainie and Barry Wellman describe networks of connected individuals, each of whom is at the centre of a constellation of their own networks as well as being a part of those of many other people:

> People are becoming more aware that each individual is at the center of his or her own *personal network*: a solar system of one to two thousand and more people orbiting around us. Each person has become a communication and information switchboard connecting persons, networks, and institutions. At the same time, each person has become a portal to the rest of the world, providing bridges for

their friends to other social circles. With the size and complexity of these networks, each networked individual has to balance out collective and interpersonal commitments in unique ways. Facebook is a good example: It consists of millions of interlinked personal networks, each 'home page' connecting to 'friends' and interests. (Rainie & Wellman 2012: 55)

This kind of 'networked individualism' is a characteristic of social network sites. In their 2008 discussion of these, boyd and Ellison point to the importance of the pioneering social network site SixDegrees, which launched in 1997. Snapshots of the platform are preserved at the Wayback Machine. In one of these, its self-description from April 1999 still sounds very contemporary in its use of the words *communicate, share* and *connected*, and in its juxtaposition of *personal* with *millions of other members*:

> Inspired by the theory of six degrees of separation, sixdegrees is your personal on-line community where you have the ability to interact, communicate and share information and experiences with millions of other members from around the world, all of whom are connected to you.

But the web environment of the late 1990s was not yet one in which such a network could cross the kinds of demographic boundaries that Facebook has done to reach its current position where one in every five people on earth use it regularly, and SixDegrees closed within a few years. Not everyone in the late 1990s yet had enough friends who were also online to enable network effects to kick in. And the practices of making, sharing and commenting on content – especially online video – weren't yet developed enough for any but the most hardcore. And as Kirkpatrick (2010: 69) points out, even uploading profile photos was not yet practical for many users as there just weren't that many digital cameras yet in use, which made it harder for people to connect with those they knew (which Jane Doe was the one you went to school with?). The lack of photos also made the entire network less attractive than one built around people's faces. But SixDegrees mattered because it brought together existing elements of online culture into something that was a recognisable precursor of contemporary social media, including personal profiles and buddy lists from chat and messaging services. It was an early example of how online media could be used not just to create community, but to develop networks for the collaborative performance and presentation of identity.

Marshall (2014) offers a useful distinction between what he calls representational and presentational media. By *representational* media, he describes the established media industries of the mass production of popular culture (cinema, broadcasting, recorded music, newspapers and magazines, games): 'It is representational in the sense that, through its stories, narratives, and images, these media forms attempt to embody a populace. The stories, in all their manifestations, represent a culture' (Marshall 2014: 160). By *presentational* media, he describes the ways in which media are now 'performed, produced and exhibited by the individual'. By creating, linking to or commenting upon some item of media, the user is also establishing a performance of self – a presentation that foregrounds the *individual* in contemporary communication rather than the *audience*. The individual is both presenting and performing versions of themselves, but is also doing so within networks.

On some platforms, this is explicit. LinkedIn, for example, on which one crafts one's CV for public display, and develops a network of professional connections with whom one might share endorsements for particular work skills or even write a public reference. LinkedIn has been open since 2003, and became a publicly traded company in 2012. As of July 2015, it claimed more than 360 million members in more than 200 countries and territories (https://press.linkedin.com/about-linkedin), making it a major presence in the social media environment. Employers and recruiters use LinkedIn to search for possible candidates, while users try to present themselves in their most marketable light. LinkedIn does not see the kinds of over-sharing common to other platforms, through which users face the problems of negotiating collapsed contexts that separate their different offline and online networks (Meyrowitz 1985, Wesch 2009, Marwick & boyd 2010). LinkedIn uses what has been described as a 'gated-access' approach to establishing connections with other users (Papacharissi 2009), in that users are discouraged from adding people to whom they cannot demonstrate an existing connection of some kind (colleague, classmate and so on), and there is also a function to request introductions to users who are not part of one's network if there is a mutual connection. The presentation of self on LinkedIn is strictly business.

Dating sites and apps, in contrast, demand a quite different kind of self-presentation, in which the user simultaneously tries to present themselves in the way they think will be most attractive, while trying at the same time to invoke a very specific imagined and desired audience (Smaill 2004, Arvidsson 2006). Matchmaking and hook-up apps like Tinder or Grindr combine this with geolocation and chat functions to narrow the search to a particular environment. Facebook in fact resembled a dating website in some respects for some years, and in creating a profile users are still asked to indicate whether they are 'interested in' men, women or both. Options that have been removed over the years include the ability to search for new people in specific locations by gender and relationship status (which include, among others, 'single', 'married' and 'it's complicated'), as well the option to indicate what one is 'looking for' – these used to include 'random play' and 'whatever I can get'. When adding a new friend, Facebook used to ask how you knew each other, and provided a standard fill-in-the-blank option to select 'We hooked up and it was _____'. The unlovely option to *poke* someone remains a part of Facebook today.

Profiles have antecedents in dating websites, personal homepages (Papacharissi 2002, Cheung 2007) and online communities of interest that form around particular topics (Rheingold 1993). But a user's social media profile is not always a self-representation, but instead one that others collaborate on developing through using the service (Ellison & boyd 2013). A user's presence on a platform like Facebook is one in which that user's friends collaborate in developing the presentation of self that is the profile – every comment, every 'like', every post on another user's Timeline, is a contribution to how that other user is represented to others on Facebook.

The popularization of the mobile internet that was driven by smartphones makes the internet less about connecting computers and more about connecting individuals. Personal communication is not necessarily just one-to-one, and can be scaled up within networks, so that it takes on a public quality. And on social media, each individual is at the centre of their own mobile network of networks – the people with whom one interacts on Facebook may be different from those one prefers to follow on Twitter, and each of those may be quite different from the professional constituency to whom one pitches one's work identity on LinkedIn, or the kind of person one hopes to find when swiping on Tinder. None of these people is an audience or a group, but rather in each case each connection is a part of just one of an individual's own network of networks.

Platform + Database

YouTube was created in 2005. Ten years later, it's hard to remember the web without it. Was there ever a web without Keyboard Cat? Were fails epic back then? YouTube very quickly became a central hub of popular culture, with prominent moments from 'Leave Britney alone' to 'It gets better' becoming catchphrases on a scale that could previously only be managed by the very biggest broadcast TV shows. Now it is unremarkable for leading politicians to launch election campaigns on YouTube, or for the service to compete with broadcasters for the rights to stage campaign debates. News stories are frequently broken, sustained or suddenly upturned by video evidence uploaded to YouTube by bystanders with smartphones (Allan 2013, Thorsen & Allan 2014). It has made possible new approaches to advertising (*I'm on a horse*), and to activism and advocacy (*Kony 2012*). It has spawned entire new genres (unboxing and haul videos) and enabled entirely new audiences for genres that had previously been limited to particular kinds of specialist community (supercuts, videogame speedrunning). And of course, YouTube has made possible a whole new kind of self-branding entrepreneur (Marwick 2013a), from PewDiePie, who earns a reported US$4.7 million annually from YouTube ads alone (Kang 2015), to Zoella; the more than 8 million subscribers to Zoella's main channel, on which she offers hair and beauty tips and shows off what she's bought at the shops, helped her ghost-written debut novel become the UK's fastest-selling book of 2014.

But, for context, think back to just another ten years before the site launched, and the improbability of YouTube is striking. Picture yourself in 1995, trying to pitch the concept for YouTube to a broadcast-model media mogul like Rupert Murdoch. Murdoch was then – and still is – head of one of the most powerful, influential and genuinely global media corporations in the world. He had built an empire, first from news-papers, then from television, then film and book publishing (Shawcross 1992, Wolff 2010). His corporation ran household-name brands such as *The Simpsons*, *The Sun*, Twentieth Century Fox and Sky. There was almost nobody on earth more successful at making money from public communication. So you'd take him your idea for YouTube.

We're going to build this really huge website, you'd tell him, *and it's going to offer free access to every music video ever made. And not just that. It will also have every movie trailer ever made, every big news story, every TV and cinema commercial from the last forty years, the best bits of every football match, the standout scenes from every film and every episode of every TV show, and all available film of cats. We think we can make global superstars out of Korean rappers doing novelty horsey dance moves – something like that could get watched more than 2 billion times. And – get this! – it will also have videos of everybody's birthday parties!*

Murdoch would likely have called for security to have you escorted from the building. But then again, not many people really got the web in 1995 – even Bill Gates took a while to see its potential. And *hype* was the native language of the web from the start, as some of the sharper commentators at the time pointed out (Barbrook & Cameron 1995, Dery 1996, Wark 1997). So a figure like Murdoch, who had built his empire through business models of both mass distribution and enforced scarcity, would have had lots of quite natural objections. *Who owns all those rights?*, he might have asked. *Who wants to see videos of everybody's birthday parties? How much is the electricity bill going to be? And what's with all the cats?* Those would all have been legitimate questions – some of them still are.

And another basic objection to this fantasy sales pitch of 1995 would very likely have been about the enormous human resources and working hours required to source, compile, convert, upload, organize, title, tag, subtitle and caption those many hundreds of millions of hours of videos. *Who's going to do all that work and how much would we have to pay them?* The answer, which nobody really saw coming in the 1990s, was that we would do all that ourselves for free. And more than that, we would *make* videos ourselves and upload those to YouTube too.

YouTube remains the best example of what came quickly to be called *Web 2.0*. Web 2.0 was both marketing hype and business model (Lovink 2011, Marwick 2013a), but it also captures a particular moment in the first decade of the twenty-first century, in which a new wave of popular websites came to rapid prominence and shifted the narrative of what the web was about. YouTube, along with Blogger, Flickr and others, was a site for what began to be called user-generated content (UGC). This is a label that is sometimes used in ambiguous ways, but was usefully defined by the OECD (2007: 18) as media material that: first, is published in some way (so making a video and then just keeping it under your bed doesn't count); second, involves a certain amount of creative work or contribution (so just clicking *like* on that John Oliver clip doesn't count); and third, is made outside of its creator's professional work practice or routine (so your Harry Potter fan fiction might count, but J.K. Rowling's would not). The rapid success of YouTube led to its purchase by Google in November 2006 for US$1.65 billion, an event and a sum of money that no doubt had something to do with *Time* magazine's selection the following month of *you* as its Person of the Year:

> for seizing the reins of the global media, for founding and framing the new digital democracy, for working for nothing and beating the pros at their own game, TIME's Person of the Year for 2006 is you. (Grossman 2006)

But this rapid mainstreaming and commercialization of YouTube contributed to the site changing in ways that weren't always in tune with the elements that had contributed to its initial appeal. The ever-rising scale of YouTube's reach, and the speed with which established commercial media recognized and moved in on its potential, meant that, as van Dijck (2013: 117) put it, 'ordinary users never really rivaled mainstream pros'. The 'most viewed' videos of all time are no longer home-made novelties but are now expensive music clips by the likes of Katy Perry and Rihanna. True, this picture is complicated by YouTube's 'Partner Program' which shares advertising revenues with pro-am YouTubers whose channels attract significant numbers of subscribers (Burgess 2013). But at the same time, we should also be careful to recognize that YouTube is not broadcasting, and the value its users derive from it should not be reduced to a twentieth-century fixation on Top Ten lists. This is a common error in discussions of networked digital media – to assume that something only matters if it can draw a large audience (as in Hindman's 2009 book on blogs, for example, or Castells's unpleasant term 'electronic autism', Castells 2009: 66). But your video that only gets six views is still worth posting on YouTube, if those are the six people you wanted to see it, or if those six people can take something from it.

David Gauntlett argues that Web 2.0 was best characterized by the ways in which its best known sites enable previously disparate individuals to 'come together to work collaboratively in a shared space' (Gauntlett 2011a: 5). He offers the analogy of the early web with its personal homepages as lots of separate gardens, tended by individuals, whereas Web 2.0 was more like a community allotment. The more people join in and take part, the better the space gets, the more variety and depth it has, the more range and utility it can offer. So, seen from this perspective, Web 2.0 was about enabling online collaboration on an enormous scale, and offering a platform for anyone who wants to contribute their resources to a project that will be more than the sum of its parts. For many commentators (such as Delwiche & Henderson 2013), Web 2.0 was about what Henry Jenkins (2008, 2009) labelled *participatory culture*. It's important to note that Jenkins does not suggest that Web 2.0 sites like YouTube created participatory culture. Rather, he argues that: 'the emergence of participatory cultures of all kinds over the past several decades paved the way for the early embrace, quick adoption, and diverse use of such platforms' (Jenkins 2009: 109). He's absolutely correct in pointing out that people had been finding ways to create, communicate and circulate their own media long before YouTube (Duncombe 1997, McKay 1998, Downing 2001, Atton 2002, Meikle 2002).

But we should be clear that the term was originally coined to label an emerging business model, not a culture. 'We should judge Web 2.0 for what it is', cautions Geert Lovink (2011: 4), 'a renaissance in Silicon

Valley'. The label *Web 2.0* is generally credited to Tim O'Reilly, who applied it to those internet projects that were having some degree of success in the wake of the dot.com collapse of 2000. O'Reilly's original discussion of Web 2.0 (O'Reilly 2005) brought together a range of tools and services that perhaps had as many points of difference as they had things in common (including Google, BitTorrent, Wikipedia and Flickr, for instance). But the common points included providing a software service rather than selling a software product. They included an 'architecture of participation', which makes the service better the more it is actually used (search results, for instance, which become more precise the more data the search engine has – including previous searches). They included developing services that could be used across multiple devices, something that was to become crucial with the rise of the smartphone. And they included the importance of the database as the engine of the successful Web 2.0 business model: YouTube is not just a database of videos, but also of its users' viewing histories and preferences, their search records and their interactions with others on the site. All of these become fuel for YouTube's advertising business (an approach that we will discuss in more detail in Chapter 2).

Before the coining of the term *Web 2.0*, there was no concept of a precursor *Web 1.0*. Nobody spoke of Web 1.0 – there was just the web. But after the concept of Web 2.0, it became necessary to construct a retrospective model of what Web 1.0 had been: a reductive characterization which involved eliding all kinds of inconvenient messy complexities. And after Web 2.0, it also became inevitable that people would start to talk about, look for or devise contending versions of Web 3.0 and beyond (a quick search on Google for *Web 4.0*, whatever the hell it may be, brings back 143,000 results; more, no doubt, by the time you read this). Tim O'Reilly and John Battelle topped even this with their move to *Web Squared* (O'Reilly & Battelle 2009).

Matthew Allen (2013) argues that we should see Web 2.0 as 'rhetorical technology, through which the computing industry attempted to change the way we think of the internet' (Allen 2013: 264). It was to think of the web as a platform, and the discourse of 2.0 meant bringing together transformation (*it's an upgrade*) with continuity (*it's still the web, just different*). And so other contending interpretations of Web 2.0 now take place within this 'discourse of versions', in what Allen describes as 'a fight to define the future, though control over the meaning of the past and the referential present' (Allen 2013: 270). To tell the history of the web as a teleological narrative of Web 1.0, 2.0, 3.0 and so on and on is to try to influence that very narrative, through directing its development along lines that suit one's own ideals or business plans. The term *social media* does similar work, and brings together transformation and continuity in a similar way, with its *media* positioning itself within the familiar, while its *social* modifies this in a claim to change.

Nancy Baym (2011), similarly, has pointed out that not only was UGC central to the web from the beginning, but that internet communications before the advent of the web – such as Usenet – offered *only* user-generated content. There was no professional commercial content with which to contrast the idea of UGC (see also Lobato *et al.* 2013). Some of the most important projects of the 'Web 1.0' era were built around UGC, from GeoCities to Indymedia. Web 2.0 exemplar Blogger launched in 1999, before the dot.com collapse, while Amazon had been soliciting its users to contribute book and product reviews for years before these were retconned as UGC.

But YouTube and the Web 2.0 moment did two things. First, it made this kind of collaborative, de-professionalized, everyday creativity, posting and sharing into something that was both mainstream and pervasive. GeoCities and Indymedia were pretty niche, but YouTube is ubiquitous. And second, YouTube and the other successful Web 2.0 operations demonstrated a business model that would go on to underpin social media. As in my earlier observation about Facebook, YouTube found a way to make money by becoming a media company that does not itself produce any media. Rather, it provides a platform for others to do so. And in so doing, its users build the database of content and personal information from which the company makes its money.

In some cases, providing such a platform is the basic affordance offered by the service, in the way that a photo-based social media tool allows its users to upload photos. In other cases, such as that of Facebook, it is a much larger and more complex set of affordances, built around the provision of an Application Programming Interface (API) which allows third-party software developers to produce add-on services, such as games, to run on the platform provided by the social media firm. Facebook also, of course, offers tools for its users to upload or provide links to media material of various kinds, as well as to express themselves through writing or images. This dimension of social media is about publishing – the platform provides a means for the user to republish found material with or without additional comments, or to distribute user-generated content.

Tarleton Gillespie has teased out the multiple meanings of *platform* in this kind of Web 2.0 discourse, and the ways in which it sometimes suggests a technical system (as in the iPhone or Android platforms for developers) sometimes suggests a system of opportunity (a platform for advertisers), and sometimes suggests a system of empowerment for its users, who can use it to find and express their voice (a speaking platform). Gillespie argues that the uses and ambiguities of *platform* offer YouTube (and its parent Google) the means to not only present but also to disguise its operations.

> This discursive positioning depends on terms and ideas that are specific enough to mean something, and vague enough to work across multiple venues for multiple audiences. To call one's online service a platform is not a meaningless claim, nor is it a simple one. Like other structural metaphors (think 'network', 'broadcast' or 'channel') the term depends on a semantic richness that, though it may go unnoticed by the casual listener or even the speaker, gives the term discursive resonance. (Gillespie 2010: 349)

In this analysis, the connotations of platform – *a raised stand for speaking, a political party's manifesto, a computer operating system* – overstate the ways in which YouTube is different from older media operations and understate the ways in which it is similar to them. These similarities would include its reliance on advertising, and its resulting susceptibility to commercial and regulatory pressure. Gillespie's argument is that the uses of *platform* by social media firms obscure such pressures rather than illuminating them. A similar argument can be made about the uses of the word *share* by social media firms, and will be explored in Chapter 2.

Public Media + Personal Communication

Let's return to that small example from the start of this chapter, where Facebook had suggested someone using the name of the eighteenth-century thinker Jean-Jacques Rousseau as a possible new friend, and the beginning of the exchange beneath that image between me and my Facebook friend Andrew. To recap:

ANDREW: Graham, did you coin the phrase, 'Man is born free, and everywhere he is on Facebook'?
ME: I did, Andrew, although Rousseau had done most of the work on it before I got there.
ANDREW: heheh. Is it OK if I use/cite this wonderful rhetorical coinage in a piece I am writing?
ME: Absolutely :-)
ANDREW: Great. I am going to take a screen shot of it, so your name will appear. Is that OK?
[continues ...]

The very banality and unexceptional nature of this exchange in this context tells us a lot about how people communicate on social media, and about what makes such media distinctive. The exchange brings together an element of public communication with an element of the personal in an environment of uncertain visibility.

The initial post is, on a *very* small scale, an example of the broadcast model of communication – what Thompson (1995) calls 'mediated quasi-interaction'. It's addressed to no one in particular. There is no specific imagined audience, beyond the set of everyone who can see my posts on Facebook. It's not aimed at anyone specific, in the way that a phone call or a text would be. At the same time, it does recognize those people who can see my posts on Facebook as likely to get the reference and get the joke (although it would also be possible to get one or the other but not both). And in this, as Scannell (2000) has argued, it addresses the general *anyone* of its intended audience as *someone*, without knowing quite who that someone is. The public and the personal converge.

The follow-up conversation below the image is an example of what Thompson calls 'mediated interaction'. It uses a technical medium of some kind, in this case Facebook on our respective devices, mediated by wireless networks or broadband cables. It's also two-way communication, or indeed more than two-way, with possibilities for a great many people, in principle, to join in. Facebook's interface is structured to prompt such interaction, with every post we view coming with clickable options to *like* or *reply*, and with our profile pictures already lined up next to a text box reading 'Write a comment' on each post that we view.

An important aspect of such communication is that it involves people who are not together in the same space at the same time, and this connects with a certain absence of cues as to how each comment is to be read. So unlike face-to-face communication, we have no access to tone of voice or facial expression or body language, and so we have only the text to go on. There is a certain tension in all online posts, as was observed back in the days of Usenet and listserv cultures (Connery 1997). On the one hand, posts are written texts, and as readers, we tend to expect that means they're finished thoughts; on the other hand, a comment on a social media thread may be a throwaway remark, of the kind that we might revise as soon as it left our mouths in conversation. In conversation, it's fine to say *wait, that's not what I meant*. In writing, that's harder (although Facebook now allows users to edit both posts and comments). The cues that we associate with both writing and speech are absent in a social media environment. This is why misunderstandings online are so very common, and why both Andrew and I make small gestures in our exchange to signal our attitude to each other, Andrew with his *heheh* and me with my :-). Because we're not present in the same space, words like *here* and *there*, or *this* and *that*, can't be used with quite the same precision, as we can't both see what the other is pointing to when they say *this*. So note Andrew's retyping of the full caption of my image at the start of the exchange, rather than writing *this*.

And a further central element to social media communication is that both the public and the personal aspects are visible to others who are not otherwise a part of the interaction. At times they may announce their presence by clicking *like* on one line of an exchange or even by sharing it. This in-principle visibility is a fundamental part of what makes social media a distinct experience from other forms of communication. It brings with it new kinds of demands for new kinds of ethics in everyday life, as we negotiate each other's communications and each other's public identities in making use of these in our own social media presentations of ourselves. Andrew's asking for permission to reproduce the image and to identify me by name is one recognition of those daily ethics of visibility. We'll return to this question of a social media ethics of visibility in more detail in Chapters 4 and 5.

This convergence of the public and the personal in a context of unpredictable visibility has brought with it new dilemmas, possibilities and risks for relationships. Daniel Miller's anthropological study *Tales from Facebook* offers fascinating narratives of people watching their own relationships unravel as a result of their own behaviour on Facebook. Again and again the convergence of public and personal is the problem – not least in being able to tell which is public and which is personal. 'You can't say that the photos on someone else's Facebook site were posted specifically for you to see, but neither can you say they weren't. Once there, they are part of your social life' (Miller 2011: 171).

The rise of social network sites, and the Web 2.0 business model and the cultural practices that it made possible, are two of the three pillars on which social media have developed. The third is the rise of the smartphone, which brings public and personal together in new alignments. Smartphones exemplify the convergence of communications, computing and content. And they bring mobile devices firmly onto the agenda of communication research and scholarship (Goggin 2012, Goggin & Hjorth 2014). Communications regulator Ofcom reported in August 2015 that 66% of UK adults owned a smartphone, which represents very rapid adoption of a kind of device only available for less than a decade (Ofcom 2015a: 3). There are long prehistories of mobile telephony, but recognisable mobile phones were first introduced commercially in the 1970s and 80s (Goggin 2006, Green & Haddon 2009, Ling & Donner 2009). While it too had its antecedents (Goggin 2011), it was the launch of the first Apple iPhone in January 2007 that inaugurated the smartphone era:

> The iPhone represents a distinctive moment, both in the very short history of mobile media and in the much longer history of cultural technologies. Like the Walkman three decades earlier, it marks a historical conjuncture in which notions about identity, individualism, lifestyle, and sociality – and their relationship to technology and media practice – require rearticulation. (Hjorth *et al.* 2012a: 1)

Apple's introduction of the App Store the following year made possible new approaches to designing, selling and using software, and made every iPhone infinitely customizable. Each mass-produced phone is also a one-off personalized extension of one's daily life. But, as several commentators have pointed out, an iPhone is also a tightly controlled system, which the user is unable to personalize by hacking or changing the code in the way they could with any other computing device; you can install any software you want, so long as it has passed through the gatekeeping systems of the App Store (Zittrain 2008, Goggin 2011, Hjorth 2012). For many, probably most, users, messing around with their phone's software is not something they would want to do anyway. They want something that works. Ben Goldsmith (2014) points out the paradox that this closed and tightly controlled operating system has nonetheless become the platform on which developers have built more than a million different apps. But the closed black-box operating system is nonetheless an example of how the contemporary networked digital media environment manifests tensions between closed proprietary systems and open source ones (including the category of open proprietary systems such as Android).

Smartphones are central to the convergence of public media with personal communication. As Vincent and Fortunati point out, every phone becomes a repository and a vehicle for its user's emotions and relationships. 'Held near to or on the human body', they observe, '[the phone] plays a vital role in the emotional identity of the user, as well as assisting in the emotional management of the ups and downs of everyday life' (Vincent and Fortunati 2014: 317). A phone also, of course, offers multiple portals through which that user can connect with others, including the unknowable audiences of social media platforms. A photo taken with one's phone can be shared with personal contacts through the built-in address book and its integration with SMS and MMS and email, or it can be shared straight to the limited personal network of one's friends or followers on whichever social media tools one has chosen to install, or published to any or all users of Tumblr, Instagram, Pinterest, Flickr, Facebook, Twitter or many more. Personal moments, however trivial, can be shared with specific or imagined audiences, as in the internet meme that reappears whenever a major platform goes offline for any time at all, in which an anguished hipster clutches their phone and says *Instagram is down – just* describe *your lunch to me*. The emergent genre of the selfie – a form that captures social media perfectly, and which we will discuss further in Chapter 5 – can be used to share not just the personal but also the intimate. The phone can be used to personalize one's experience of public space, by playing music through headphones to provide a customized soundtrack; and it can also be used to draw in sounds and images from that public space for later personal use, by for example using Shazam to pursue an interesting song heard in a café (Crawford 2012). *Listening*, as Crawford argues, is a useful frame in which to consider social media habits, as we drop in and out of Twitter or Facebook to catch what people are saying, or tune in and out as our attention shifts.

But smartphones are intimate in other ways as well. The apps we install on our phones collect ever more information about our personal communication and behaviour. For instance, installing Facebook's app on your phone means giving it permission to do a lot of things, including read and modify your contacts, add and edit events in your calendar, read your texts, take pictures and video, record your physical locations and your network connections, read your phone call log and call your contacts directly, and prevent your phone from going to sleep. Many other apps are just as intrusive (see the analysis by Share Lab 2015 for more). Apple's Siri agent will rummage through your email to try to identify the number of any unknown caller. Spotify records not just your location, but how fast you're moving to your next one, and whether you're walking or running to get there.

Smartphones expand the range of ways in which people can experience being present in the same space at the same time (Hjorth *et al.* 2012b) and can complicate our understandings of what it means to be present with someone (yet swiping on Tinder) or absent (yet chatting on WhatsApp). Licoppe (2004) describes the phenomenon of 'connected presence', through which we maintain relationships by the continuous exchange of communication, rather than waiting until we're present in the same space at the same time to catch up. Those moments of physical co-presence and those moments of absent mediated interaction become threaded together in a coherent relationship, managed and maintained through mobile media. I attended a wedding in 2014 in which the adult daughter of the bride watched the ceremony from the other side of the planet through FaceTime and appeared in some of the formal wedding pictures, as the bride held up the phone for the photographer with her daughter's face filling its screen, while the daughter commented aloud on who she could see in the crowd.

Conclusion

The social media convergence of public media and personal communication was not invented by Facebook. Facebook was not the first to use the database business model or to offer a platform for users. And it was certainly not the first network. But Facebook has so far been the firm that has best been able to capitalize on the affordances of social media. It has exploited the database and platform elements of the Web 2.0 business model by continuing to draw in new markets: it has been very strategic in this from the beginning, when its phased addition of new universities to its closed network gave it a sense of exclusivity and created demand. And it has its sights set on developing internet infrastructure in parts of the world that have not yet been able to gain reliable access, with a view to making the firm synonymous with the net. It has continued to expand the range of media types that users can post to the site (photos, videos, gifs) in order to undermine rivals that specialize in one type – Flickr's claim to be the world's largest photo-sharing site was killed years ago by Facebook, and photos were not even Facebook's core proposition. Facebook has been relentless in adding new affordances for its users to commit more of their lives to its servers. Its ascent coincided with the arrival of the smartphone and tablet, and with greater availability of both wireless and broadband networks. Its timing, its simple fill-in-the-blanks interface, and its provision of a free service all helped Facebook to see off earlier leading platforms, some of whose names now echo from the past like half-remembered bands – Friendster, Bebo, Friends Reunited and MySpace among them. So having defined social media, the next chapter turns to focus on Facebook as the leading example of the sharing industry.

Chapter 2

The Sharing Industry

The word *share* is at the heart of social media. It appears as both a link and an imperative verb under every Facebook post, every YouTube video, every story on the websites of the *Daily Mail* or *The New York Times*. Social media tools from Twitter to Tumblr highlight possibilities of sharing, and with it possibilities of connection. Instead of simply watching, listening or reading, we are urged to share ideas and images, information and entertainment, stories and songs with self-selected networks of friends, contacts and our own personal audiences. From Spotify playlists to the BBC iPlayer, from BitTorrent to *The Guardian*'s opinion page, we are encouraged to communicate, cooperate, collaborate and *share*. Sharing is part of what's social about social media.

But the word *share* is also the very word that the established media content industries have mobilized against as a threat. The practices of file-sharing break open the business models of the music, TV and film industries. Newspapers find their online content accessed, circulated and archived by advertising-driven firms such as Google, and by individual users, all of which challenges the news industry's business models and brand profiles. Content industries lobby for the criminalization of sharing, and for regulatory models and technological interventions that will inhibit it. File-sharing portals such as The Pirate Bay, EZTV or Isohunt disappear and reappear with new URLs, as though in some kind of regulatory whack-a-mole game. And while online sharing opens up new social possibilities, new kinds of networks and new forms of distributed creativity and collaboration, it also opens social media users up to new forms of visibility, exploitation and surveillance.

So it's immediately clear that the word *share* operates in many different ways. Raymond Williams identified *share* as one end of the spectrum of meanings of *communication* (Williams 1983: 72–3). Williams traced the meanings and uses of *communication*, finding the one-way sense of *transmit* at one end of its spectrum, and *share*, with its connections to the common root word of both *communication* and *communion*, at the other. And the various senses of *share* suggested in the previous two paragraphs point to how different uses of this word are caught up in attempts to find new media business models for the networked digital environment. For older and newer media industries alike, sharing is both opportunity and threat. And it can be seen as both of those for their users as well. This is captured in the premises of one of the first authors to engage with questions of sharing in the then-emerging social media environment, Charles Leadbeater, who wrote that 'The biggest change the web will bring about is in allowing us to share with one another in new ways and particularly to share ideas' (2008: 6). But this sharing of ideas was to have an economic function, as our individual acts of sharing would come to define us in an economy built around creativity and innovation: 'In the economy of ideas that the web is creating, you are what you share – who you are linked to, who you network with and which ideas, pictures, videos, links or comments you share' (Leadbeater 2008: 6). The idea that *you are what you share* is one that has gathered force since then, although the idea that this is part of an *economy* of ideas is not always front and centre in the enthusiastic promotion of sharing by social media platforms.

Sharing, as Nicholas John (2013) points out, has become established as a central term of media and communication since the emergence of the Web 2.0 business model in the early years of this century. He traces how it has come to be used in relation to very general and abstract qualities, as in exhortations on websites to *share your life* or *share your world*. He also notes its use with no object at all, as in *sign up and share* or *log in and start sharing*. And he shows that it's now used in relation to social and communicative activities that were formerly described in different ways, so that acts of self-expression are now things to be *shared*. By 2009 the word had become so central that Manuel Castells could declare that 'In our society, the protocols of communication are not based on the sharing of culture but on the culture of sharing' (Castells, 2009: 126). Matthew David (2010) and Stephen Witt (2015) explore the implications of file-sharing for the music industry. Meikle and Young (2012) identify sharing as one of a set of specific shifts in media audience behaviour that were made possible by the convergence of content, computing and communications. Joshua Green and Henry Jenkins discuss the active ways in which audiences choose to share and connect, and the 'series of socially embedded decisions' that each moment of sharing involves, including:

> that the content is worth watching; that it is worth sharing with others; that the content might interest specific people we know; that the best way to spread that content is through a specific channel of

communication; and, often, that the content should be circulated with a particular message attached. (Green & Jenkins 2011: 113–14)

This range of scholarly attention is in part because the word *share* is open to such a very wide range of connotations.

Share and Share Alike?

To *share* can be to separate and divide, and this is the original sense of the word in English – to cut something tangible into smaller portions to divide with others. But in digital media it can also be to copy and multiply. Copying is, of course, one of the most basic intrinsic functions in any general purpose computer – CTRL + C. And it pairs naturally with paste – CTRL + V – which means that the act of copying and sharing intangible items becomes second nature. One example of this second nature response is that the BitTorrent protocol assumes that the user is simultaneously uploading to others as well as downloading – a reciprocal return is encoded in the software. So to share can be to take something without paying, but it may also be implicated in other forms of exchange, in which the user is to return the gift (Mauss 1954). Sometimes there can be an ideological dimension to this. The late Aaron Swartz, who helped develop RSS and Reddit, wrote in his 'Guerilla Open Access Manifesto' of 2008 that: 'sharing isn't immoral – it's a moral imperative. Only those blinded by greed would refuse to let a friend make a copy' (Swartz 2008). (Swartz killed himself in 2013, while facing 35 years in prison on charges of having downloaded an archive of academic journal articles.) And users can also share something of which neither actually has a copy, such as a Spotify playlist or a YouTube video. So there is an important reciprocal dimension to sharing, just as the exchange of gifts is at the basis of other forms of social interactions. All of these senses of *share* can be about identifying the individual that is at the heart of their own self-selected social media network of friends, contacts or connections. And moreover, all of these instances of sharing may be made visible, as others join in observing or commenting on our actions within the network.

To share can be about imparting information. On social media platforms such as Facebook, it can variously be about posting images, links and ideas. Or it can be about phatic or ritual communication – about developing, maintaining or repairing relationships. Sharing online can be the performance of versions of oneself, as we display our tastes and opinions for others, circulate things we find meaningful, or curate public collections of music or images that matter to us. To share can be to affirm someone, or it can be about looking for or offering a moment of communion, as we connect with others through meanings, through opinions and through emotions. So sharing is social. We share things online in the hope that others will not only see them, but will also share in the meanings that we've made from those things. A post that draws no *likes* or comments is disappointing, and a post that draws only snarky WTF responses is disappointing too, because the meaning we sought to share has not been reciprocated.

And what we share becomes commodified by Facebook – for Facebook, *share* has become a metaphor for *sell* (a point also made by Fuchs 2011, van Dijck 2013 and John 2013). And this metaphorical usage is spreading beyond social media platforms into the wider culture as well. In the UK, the National Health Service chose to emphasize the *sharing* of patients' medical information in its promotional materials distributed to millions of homes to explain controversial new databases of patient information: information which many were concerned could be sold to insurance companies once it had been *shared*.

On social media platforms, all of these senses of share converge. So one way to understand social media is as *the sharing industry*. And in that sense, we shouldn't overlook one further meaning of *share*, which is that denoted by owning shares in a company. Facebook's share price is tied to the amount of information its users are willing to share with it. On social media, our shares boost other people's stocks.

This chapter takes Facebook as a case study in the sharing industry of social media, and explores the tensions and contests that characterize its relations with its billion+ users. It examines social media in relation to discourses of sharing, by focusing on Facebook's 'mission statement'. The chapter traces how the key propositions from this very short mission statement – two sentences, forty-eight words – iterate throughout the company's diverse communications with its various publics. The language of this mission statement appears across the full range of Facebook's communication strategy, including in media releases, in published interviews with Mark Zuckerberg, and in its annual reports to shareholders. In this chapter, I draw on tools from Critical Discourse Analysis (CDA) to examine how the company Facebook represents itself to the world through its uses of *sharing* in such official pronouncements. And I trace how Facebook has developed its affordances for sharing media content, opinions, emotions and personal histories, throughout its decade online, as it seeks to exploit all of these for commercial use.

The Case of Facebook

If the sharing industry builds upon the provisions of networked database platforms that combine public with personal communication, how does it do this? In its annual report to shareholders for the year ending 31 December 2014, the company claimed that 1.39 billion people used Facebook by that date – one in five of the world's population. And while it's common to hear people say that Facebook is on its way out, this vast number in fact represented a 13% increase in users since December 2013. Facebook reported that 526 million of its monthly users accessed their site only through a mobile device, and projected that mobile users would continue to be a main driver of its business, suggesting there is still considerable scope to recruit still more users (Goggin 2014). In order to create new markets for expansion, the company is involved in initiatives to expand net access and connectivity in developing countries, through its Internet.org joint venture with mobile phone companies including Samsung (van Dijck 2015).

From all of this use, Facebook declared revenues of US$12.466 billion for 2014, up from US$7.87 billion in the previous year. The bulk of these revenues (92% in 2014) come from advertisers, who can pay to place ads in users' news feeds, as well as on other platforms owned by Facebook, such as Instagram; Facebook also owns the WhatsApp messaging tool and its own Messenger platform, among other interests including the Oculus Rift Virtual Reality system. Revenues also come from developers, who incorporate Facebook's data and services into their own businesses (games, notably); from marketers of various kinds (direct marketers, brands); and through providing other kinds of advertising services, campaigns and analytics beyond displaying ads in news feeds:

> Our ads let marketers reach people on Facebook based on a variety of factors including age, gender, location, and interests ... When marketers create an ad campaign on Facebook, they can specify their budget, marketing objectives and the types of people they want to reach. Facebook's ad serving technology then dynamically determines the best available ad to show each person based on those dimensions. (Facebook 2015: 5)

While a user's age and gender can be captured when they sign up, their location and interests may constantly change. So in order for its advertising business to develop, Facebook has to keep prodding each user to provide fresh information about themselves (after eight years of heavy use, I still get messages appear on my Timeline saying my profile is only '82% complete'). Each visit to Facebook brings new such prompts to connect with 'people you may know', to join 'suggested groups', to 'like' pages that have been liked or launched by friends, to respond to notifications or to update that status. *What's on your mind?* the site asks when the user logs in. Each of these gestures to the user to add another detail is driven by the need to sell ads. Facebook's business model depends on its users constantly updating their presence in its database, because it is access to this database of personal information that Facebook has to sell.

So since its launch in 2004, Facebook has continually expanded its range of affordances for users to add different kinds of information about themselves – or, as the company prefers to put it, to *share*. Each such expansion has often brought significant objections from users, who sometimes just get used to it, or who sometimes force Facebook to row back from their latest limit. This has resulted in an ongoing series of controversies about privacy and visibility, which stem from users being positioned by Facebook to share ever more access to their data and information, at times in ways which have confused or surprised significant numbers of those users.

Here are some of the most important of these expanded affordances. In 2006, Facebook introduced the news feed, in which friends' activities were collated into a shared space for the first time. This drew together in a single stream all kinds of information that had already been accessible, but that users had previously had to seek out by visiting their friends' profiles (see Solove 2007). In the same year, the company began the implementation of *share* buttons on other websites (see Kennedy 2013). In 2007, Facebook offered the disastrous experiment of its Beacon service, in which commercial transactions between a user and a number of prominent services such as Amazon were published to that user's friends (discussed in boyd 2008 and van Dijck 2013). In 2011, Facebook introduced the term *frictionless sharing*, to describe functions through which apps such as Spotify or *The Guardian* were able to publish updates about users' activities within those apps on those users' own feeds. In the same year, the company reinvented everyone's profile as their Timeline. The Timeline extends back across the user's whole life, not just their activity since they joined Facebook, and so users are prompted to add information about their whole biographies. And in early 2013, Facebook introduced sharing icons to status updates, so that users could illustrate their posts with simple emoticons or drop-down menu items. This facility led to the indelible FAQ on Facebook's 'help' pages of *How do I share my feelings?*

The choice of the word *sharing*, observes Jenny Kennedy (2013), is always *strategic*, with the term's multiple semantic possibilities at times obscuring the symbolic power contests that its uses enact. José van Dijck argues that *sharing* is 'an evolving norm', taking the phrase from Mark Zuckerberg, who applied this same description to privacy (van Dijck 2013: 46). How, she asks, has a particular ideological sense of *sharing* come to dominance in the Facebook era? This particular sense, for van

Dijck, is a double one, in which sharing means users distributing personal information to each other *and* also that information being sold on to third parties. Her main emphasis is on this second sense, and on how Facebook has worked to shift its users' expectations of their own control over their own data. So Beacon, for example, failed, in van Dijck's analysis, because the company was so clear about what it was doing and about which other companies were involved. Users, she argues, just were not ready for this in 2007. It was too unfamiliar, too radical, too abrupt.

So Facebook sought to change the users' expectations and behaviour, rather than modifying its own corporate strategy. One way that it did this was through the coding of the platform and the affordances that it offers. The introduction and expansion of Facebook's Application Programming Interface (API), which allowed other developers to create tools for use on Facebook, helped to shift users' perceptions of the platform to being one which was now engaged across the whole internet, rather than being a secured walled garden. The introduction of the *like* button, for example, and its installation across hundreds of thousands of websites was crucial in adjusting users' sense of sharing (van Dijck 2013: 49). So even though Facebook is collecting all the information generated by its users' visits to sites with *like* buttons installed (even when those users are logged out of Facebook), it no longer appears to be at the visible centre of the transaction in the way that it did with Beacon. Because of the very ubiquity of the thumbs-up *like* button, and because the apparent or *visible* part of the transaction is a user sharing info with their *friends*, rather than with a third party or with Facebook, *Inc.*, users have been more accepting.

Do You Work for Facebook?

All media are implicated in work. We recognize as labour or employment certain visible kinds of media work such as the roles of journalists, film-makers, broadcasters, musicians and photographers. But as Downey (2014) reminds us, there are also many kinds of hidden histories of information work, going back to nineteenth-century and early twentieth-century telegraph messengers and telephone operators, through many decades of changing demands on librarians and information curators, and on to various kinds of real-time stenography, from courtrooms to TV captioning and live tweeting and blogging. Flows of information always have to be guided by someone. To focus on the industrial aspects of social media, as this chapter does, means situating its argument within a broader set of arguments about labour in the social media environment.

There are very real issues surrounding labour in the networked digital media environment (Scholz 2013). At one end of the spectrum, there is the exploitation in the Chinese gold-farming industry in which people are paid to play videogames on behalf of others who want their game character to reach a certain level (Zhang & Fung 2014). At another end of the spectrum, there is the tax avoidance of global media corporations, which undermines the public services and infrastructure available to their workers. There is the exploitation of those who assemble our devices, and of those who produce the raw materials that are used in their manufacture. There is the exploitation of those who work in the creative industries, and whose labour is to create ideas and concepts that can be turned into intellectual property by someone else. And there is also a complex literature that argues our very use of Facebook or similar platforms in itself constitutes unpaid labour.

The raw materials of our communications devices may be extracted at considerable human and environmental cost. The smartphones, tablets and laptops that we use to check our Facebook notifications or to *like* our friend's new Instagram post are made of metals and minerals that have been mined in Latin America, Asia or Africa under conditions that would perhaps make us drop our devices if we were to see them for ourselves. For example, the mining industry of the Democratic Republic of Congo, which is a key source of one fundamental mineral used in the manufacture of media devices, is reportedly dominated by mercenary-run, military-backed mining operations that have been known to control their workforce through slavery, rape and mutilation (Maxwell & Miller 2012: 93–4).

The workers who use these raw materials to assemble our devices may do so under grim conditions, such as those reported for workers employed by Foxconn factories in China (Fuchs 2014a: 182–99). Foxconn is the fifth largest corporate employer in the world, with a workforce of over a million people who assemble the smartphones and tablet devices that so many use to access social media, including the iPhone and iPad, and other glamorous convergent devices produced for Amazon, Microsoft, Sony, Nintendo and various phone companies. But the conditions under which these devices are manufactured are in stark contrast to the worlds of stylish pleasure and rewarding communication invoked by the adverts for these brands. Fuchs (2014a) offers a sobering list of the names of young employees of Foxconn who committed suicide in 2010 by jumping from company buildings. Foxconn wrapped its workers' dormitories with nets to dissuade copycat suicides. Researchers interviewing Foxconn workers have underlined this cluster of suicides with reports of horror stories of harsh conditions, hours and management (see the website of the Hong-Kong-based workers' rights organization 'Students and Scholars Against Corporate Misbehaviour' at http://sacom.hk). Jack Linchuan Qiu (2012) writes of visiting numerous injured Foxconn workers in hospital who had lost their fingertips producing digital media devices – a cruel accident with a bitter twist when so many of those devices use touchscreens.

Meanwhile, the media environment of which social media have become such an important part is an increasingly precarious one for anyone trying to start or develop a career (Deuze 2007). Unpaid internships more and more replace the paid internships that have themselves replaced entry-level jobs (Ross 2013). Those who do have jobs to maintain find that networked digital communications penetrate the walls that used to separate work from home. Social media tools do not just bring together public and personal communication, but they also bring together the 'public' time we spend on the job with the 'personal' time we reserve for ourselves. Melissa Gregg (2011) coins the harrowing phrase *presence bleed* to capture the ways in which communications mean that work tasks and demands can no longer be confined to specific workplace locations or scheduled hours, and to capture the accompanying sense of anxiety. Can you ignore the 11 pm email from your boss, if she can see you're awake because you're posting on Facebook? Moreover, the creative industries of which social media are a part, practise a particular form of exploitation of their own. The creative industries are those that produce intellectual property (DCMS 2001, Hartley 2005, Hartley *et al.* 2013). They take their workers' creativity, talent and ideas – their words, their images, their code – as their raw materials, and transform these into copyrights and patents to be controlled for the financial benefit of their shareholders (Wark 2004).

There is also a prominent line of argument that to use social media is to provide unpaid labour for the social media firm (different perspectives on this can be found in Miller 2009, Gauntlett 2011a, Arvidsson & Colleoni 2012, Fuchs 2014b, 2015b, and Bolaño & Vieira 2015). This position asserts that social media firms are able to realize profits because their users create all the content for free, so this makes those users into exploited workers. This line of argument draws upon Dallas Smythe's 1981 discussion of TV viewers at the peak of the broadcast era. Smythe argued (correctly, in my view) that TV audiences are a commodity, and that TV networks provide programming in order to attract audiences that they can sell to advertisers. He also argued (incorrectly, in my view) that watching TV constitutes unpaid labour, and that as viewers we are doubly exploited, as both commodity and uncompensated worker. His argument begins to strain when it requires that the commodity is also labouring at the same time. Certain types of work do involve the person doing the labour also being the commodity: sex workers or slaves, for example; but sex work or slavery seem extreme analogies to apply to people sitting down to watch *Doctor Who*. The argument that the viewer is a commodity is a solid conclusion that can be drawn from looking at the relationship between the viewer and the TV network. But the argument that the viewer is an unpaid labourer, in contrast, does not look at that relationship. Instead, it starts with unpaid labour as its conclusion, because it wants to argue that Marx's analysis of surplus value applies, and so then tries to extend it back to the TV viewer as its premise.

To extend Smythe's analysis to social media likewise requires us to accept that what we do on social media is best understood as labour in the first place. And it likewise involves starting from the conclusion and then working backwards to the users and their daily interactions with a service like Facebook. I have a lot of sympathy for arguments that social media exploit their users, as I'll argue below and again in Chapter 6, but that relationship is not best characterized in terms of labour. To use Facebook is to become Facebook's commodity, not to become part of its workforce. Facebook users are the raw material for the product that Facebook sells, which is information about those users. There is certainly an element of exploitation in this arrangement, as I'll discuss further below. And there are elements of risk for the users, who are unable to be confident that their data is safe with Facebook (we'll return to this in Chapter 5). In terms of affect and meaning, and pleasure and engagement and a sense of connection with one's friends, many people may feel that allowing Facebook to use their data for ads is a decent bargain. My concern in this chapter is that they be clear about the nature and terms of that bargain.

Critical Discourse Analysis and Symbolic Power

Facebook has built a formidable business and number of users. Its interface has very often allowed the company to keep growing. In part, this comes down to the uniform, neutral design of the page, with everyone's Timeline built on the same template. This offered a point of contrast with MySpace at the time of its brief dominance, as MySpace users could customize the look of their page by tweaking its code or pasting in add-ons that often gave the site a garish tone; it was fun, but it wasn't going to draw one in five of the world's population to join in. The downside, though, is that Facebook's uniform design can be seen as enforcing what Jaron Lanier has called 'multiple-choice identities' (Lanier 2010: 48), as each user's self-presentation of personal identity becomes a matter for drop-down menus and lists of 'favourite quotes'.

Other important dimensions of Facebook's interface include its choice of key words. The use of *share* is one strategic success, and I'll explore why below, but so too are the choices of *like* and *friend*. The choice of *like* seems obvious, even inevitable, with hindsight. But as Pariser in *The Filter Bubble* points out, it was a choice made from among options:

> the team that developed the Like button originally considered a number of options – from stars to a thumbs up sign (but in Iran and Thailand, it's an obscene gesture). For a month in the summer of 2007, the button was known as the Awesome button. Eventually, however, the Facebook team gravitated toward Like, which is more universal. (Pariser 2011: 149)

Friend, similarly, offers positive and universal connotations, just as *like* does. This choice was not an innovation of Facebook's, but still offered the company an advantage over those opting for *contacts, connections, followers* or *buddies* instead. This advantage comes not just from the positive connotations of *friend*, but also from the lack of precision with which that word is often used. The word *friend* is malleable and often ambiguous in many contexts, not just on Facebook (Bucher 2013, Lambert 2013). But Facebook has made its meaning into something that every user now has to negotiate as they weigh up whether to accept invitations or whether this or that individual should get to see their photos. danah boyd highlighted the layered ambiguities of the word *friend* in an early analysis of social media:

> What constitutes a friend? In everyday vernacular, a friend is a relationship that involves some degree of mutual love or admiration. Some people exclude sexual partners and family members from this category while others talk about how such an individual is also a friend in order to indicate a degree of trust. For sociologists, friendship is an informal category without clear boundaries (like 'co-workers') or mutual responsibilities (like 'family'). (boyd 2006: unpaginated)

As with *friend* and *like*, the apparently simple and positive meaning of an everyday word such as *share* becomes bound up in a network of ambiguities and strategic nuances as it becomes a more central part of Facebook's interface and public presentations. Each of these words is a crucial part of how Facebook represents itself to the world.

How, then, does this entity which has grown in just over ten years to engage over a billion people represent itself to the world? This chapter examines a key Facebook text by using tools from Critical Discourse Analysis (CDA) (Fairclough 1995, 2003, Garrett & Bell 1998, Hansen & Machin 2013, Hodge & Kress, 1993, Jäger 2001, Wodak 2008). CDA is an established qualitative approach that offers a range of powerful mechanisms through which to identify how particular effects are achieved through discourse, defined here as 'socially constructed knowledges of (some aspect of) reality' (Kress & van Leeuwen 2001: 4). While its exponents most often frame CDA as a means to uncovering the ideological elements of texts, this chapter considers not ideology, but rather how Facebook represents itself as an instance of *symbolic power* relations.

Symbolic power, for Pierre Bourdieu, is 'a power of constructing reality' (Bourdieu 1991: 166). It's the ability to persuade, to endorse, to define, to name and in so doing to influence others (Thompson 1995). It is, as again Bourdieu has it, the business of 'making people see and believe' (Bourdieu 1991: 170). James Carey once argued that reality is 'a scarce resource' – scarce, he went on, because 'so few command the machinery for its determination. Some get to speak and some to listen, some to write and some to read, some to film and some to view' (Carey 1989: 87). In the social media environment, a quarter of a century on from Carey's observation, the capacity to communicate to various kinds of public is now much more widely distributed. But its distribution is uneven and unequal. Large media organizations with the resources on the scale of a Facebook are able to exercise disproportionate resources of symbolic power.

Melucci argues that in a society in which information is central, 'the power of information is essentially the *power of naming*' (Melucci 1996: 228, emphasis in original). It's in this way that the news industry, for instance, tries to define for us the way the world is by nominating which stories, which issues and which perspectives we should be thinking about each day. With the strategic use of *share* in so many of its activities, Facebook is engaged in efforts to name and define the daily communicative practices of its billion users on its own terms, using its enormous resources of symbolic power to define the scarce resource of reality for its users. So the word *share* matters.

A word, first, about what Critical Discourse Analysis is and how it's useful for understanding the way a major social media firm represents itself to the world through its uses of the word *share*. For Fairclough (1995), CDA has three dimensions – the analysis of texts; the analysis of discourse practice ('processes of text production, distribution and consumption', p. 2); and analysis of 'discursive events as instances of sociocultural practice' (ibid.). In this chapter, I don't engage with processes of textual production. Rather, I draw upon the approaches to textual and discourse analysis presented in Fairclough (2003) and Jäger (2001), and

I augment these with specific concepts of lexical and grammatical analysis drawn from Fowler (1991) and Hansen and Machin (2013).

What this means in practice, is that I address a series of questions to the text. I ask about the choices of words, or lexical level, first of all. I ask about how those words are combined through larger syntactic and grammatical choices at the level of the paragraph. I also consider not only what is actually present in the text, but also what has been omitted, elided or – and this is crucial – assumed (Fairclough 1995: 5). And I ask about the intertextual relations of the text with others. Textual analysis combines linguistic and intertextual analyses. Fairclough (1995: 189) argues for the importance of analysing intertextuality in order to understand the relationships between texts and their various social contexts. The intertextual bridges the gap between text and context, and the intertextual qualities of a text are made manifest in that text's language. And this allows us to trace meanings across more than one text. 'Any text that has slept with another text', observes Robert Stam, 'has necessarily slept with all the texts the other text has slept with' (Stam 2000: 202).

So my discussion below summarizes the answers to the questions I asked of certain key texts produced by Facebook. These were questions at the lexical, textual and intertextual levels. Each of the Facebook texts discussed below is of course intended to promote Facebook to various constituencies, so the analysis is not intended to reveal *what* Facebook is doing (promoting itself) but rather *how* it accomplishes its self-promotion. At the *lexical* level, I wanted to consider which word choices, or patterns of word choices, are most significant in suggesting preferred meanings to the reader. I also wanted to think about how generic, aggregate or pluralized terms (such as *people*) suggest or elide different meanings. At the *textual* level, I asked how the relationships between clauses, and those between sentences and paragraphs, contribute to suggesting preferred meanings. I looked at who or what is represented as *acting*, and who or what as *being acted upon*, and whether there are significant uses of passive verbs, or of nouns changed into verbs (both of which can hide who's responsible for doing the action, which would be revealed by an active verb). I asked how the text expresses degrees of certainty. I asked especially about what kinds of assumption or presupposition structure the text, and what kinds of power relationships these suggest. And I asked what's missing or omitted. And at the *intertextual* level, I asked about things like: the genre of the text; about how certain elements recur in other texts and how they change; and about how non-lexical elements (such as colour, design, image, audio, moving image, hyperlinks) contribute to creating meaning. The results of all this are brought together and discussed below when I explore what we can see if we ask these questions of Facebook's own self-description, its 'mission statement'.

Facebook's Mission

Facebook's mission statement is a very important text, through which Facebook represents itself to the world in its own self-description on its own website:

> Founded in 2004, Facebook's mission is to give people the power to share and make the world more open and connected. People use Facebook to stay connected with friends and family, to discover what's going on in the world, and to share and express what matters to them. (http://newsroom.fb.com/Key-Facts)

This text appears in a section of the site headed 'Newsroom', reached by following the 'About' link on Facebook's own Facebook page. The design and interface are the same uniform blues and greys that characterize each individual's basic Timeline. And even though almost everything else on Facebook is clickable, this mission statement contains no hyperlinks. It stands alone. These are just two sentences, but they tell us a lot about what is important in how the company presents itself. They tell us about its relationship with its users, and what it chooses to omit or elide. These two sentences invoke a model of a world, and they self-consciously present Facebook as an articulation of that world.

In the first sentence, the subject is *Facebook*, which has a *mission*. It seeks to *give people the power* and to *make the world more open and connected*. In the second sentence, the subject is *People*, which is the most general and perhaps the most neutral term available in this context – not *users*, because that would construct a different kind of relationship with Facebook here. And *users* would be only a subset of *people*, whose very global quality makes it an attractive choice of word for the company. And not *customers* or *clients*, because Facebook is a business-to-business operation, whose customers are advertisers, marketers and developers, not those who use it each day to *stay connected* or to *share and express*. *People*, in this statement, *use Facebook* – there is no mention of Facebook using people.

What's more, those uses that people are said here to make of Facebook are presented in a very generalized fashion. They omit almost all of the nuances that make the network such a fascinating space for so many of its users. Those users are not just using Facebook to *stay connected*, *discover* or *to share and express what matters*. They are also flirting, cheating or stalking; hooking up or falling out; bickering, flaming or trolling; boasting, bullying or belittling; conforming to peer and social pressures; marketing, selling or spamming; idly or dully killing time; or any of a theoretically infinite range of communicative interactions that Facebook here distils to three.

Another important thing to note about this mission statement is that Facebook is not identified as a profit-making company. Instead, it presents itself as an institution with a *mission*, and proudly leads with the date it was *founded*, in a style that speaks less of new tech firms and more of venerable institutions such as Harvard (where Facebook itself was started). Rather than identifying Facebook as a commercial operation, the relationship between the two sentences frames the platform as a public good. The first revolves around the things that Facebook does for people, the second around the uses that people find for Facebook. Any reference to Facebook as a commercial entity is elided. If this sounds as though it doesn't matter, then consider how differently the mission statement would read if Facebook were explicitly identified as a commercial operation:

> Facebook Inc.'s mission is to give people the power to share.

A simple commutation test on the word *mission* underlines this:

> Facebook's *business model* is to give people the power to share.
> Facebook *generates revenue* by giving people the power to share.
> Facebook *makes money* by giving people the power to share.

Each of these would be an accurate description of how the company works, and would be a defensible alternative to the chosen term *mission*. But each would construct the relationship between Facebook and its users in a very different way.

Why does this matter? It matters because Facebook is always careful to frame its relationship with its users as a matter of *choice* and one built on the strategic lexical selection of *share*. Facebook sells to advertisers the information that we have *chosen to share* with the company. But the company presents itself as operating for different reasons and in a different pattern of relations with its users – it *gives* them things, rather than *takes* from them; people *use* Facebook, rather than *are used by it*. Of course, it's unlikely that many of Facebook's users imagine the company operates entirely out of altruism; many of those billion+ users may have quite sophisticated understandings of its use of advertising and their personal information. Nevertheless, their uses of the platform, and the choices they make in relation to it, take place within what Facebook constructs as a discourse of altruistic and visionary utopianism. Those uses and choices are claimed to be part of a *mission* to *give people the power to share* and *make the world more open and connected.*

Facebook is the main example in this chapter, but it's not unique: rather, it's a major part of the broader sharing industry of social media. The mission statement of this industry is a genre in its own right. And those of other social media firms resonate with Facebook's in certain key ways. Here are four major examples of the genre. Notice how much they share.

YouTube

Launched in May 2005, YouTube allows billions of people to discover, watch and share originally-created videos. YouTube provides a forum for people to connect, inform, and inspire others across the globe and acts as a distribution platform for original content creators and advertisers large and small. (https://www.youtube.com/yt/about)

LinkedIn

Our mission is simple: connect the world's professionals to make them more productive and successful. When you join LinkedIn, you get access to people, jobs, news, updates, and insights that help you be great at what you do. (https://www.linkedin.com/about-us?trk=hb_ft_about)

Twitter

Our mission: To give everyone the power to create and share ideas and information instantly, without barriers (https://about.twitter.com/company)

Instagram

Instagram is a fun and quirky way to share your life with friends through a series of pictures. Snap a photo with your mobile phone, then choose a filter to transform the image into a memory to keep around forever. We're building Instagram to allow you to experience moments in your friends' lives through pictures as they happen. We imagine a world more connected through photos. (https://instagram.com/about/faq/#)

These all make similar claims and use similar language to the Facebook example. All promise global reach – *the world, billions of people, across the globe, the world's professionals, everyone, a world more connected, without barriers.* Of these examples, all use *share*, except LinkedIn, taking advantage of the word's many possible nuances, from sharing-as-publishing (YouTube, Twitter) to sharing-as-phatic-communication (Instagram). And all use *connect*, except Twitter, combining connotations of networking and communication. All of these mission statements highlight possibilities of the new – users will *discover* and *inspire*; they will get *insights* and *transform* images into memories *to keep around forever.* Of the five, only YouTube acknowledges the purpose of all this – advertising. And even here, YouTube elides certain key details, stating only that it *acts as a distribution platform* for advertisers, rather than selling those advertisers access to its users.

Facebook's mission statement, like the others above, is an artefact of promotional culture. So of course it presents Facebook as the solution to a series of implied problems. These implied problems rest upon an important series of assumptions. Fairclough (2003: 55–61) distinguishes between three different kinds of assumption: *existential* assumptions (the presupposition that something exists); *propositional* assumptions (the presupposition that something can or will be or indeed is the case); and *value* assumptions (presuppositions about what is desirable or good). Value assumptions are a clear mechanism for the exercise of symbolic power, and Facebook's mission statement is built upon a sequence of such assumptions. Every key clause of its two sentences responds to unspoken assumptions about what is good and desirable.

The implicit problem in the first sentence is that the world is insufficiently open and connected because people lack the *power to share.* The solution is Facebook. In the second sentence, there are three implicit problems – people need a way to stay connected, people need a way to find out what's going on, people need a way to express themselves – the solution to each of which is Facebook. This matters because of the ways in which it frames Facebook's users in relation to the company's business model, and how *the power to share* is at the heart of this. The language of the mission statement asks us to accept the assumption that people do not have the power to share and need Facebook to give it to them; and it asks us to accept the assumption that sharing on Facebook will indeed make the world more open and connected; and to accept the assumption that a more open and connected world would be a good thing. The assumptions pile up in the second sentence – that people are unable to stay properly connected with family and friends without the service; that Facebook is a key means of learning about the world; and that the things that people share on Facebook are indeed those things that matter to them. Each of these implicit value assumptions establishes the ground on which Facebook seeks to persuade the reader of its importance.

To focus in more detail on just one of these, the value assumption that *open* is a good thing and that it pairs naturally with *connected* is a distinct strategic choice. There is much in digital culture that makes use of positive connotations of *open*, from open access journals to open source software. But in these cases, *open* has a specific adjectival function to modify a particular term in the name of a particular practice. In contrast, in Facebook's mission statement, *open* has a much broader adjectival function, modifying *the world*. But the value assumption that a *more open* world is a desirable thing depends on just what is being opened. Would this more open world include open medical records? Open voting histories? Open bank accounts? The revelations facilitated by whistle-blower Edward Snowden of US security agencies' systematic, wholesale and indiscriminate hoovering of electronic communications worldwide could be held up as one example of a very different vision of a *more open* world (and we'll come back to that example in Chapter 5).

Facebook's mission statement is marked by carefully achieved effects of clarity and persuasive force. But there is one intriguing ambiguity in the first sentence. The relationship between the two clauses joined by that first *and* is open to more than one reading: *Facebook's mission is to give people the power to share and make the world more open and connected*. Does that first *and* mean that Facebook's mission has two distinct components: not only (a) giving people the power to share, but also (b) making the world more open and connected? Or does it mean that making the world more open and connected is a causal consequence of giving people the power to share? Or that sharing and making the world more open are consequences of the same power (*the power to share and make*)? Mark Zuckerberg resolves the ambiguity in a 2010 blog post by writing 'When you share more, the world becomes more open and connected' (quoted in Kennedy 2013: 130). The value assumption that posting on Facebook in itself makes the world a better place is both a breathtaking proposition and a strong example of the exercise of symbolic power, as Facebook attempts to redefine *share* for its own commercial purposes.

Mission Creep

This section of this chapter elaborates on the intertextual dimensions of Facebook's mission statement by considering how its key elements iterate and recur throughout different aspects of the company's public communications. Three texts have been chosen to illustrate how Facebook reframes its mission for different imagined audiences. First, for journalists, as it presents a new development in a media release. Second, for readers of *Wired* magazine, as one kind of general public, if one with an elevated degree of interest in media and technology. And third, for its shareholders, as it frames its business in its first annual report.

Media Release

In a media release of 10 April 2013 (Lindsay & Yung 2013), Facebook announced new affordances which allow users to include a range of emoticons within a status update and to have these link to other Facebook pages maintained by products or brands:

> Starting this week, people can express what they're watching, reading, listening to, eating, drinking or how they're feeling in status updates.
> For example, if you share that you're watching a movie like *Jurassic Park*, your post will contain the movie icon and a link to the movie's page.

In other words, an individual user's status update can now incorporate branded advertising. This is not made explicit, but is instead presented in the language of Facebook's mission statement – *express* and *share* – and positions the company as fulfilling an unmet need. Before *this week*, the text implies, it was not possible for users to express what they were doing or how they were feeling by writing those things in the status box. Again, Facebook is the solution to an unimagined problem. Facebook again presents itself as a public good without any apparent explicit means or need to generate income through the provision or imposition of the kinds of service introduced in this text.

Magazine Interview

In a 2013 interview with Steven Levy of *Wired* magazine to promote Facebook's smartphone Home platform, Zuckerberg speaks of his company's 'social sharing mission' (Levy 2013). Here again *sharing* is a *mission*. And here again what is actually being discussed is in fact a highly competitive business model:

> One of our big challenges over the next few years will be figuring out our relationships with companies that clearly have the same kind of social sharing mission.

In the interview, Zuckerberg builds an analogy with the widely understood computing maxim known as Moore's Law, through which technological advances enable processing power to double roughly every two years. In comparison, he describes Facebook's *law of sharing*:

> our equivalent of Moore's law, which states that the average amount of information that a person shares doubles every year or so.

And he elaborates:

> Sharing is not just about status updates doubling every year. It's made up of all these different trends. In the beginning, people shared by filling out basic information in their profiles. Then we made it so that people could update their status. Then came photos. Now people are sharing through apps like Spotify. We talk about the Moore's law of sharing, but we never meant that all this will happen on Facebook – it will happen in the world. Our challenge is to make that happen on Facebook.

To let the Biblical echoes of 'In the beginning' pass without further comment, Zuckerberg here presents Facebook not as driving these practices, but as responding to them. Facebook, in this view, is not acting but is being acted upon, as though attempting to meet a public demand that exists in the abstract but which has been without a vehicle for its realization before now. This is difficult to accommodate alongside the company's historical pattern of pushing the limits of the acceptable, and then climbing down when user push-back makes it tactically advisable to do so.

Annual Report to Shareholders

In May 2012, Facebook went public, and its first annual report to its resulting shareholders was made available in January 2013. It's a significant document in Facebook history. It opens with a one-page statement from Mark Zuckerberg, which rephrases and restates the company's mission statement in its second paragraph:

> Our guiding compass is our mission: to give people the power to share and make the world more open and connected. This is why we are here. We try to help you stay connected with everyone you care about, give you a voice to share what's important to you, and hopefully make the world a little smaller as a result. (Facebook 2013: 3)

The text once again frames Facebook as the solution to implicit problems, using phrases such as *we can help, our mission* and *new opportunities to serve the world in new ways*. It once again frames Facebook as a public good rather than a public company, using phrases such as *we can help connect, help everyone in the world get connected* and *our guiding compass is our mission*.

But the full 500-word text is significant for what it makes explicit to the company's shareholders that it withholds from other audiences of its other public-facing statements. In the verbs it uses this time, Facebook is the actor for this audience, not the acted upon. In reviewing the company's year, Zuckerberg reiterates terms such as *we connected, we transformed* and *we transitioned*. This time, in this context, the company is not responding to unmet needs, but is the initiative-taking actor. This is communicated with a high degree of certainty and persuasive force, so that interacting with others through technology is expressed as *It's natural and it's how we're wired*. Above all, and unlike in the company's mission statement, or the other texts discussed above, here Zuckerberg is explicit about the company's business model. To use Facebook, he writes, is to *join the modern knowledge economy*:

> We feel it is a great opportunity – as well as our responsibility – to help everyone in the world get connected and join the modern knowledge economy. We can establish Facebook as one of the great economic engines of our time. Small businesses will be able to acquire new customers and build deeper relationships than ever before. Great brands will be better able to tell their stories and build meaningful connections with consumers. E-commerce services will be able to sell products inline as millions of people discuss them. Developers will have the tools to remake every product category and deliver new experiences to people everywhere. (Facebook 2013: 3)

So there is a significant difference between the ways in which Facebook represents itself to different imagined publics. It frames itself as responsive, offering a public service as its mission, in its own public statements, including its own Facebook page and in interviews. But it frames itself as active and dynamic, driving the modern knowledge economy with its database business model, in its statements to shareholders.

Facebook, then, articulates its identity to different imagined publics in different permutations of the same constituent terms. This is something that we all do in our own daily lives. Each of our identities works through the presentation of different aspects of ourselves in subtly different ways in different situations – some formal, some less so; some intimate, some remote; some serious, some not. 'I am large, I contain multitudes', as Whitman had it in *Song of Myself* (Whitman 1973: 88). As far back as the sixteenth century, Montaigne was exploring this sense in which each of our identities is plural:

> Every sort of contradiction can be found in me, depending upon some twist or attribute: timid, insolent; chaste, lecherous; talkative, taciturn; tough, sickly; clever, dull; brooding, affable; lying, truthful; learned, ignorant; generous, miserly and then prodigal – I can see something of all that in myself, depending on how I gyrate; and anyone who studies himself attentively finds in himself and in his very judgement this whirring about and this discordancy. (Montaigne 1993: 128)

We each choose to make certain elements of ourselves visible to certain people in certain situations, and we choose to reserve other elements of our identity from others in other situations (Goffman 1959, Meyrowitz 1985). Each of us manages, maintains and protects our own reputations as best we can. Each of us has to negotiate the challenges of 'trying to be in public without always being public', as Marwick and boyd (2014: 1052) have it. But Mark Zuckerberg himself, we may note, has spoken out against this fundamental dimension of social behaviour, on the grounds that it undermines his business model.

In *The Facebook Effect*, company biographer David Kirkpatrick describes Mark Zuckerberg repeating several times in an interview with him 'You have one identity'. Zuckerberg expands on this: 'The days of you having a different image for your work friends or co-workers and for the other people you know are probably coming to an end pretty quickly' (Kirkpatrick 2010: 199). This kind of 'context collapse' is indeed a contemporary concern (Wesch 2009, Marwick & boyd 2010), not least thanks to Facebook. But then Kirkpatrick quotes Zuckerberg as saying something more problematic: 'Having two identities for yourself is an example of a lack of integrity' (Kirkpatrick 2010: 199). Facebook's use of the key terms of its own identity – *share, mission, open, connected* – is consistent. But the degree to which the company is explicit about what these mean for its billion+ users and for the information that they reveal to Facebook is noticeably less consistent from one form of public address to another. Shareholders get a different message than people who share. Mark Zuckerberg may or may not consider this an example of a lack of integrity.

Conclusion

This chapter has examined Facebook as the leading exemplar of a new communications system built upon affordances and discourses of sharing. In Facebook's rise to pre-eminence, and its refinement of the data-mining advertising approach, we can see the contours of a new media model – the sharing industry. The ways in which this sharing industry is adopted and adapted by its users depend on the ways in which it is communicated to those users. And the ongoing controversies about each expansion of what users are expected to *share* through Facebook reveal the tensions and contests that characterize its relations with its billion+ users. In the ways that it represents itself to different kinds of particular imagined audiences, Facebook demonstrates what it is prepared to acknowledge and what it prefers to leave unspoken about its relations with those billion+ users. And it reveals its intentions towards the opinions and emotions, memories and images, messages and relationships that those users embed within Facebook each and every day.

Chapter 3

Remix Cultures

Here comes Pharrell, mouthing the words to his song 'Happy', stepping towards the camera as it tracks him down an alleyway. And now here come lots and lots of other people as well, all singing, dancing and clapping along with the song, one after the other, stepping towards the camera that endlessly pulls backwards as though to draw still others into the frame – a bearded guy out for a run; a woman in a pink dress, clutching a tiny dog; a laundry worker folding towels; all caught up in their fleeting 'Happy' moment as part of Pharrell's video. But now, here come yet more people, all starring in their own DIY versions of that music video – thousands of them, lip-syncing the words as they dance through the streets of their own towns, remixing the original clip into thousands of new contexts. In 2013, Pharrell Williams had three of the biggest hit singles of the year, collaborating with Daft Punk on 'Get Lucky' and with Robin Thicke on 'Blurred Lines'. But it was the music video for his own song 'Happy' that went on to generate one of the biggest internet memes of that year, with thousands of remixed versions of the original video created, shared and circulated across social media.

The original video appeared in November 2013, when Williams put up the website *24 Hours of Happy*, claiming its clever editing as the first 24-hour music video (the 24-hour version of 'Nyan Cat' had got there two years before him, but it was still an interesting device). A more conventional four-minute video followed, and it was this that was answered by thousands of video responses, in which people made their own 'Happy' clips. The original clip has some clear elements that are easy to reproduce: the black-on-yellow title card at the beginning, the backwards tracking camera movement and the song itself as both soundtrack and structure. The 'Happy' video connects with some of the fundamental elements of YouTube's popular culture (Burgess & Green 2009). Viewing videos is not the only draw for many YouTube users, who also use the platform as a space for comment and discussion, for curation of favourite videos, for the performance of personal taste and for the making and sharing of video responses to other clips – videos that directly refer to their original source, acknowledging this source as a call to creative action. 'Happy' offers an excellent resource for such video responses: the original video of passers-by dancing in the street provides a clear template for responses, requiring no special choreography skills, while as a music video the soundtrack comes built-in, even indicating peaks and climaxes. The yellow title card can be used to announce the location of the clip's creators, while hashtags simplify the practice of promoting and circulating a 'Happy' video, enabling its creators to situate it within this existing context for others to find.

Many of these response videos are themed around a particular city or place, with the typical title 'We are happy from Sydney' (or Paris or Abuja and so on and on). One website tries to collate all these response videos on a single clickable world map; as of July 2015, this site had linked to almost 2,000 versions of 'Happy' from over 150 countries, from Quito to Khartoum, from Ulan Bator to Glasgow (http://wearehappy-from.com). And as well as the geographically themed 'we are happy from …' versions, there are still more 'Happy' videos that take a different angle on remixing the clip. There is a version from the planet Tatooine – or at least according to the members of the Tunisian *Star Wars* fan society. There is a whole sub-genre of versions recorded within the game *Minecraft*. There are porn versions (Rule 34). There are versions built around dancing dogs, and a rather larger number starring cats. And there is one with the now very familiar music edited out of Pharrell's own version, and with ambient sound effects such as dancers' footsteps added instead.

Each of these is an example of the genre that Vimeo founder Jakob Lodwick named 'lip dubs' – filmed performances of non-professional singers and dancers miming to well-known songs for sharing online (Shifman 2014: 105–7). Some of these coordinate many hundreds of people, and work as tourism promotion for their location or recruitment promotion for their university (try the version of 'Don't Stop Me Now' by students at Trinity College, University of Western Australia); others focus on a small group of friends (the 'Happy' video from Cali in Colombia features just two guys). One of the most popular videos of YouTube's early days was a bedroom lip dub of the Pixies song 'Hey' performed by two young Israeli women called Tasha and Dishka (who some years later went on together to direct the official video for a Pixies single). At their best, these lip dub performances evoke a feeling of shared joy; they both make possible and record a shared participatory experience.

As a music video, 'Happy' is of course a commercial tool: an artefact of promotional culture designed to maximize sales of the recording, which was itself originally created to promote the animated film *Despicable Me 2*, on whose soundtrack it first appeared. But the range of responses that the video has provoked point to a more complex set of motivations to join in. 'Happy' works through not only being adopted but also adapted. Some user-created 'Happy' videos may be made just for the lulz, but other versions are carefully crafted promotional showcases for a particular town's tourist industry (I don't just want to visit the city of Split in Croatia after watching its take on the song – I want to live there). And still others use the format to comment on, critique or participate in a political situation in their own country.

In some cases, this is deliberate and explicit – the 'Happy British Muslims' version; the 'Porto (un)Happy' version from Brazil, designed to highlight the run-down state of the city even as billions were spent on stadia for the World Cup; or the 'Happy from Gaza' version. But in other cases, participants in the 'Happy' craze found themselves caught up in political complications that they were unlikely to have seen coming. In May 2014, a group of six young Iranians uploaded a 'Happy from Tehran' clip to YouTube. The clip is entirely typical of the genre, with the six dancing and miming along with the song in and around a Tehran apartment building. Rather less typical of the genre was the police reaction, with all six, along with the director of their video, arrested on the same day for violating laws that ban women from appearing bare-headed and dancing with a partner of the opposite sex, and made to appear on state television confessing to their 'wrongdoing'. The arrests attracted international attention, with thousands on Twitter using the #freehappyiranians hashtag. Even the Iranian president Hassan Rouhani made a veiled comment, tweeting on 21 May 2014 a quote from one of his own speeches from the previous year: '#Happiness is our people's right. We shouldn't be too hard on behaviors caused by joy'. On 19 September 2014, the BBC reported that all involved had been given suspended sentences of six months to one year in jail and 91 lashes.

The circulation and adaptation of the thousands of remixed versions of Pharrell's 'Happy' video offer an example of an internet meme. Internet memes are easy to dismiss as trivial or frivolous or just plain silly. But the examples in the previous paragraph show that they can also become implicated in political actions. They are also a clear index of the ways in which ideas, texts and images are adopted, adapted and shared through social media and beyond. And internet memes show how certain creative strategies that were once considered radical or *avant-garde*, from collage and Situationist *détournement* to digital sampling, have now become some of the basic cultural practices of everyday social media interactions. This chapter explores internet memes as forms of text and cultural practice that are central to social media.

What's a Meme?

As the 'Happy' example shows, memes are not just something which people copy. Instead, they are something that people adapt for themselves, and that they then go on to share with others. A meme is not something that is done to people – it is something that people do. This fundamental dimension is missed by the common metaphor of *viral* in relation to this kind of online circulation. Media are not viruses; media texts and images are not viruses; ideas are not viruses. Rather, ideas, images and texts are things that people choose to make and share. Internet memes circulate so widely through social media because many different individuals in many different contexts find them meaningful and choose to make them, to share them with others, and in doing so to make both their memes and themselves visible. These people have not been infected with a virus – the texts and images and ideas that they circulate do not have some intrinsic infective capacity that people are powerless to resist. Instead, they're making a remix.

In this book, I use the word *remix* in a broad sense, to describe a wide range of ways in which people interact with ideas, images and texts. While *remix* may suggest music above all, it can also describe any of the ways in which we now take digital material from one context and set it in another. I'm not thinking here only of people mashing up music or video, but of more everyday and less ambitious uses of networked digital media as well. Adding a filter to your selfie for Instagram, for instance, or embedding a film clip on your Facebook Timeline both involve reworking existing material: in the former case, changing the image itself; in the latter, setting it in a fresh context that may change the meanings that can be made from either the clip or your Timeline. *Remix* offers a broader set of relevant connotations than other possible terms such as *edit* (which too strongly suggests cutting out or cutting back, and so excludes the various senses in which things can be expanded, augmented or multiplied) or Hartley's (2000) suggested *redaction* (which too strongly suggests censoring or blacking out).

Users of social media now share ideas, information, meanings – and noise – through networks of mediated sociality. Communication through social media is an unfinished process of circulation and connection, of relationships and associations. Each new link, *like* and *share* opens up different kinds of connectivity and different possibilities for meaning, and each makes possible different trajectories for further circulation to still other people. Each connection both establishes new relations between individuals and makes visible previously invisible connections. Internet memes are forms of easily remixed texts and images that are intrinsic to this social media environment. The metaphor of the *virus* is useless in helping us to understand this.

In *Spreadable Media*, Henry Jenkins, Joshua Green and Sam Ford propose the concept of 'spreadable' as an alternative to the metaphor of the virus. These authors' analysis is clear, that the contemporary media environment is characterized by what 'the people formerly known as the audience' do (Rosen 2006):

> The decisions that each of us makes about whether to pass along media texts – about whether to tweet the latest gaffe from a presidential candidate, forward a Nieman Marcus cookie recipe email, or share video of a shoplifting seagull – are reshaping the media landscape itself. (Jenkins *et al.* 2013: 1–2)

They propose that we think of this environment through the lens of their 'spreadability model', which is intended to include the technical resources that make content easy to share, the economics governing the extent to which such circulation is enabled or constrained, the textual qualities of widely shared texts, and the social networks through which people share (p. 4). In the contemporary media environment, they write: 'if it doesn't spread, it's dead' (p. 1). But wait. So if it *does* spread, does that mean it's alive? You know, like a *virus*? As a metaphor, *spreadable*, then, just like *viral*, locates the real action within the text itself. Some texts 'are spreadable', just like some texts 'go viral'. Their proposed new metaphor fails to relocate the action where it belongs, with the people who choose to share these texts. Texts don't spread themselves, just as they don't self-replicate like viruses. Rather, they are shared by people who find them meaningful, amusing, intriguing, cute or shocking, and make a choice to involve others in this experience. 'Spreadable media' doesn't capture this, because it doesn't focus our attention on the people, but on the media themselves.

The metaphor of the *virus* has always been bound up with the word *meme*, and both have their problems. But this chapter argues that meme, while originally a word that did not need to be invented, has developed to describe in a useful way something specific to the internet environment. To show this, it's important first to distinguish between the original definition of the word meme, and the more useful contemporary application of the term to particular internet phenomena. The word *meme* was first coined by zoologist Richard Dawkins (1976) in his book *The Selfish Gene*. In that book, explaining the *gene* as a unit of biological transmission, Dawkins proposed the word *meme* as an analogous cultural unit. Meme was to be: 'a noun which conveys the idea of a unit of cultural transmission, or a unit of *imitation*' (Dawkins 1976: 206, original emphasis). Examples of memes, in Dawkins's proposal, included things like clothes fashions, catch-phrases and melodies (p. 206). But these, strangely, somehow seemed to circulate by themselves:

> Just as genes propagate themselves in the gene pool by leaping from body to body via sperms or eggs, so memes propagate themselves in the meme pool by leaping from brain to brain via a process which, in the broad sense, can be called imitation. (Dawkins 1976: 206)

Many have taken Dawkins's definition at face value and without further question. A more recent discussion of the internet by John Naughton offers an explicit definition of meme – 'an infectious idea which replicates itself' – that also presents memes as reproducing without any apparent human input (Naughton 2012: 313). In her book *The Meme Machine*, psychologist Susan Blackmore (1999) developed Dawkins's idea further, moving from reproduction to zero in on imitation as the key element, and arguing that 'a meme is whatever it is that is passed on by imitation' (Blackmore 1999: 43). But as her use of 'whatever' in that quote suggests, there are very real difficulties in deciding what is to count as a meme. From the perspective of communication rather than zoology, we might in fact wonder why Dawkins saw this as a word that needed to be invented in the first place. Because rather than adding anything new or useful to our understanding of communication, Dawkins's *meme* most often works as an unacknowledged synonym of a perfectly good word that already existed and that still works just fine. That word is *idea*.

Take, for instance, this passage from Douglas Rushkoff's 1994 book *Media Virus*, which was an early adopter of the word meme in exploring its territory of cable TV and nascent online culture:

> Each meme, especially a new or 'mutant' meme, must find a carrier – a viral shell – capable of delivering it to ready individuals, even if they are in the minority. The mass media is understandably unwilling to provide passage for memes that will be unpopular with their audiences. They are in business. (Rushkoff 1994: 196)

Replace each use of *meme* in that passage with the word *idea*, and Rushkoff's point is not only unchanged but also much clearer. His use of the words 'viral shell' also points to the problematic biological equivalence that Dawkins established from the beginning between genes and memes. Human ideas are not viruses, and they do not 'propagate themselves … by leaping from brain to brain'. Rather, they circulate through being both adopted and adapted by people.

Another early adopter of the word in relation to the internet was Mike Godwin of lobby group the Electronic Frontier Foundation, who used it in the influential 1994 article in *Wired* magazine in which he proposed Godwin's Law. Godwin's Law has become a staple of internet culture, in its identification of one way in which online discussion threads are prone to develop: 'As an online discussion grows longer, the probability of a comparison involving Nazis or Hitler approaches one' (Godwin 1994). In Godwin's article, the tendency of people online to invoke Hitler or the Nazis in discussion with someone they disagree with is itself a meme. He explains the term in Dawkins's language:

> A 'meme,' of course, is an idea that functions in a mind the same way a gene or virus functions in the body. And an infectious idea (call it a 'viral meme') may leap from mind to mind, much as viruses leap from body to body. (Godwin 1994)

But his actual article goes on to point to something more interesting. He describes how his original 'Law' of the internet has been not only adopted but also adapted by many other people, offering variations and interpretations of his original idea. For instance, one common contemporary variation of Godwin's Law is often expressed, without the original language of mathematical probability, as 'first person to bring up the Nazis loses the argument'. This is an adaptation of the original, and this dimension of people deliberately choosing to join in with the idea being shared and represented online, adapting it as well as adopting it, was to become a crucial aspect of the more contemporary sense of *internet meme*.

As the web environment developed, the usage of meme began to shift. Later in the 1990s, Canadian culture jammers Adbusters began to emphasize the word *meme* in a new sense, one which can now be seen as the emergence of the distinctly different sense of *internet meme*. Adbusters run a magazine, a popular website and various political events and campaigns, such as November's annual Buy Nothing Day. They would play a central role in precipitating the Occupy Wall Street events of 2011, to which we'll return in Chapter 6. Adbusters helped to move the meaning of *meme* away from being a rather unnecessary new synonym for *idea*, towards being a label that captured certain kinds of behaviour in the networked digital media environment. At times, true, their use of the word was a bit daft – Adbusters' founder Kalle Lasn, for example, wrote of how 'meme warfare' had become 'the geopolitical battle of our information age' (Lasn 1999: 123), and of the need to identify something called 'macromemes' and 'metamemes', without which, whatever they are, 'a sustainable future is unthinkable' (p. 124). But Adbusters were also a key group in promoting the idea of culture jamming, which connects in important ways with the contemporary sense of internet meme.

Culture jamming means taking a familiar sign and reshaping it into a question mark. Culture jammers take existing images and propose alternative meanings by editing, amending or remixing those images either with analogue tools (scissors, paint, stickers, marker pens) or digital ones (Photoshop). Culture jamming is not just graffiti, but is about political engagement and cultural negotiation. It's a practice with a pre-web history (Dery 1993, Joyce 2005), but which found a natural home online in a symbolic environment in which any image could be copied, edited and pasted into a new context, so calling into question both that original image and that new context. It can be understood as jamming in the traffic sense of getting in the way, but also as jamming in the music sense of collaborative improvisation (Meikle 2007). This is the method of Situationist *détournement* that seeks to arrest the flow of meanings rather than just add in a few more. Adbusters are open about the influence on their projects of the Situationists and their leader Guy Debord. In the 1950s, Debord and Wolman distinguished between *minor* and *deceptive détournement*. A minor *détournement* is one in which the elements have no intrinsic importance, but rather derive that importance from the new context in which they are set; a deceptive *détournement* is one in which the remixed elements are themselves of some significance, significance which is stalled or questioned by their recombination.

Adbusters were significant in using the word *meme* in encouraging their readers to rework and remix media images – particularly from advertising – in order to highlight the political assumptions through which they work. And this practice offers a bridge from Dawkins's original coinage to the contemporary sense of *internet meme*, as something that users *do* – an active engagement with digital texts and images, a critical understanding of their rules and grammar, the sharing and circulation of remixed ideas and a sense that meanings are to be made, not just taken. The distinction between so-called 'viral' content, which becomes very popular very quickly by being circulated and shared from one person to the next, and internet memes, which are not only adopted but adapted and remixed is, then, an important one (Shifman 2012, Marwick 2013b).

It's in this sense that an internet meme is a shared representation of online interaction. The rules and structures of each instantly recognizable meme are a representation of the communication practices and the particular online space in which it was developed – 4chan, Tumblr, Reddit, YTMND or YouTube, for instance – so that each new meme emerges as an in-joke, in which more and more people are able to share as it circulates beyond the space of its initial online mediation. As it becomes more widely adopted and adapted, and others share in the joke, they in turn make it their own while also participating in something more public (Baym 2010). A meme may emerge from a photo of an individual (Ridiculously Photogenic Guy, Disaster Girl, Overly Attached Girlfriend), or from a reference to a fragment of popular culture (One does not simply walk into Mordor; This is Sparta; You know nothing, Jon Snow), or from reducing some celebrity or public figure to a single trope (Ryan Gosling won't eat his cereal, Kim Jong-un looking at things), or from riffs on a repeated animal character (Honey Badger don't care, I should buy a boat cat, IKEA monkey, Hipster Kitty) or from many other cultural templates. But in every case, each meme has its own rules and its own grammar. In some cases, for example, such as the language used in lolcats or doge memes, specific uses and misuses of English grammar are a fundamental element of the meme (*I can has cheezburger?*). An individual meme is a tiny genre of text in itself, and is also a kind of game that anyone can join in (Shirky 2010). And those generally simple rules provide a framework within which each internet meme can be remixed by new participants in new contexts. The rules of each game, each meme, are simple enough to be picked up immediately, and also clear enough to provide a definitional structure. So to draw all of this together in a definition – one that I developed together with internet scholar Victoria Esteves (Esteves & Meikle 2015) – internet memes are *shared, rule-based representations of online interactions that are not only adopted but also adapted by others.*

Doge memes, for example, have certain rules. They take as their base a particular photo of a Shiba Inu dog from Japan, and add captions to these in a selection of bright colours and in the widely derided Comic Sans font. These captions use a particular *doge* grammar: *very [noun], much [adjective], wow.* These basic rules-of-the-game – the breed of dog, the colour scheme, the font, the grammar – can then be remixed into infinite new contexts. So doge memes circulate from Reddit and Tumblr and 4chan to YouTube (where a search for 'doge meme' unlocks an Easter Egg which returns the search results in doge-coloured Comic Sans), to advertisements (some branches of Subway), to political campaigns (US candidates have tweeted doge-styled assaults on their opponents) and even to public information campaigns: the US Health Department adapted the doge rules for an insurance promotion early in 2014 (*Very benefits. Much affordable*).

These kinds of public use of a meme that had first developed as an in-joke in a particular context point to some of the tensions that always surround the commercialization of subcultural activity. The very garishness of some of the key elements of the doge meme illustrate what blogger Nick Douglas (2014) identifies as an online aesthetic that he calls 'Internet Ugly', which may be used as a tactic to deter commercial appropriation. This describes the deliberate amateurism of meme genres such as Rage Comics, the unpolished manipulation of images and the standardized use of unattractive fonts such as Impact in white letters or Comic Sans in multiple colours. He points out that before the rise of the internet: 'when someone had an idea they couldn't elegantly execute, they were usually left without an audience. The near-zero production and distribution cost of the internet removes the barrier' (Douglas 2014: 329–30). The like-and-share logic of social media also means that unfinished drafts and throw-away visual responses in comment threads can now be redistributed very widely through Facebook or Twitter or YouTube, giving the rough draft the status of a finished text. In spaces such as Tumblr, Reddit or 4chan, the conscious unsophistication of graphics and images can also be read as a deliberate distancing from the more established media, and from the adver-tisers and marketers who pick memes up for re-use in commercial contexts.

F*#%ing Memes, How Do They Work?

In November 2011, students demonstrating at the Davis campus of the University of California as part of the Occupy movement staged a sit-down protest on campus. Onlookers then filmed as campus police officer John Pike casually sauntered along the line of seated students and assaulted each in the face with his can of chemical spray. The distribution of this footage caused widespread outrage and the event was quickly incorporated into the news, and as a result triggered a range of internet memes. When a commentator on Fox News in the US suggested that chemical spray weapons are 'a food product, essentially', hundreds of people were prompted to post product reviews on Amazon of one commercially available can of pepper spray: 'Accept no substitutes when casually repressing students' reads the title of the review voted 'most helpful' by more than 6,000 people:

> When I feel threatened by students, no matter how unarmed, peaceful and seated they may be, I know that Defense Technology 56895 MK-9 Stream, 1.3% Red Band/1.3% Blue Band Pepper Spray

has got my back as I casually spray away at point blank range. It really is the Cadillac of citizen repression technology.

There are hundreds of similar posts (264 'positive reviews' and 87 'critical reviews'). Taken together, they are an internet meme. Each post adopts and adapts one or more of the core conventions of this online interaction – ironic praise for the product, sarcastic references to the Fox News item, and pointed commentary on Pike's behaviour. One particular photograph that captured an indelible image of Pike – overweight, armoured, spray-can held out to his side, nonchalant body language, caught in mid-step – was adopted into countless images that circulated across Tumblr, Facebook and other spaces, and remain easy to find. The range of contexts into which Pike's picture was edited illustrates the three basic logics of such remix-based internet memes.

First, images and texts can be brought together to highlight what they have in common, or how they *complement* each other, as in the example of Pike spraying the lone Chinese protestor facing down the line of tanks in Beijing in 1989, an image that draws parallels between different state responses to peaceful protests. This kind of remix works through *recognition*, prompting the viewer to make the implied connection between the original images that are being brought together, and so seeing each differently. Similar images have Pike spraying Anne Frank's gravestone and a copy of the US Constitution, or have Pike edited into Picasso's *Guernica* and Goya's *Third of May 1808*.

Second, such remixes can instead highlight the differences between the combined texts, drawing a *counterpoint* between them, as in the many images of Pike intervening in sports events or with pop culture fictional characters, with real conflict and violence counterpointed with performed simulations or with harmless scenarios very far from police abuse. Here the characteristic impulse is *irony*, as meanings are prompted by high-lighting the distance between an aggressive, armed police officer and Winnie the Pooh, the Wizard of Oz, or the Beatles' *Abbey Road* cover. And third, such remixes can be used to *subvert* an existing idea or a standard image, taking a sign that traditionally serves as a guide and instead reshaping it as a question mark, as in the image that morphs the photograph of Pike into the Statue of Liberty, with its instant connotations of democracy and liberty upended by this single image of contemporary policing.

Remix All the Things

To remix found material is one of the essential aspects of daily digital experience (Benkler 2006, Lessig 2008, Manovich 2009). Internet memes are one key manifestation of such cultures of remix, but they draw upon long cultural trajectories of storytelling and editing, of art and computing, of *avant-garde* culture and consumer electronics, of alternative and tactical media, of cultures of copy-and-paste. The apparently novel ways in which ideas and texts circulate in the networked digital media environment of the twenty-first century have long prehistories (Lessig 2006).

Take, for example, one small internet joke that circulated in 2009, from website *Holy Taco* to the more influential and widely read *Boing Boing*, and from there across the profiles of numerous individual users of other platforms. The example is a graphic that offers a retelling of key plot points from Homer's *Odyssey* as though told on Twitter (Alt 2009). So the escape from Calypso's island becomes 'THNX for the raft! Laters!'; the Sirens episode becomes 'Hot singing chicks! KTHXBAI!'; and the story of the encounter between Odysseus and the Cyclops is summed up as 'Just saw a dude with one eye!'. It's a characteristic internet joke, of a kind that many people share across social media. It takes familiar reference points and well-known stories, and puts them in a new context for new audiences, who may in turn set it into contexts of their own – their Facebook Timeline, their Twitter feed, their blog (or, as in my case, their book).

This kind of remix aesthetic plays out on more than one level. First, the author of the Homer parody is remixing one kind of found material into a new text; and second, that remixed text itself becomes found material for social media users to incorporate into their own presentations and performances of their self and their personal taste and humour. Some critics might find this all to be too trivial for words: Jaron Lanier, for example, dismisses this kind of remix activity as 'second-order expression' (Lanier 2010: 122). He contrasts such 'fragmentary reactions' with 'first-order expression', by which he means high-order creative works which are 'something genuinely new in the world'. But one problem with this criticism is identifying what is the genuinely new and what is the reaction.

Let's take the above example of Odysseus and his encounter with the Cyclops. We first meet Odysseus in Homer's *Iliad*, the story of sulking and tantrums in one episode of the Trojan War that is one beginning of the western literary tradition (the *Iliad* also, of course, connects with much wider and much older oral traditions of storytelling). Odysseus is not the central character of the *Iliad* (that would be Achilles). He's not the story's moral centre (that would be Priam). He's not its tragic figure (Hector), or its greatest leader (Agamemnon) or even the figure from the story that most people could probably name without reading it (Helen of Troy). Odysseus is none of those things. What he is instead is the smartest guy in the story. Odysseus is the guy who can talk his way into and out of anything. In Book II of the *Iliad*, he single-handedly talks the Greek forces into staying the course for the siege of Troy when it looks as though many are ready to give up, nine fruitless years in. And when the Greeks finally defeat the Trojans through the stratagem of the wooden horse, Odysseus is the leader of the men inside the horse, and the one who resists the tricks of the Trojans outside, as they inspect the horse for dubious human cargo.

The story of the Trojan Horse appears in flashback in the *Odyssey*, the character's spin-off sequel, which records his troubled journey home from Troy to his wife Penelope in Ithaca. His encounters in the middle books of the *Odyssey* are some of the most famous incidents in myth and literature, including the song of the Sirens and his meeting with the one-eyed cannibal giant Cyclops, Polyphemus. And while Odysseus can fight when he has to (wiping out a room full of antagonists towards the end of the *Odyssey*), and while he has to rely on the supernatural help of Athena and other Olympians in some of his tightest spots, for the most part he wins the day on his wits.

The Romans too were drawn to this character, whom they called Ulysses. Some eight hundred years or so after Homer, the Roman poet Virgil remixed and mashed up both *Iliad* and *Odyssey* in his own epic of Troy and of Mediterranean wanderings. Virgil's *Aeneid* is a remix of both Homeric epics, taking the war for Troy of the *Iliad* and the chaotic wanderings of the *Odyssey*, and recombining these into a new story for Rome. In Book III of the *Aeneid*, its hero Aeneas and his crew encounter the same Cyclops, Polyphemus, for themselves, and rescue one of Ulysses's men who had been left behind in the original episode. Virgil is working here with found material; he is taking the well known and well loved, and remixing it into a new text of his own, for a new context and a new time. So is the *Aeneid* call or response?

Odysseus/Ulysses figures in other classical works too, including Ovid's *Metamorphoses*. Ovid's book is another mashup, retelling every key Greek myth and every key Roman legend in a long, shifting cycle of some 250 stories, all retold through the single metaphor of transformation. Our figure's key appearance in Book XIII of Ovid's *Metamorphoses* is when Ulysses wins the armour of the dead Achilles in a contest of speeches, a duel of rhetoric, against the powerful warrior Ajax (whom Ulysses is far too smart to fight instead). Both Ulysses and Polyphemus appear in separate episodes of Book XIII, each giving a long speech to try to sway someone round to their point of view.

This wandering trickster hero, who outsmarts rather than outfights his opponents, has drawn the attention of writers, again and again and again, for almost 3,000 years. He is an ancestor of all such figures, from Gulliver to Huck Finn to *Doctor Who* (who met him in one early adventure when the TARDIS landed at Troy). The character appears again 1,300 years after the *Aeneid* in the Eighth Circle of Dante's Hell, and later in *Troilus and Cressida* by Shakespeare, a writer who knew a story worth remixing when he saw one. Meanwhile, Odysseus was still wandering the Mediterranean and beyond, reappearing in the stories of *The Thousand and One Nights*, in the guise of Sinbad the Sailor. In his Third Voyage, Sinbad and his crewmates are also captured by a cannibal giant, whom they despatch in the same way as Odysseus dealt with Polyphemus, although without the trickster element; not quite a Cyclops, Sinbad's monster first appears with two eyes, although he has none by the time Sinbad has finished with him.

In the twentieth century, James Joyce structured his *Ulysses* around the *Odyssey*, with Odysseus, his son Telemachus and wife Penelope recast as Leopold Bloom, Stephen Dedalus and Molly Bloom. Leopold Bloom's wanderings around the Dublin of 16 June 1904 parallel Odysseus's attempts to return to Ithaca – sometimes very clearly, sometimes not so much – and there is, of course, a dangerous encounter with a fearsome giant, this time in a pub, although Joyce's Citizen is no Cyclops, and the episode ends with the hurling of a biscuit tin instead of a giant boulder.

To tell stories is to retell stories. From Homer to Virgil, from Dante to Shakespeare, from the unknown authors of *The Thousand and One Nights* to the iconic figure of James Joyce, the elements of the story of Odysseus are told and retold. Which is the original and which the remix? Homer, after all, was part of a much older oral tradition, and would also have drawn upon and remixed stories and characters that were already well known. All of these versions trade in taking stories that readers will love or at least recognize, and retelling them for a new context and a new time. All of these versions trade in remixing the familiar with the strange – updating, upgrading, rebooting. This is not something distinctive to the historical treatment of Odysseus, but is a much wider cultural pattern.

We never tire, for instance, of the story of the youngster who learns that they have a powerful destiny. We learn all over again the story of their relationship with the older mentor who offers training in arts and skills; of their relationships with their best friend and with the romantic interest with whom they form an uncertain triangle. We learn anew of their testing through a series of challenges and trials, and of the final confrontation with the forces of evil in which they save the day and everyone in it. And whether you think this paragraph is about *Harry Potter* or *Star Wars* or *The Matrix* makes no difference. The basic moves and trajectory of the story are the same, the repertoire of elements is shared, the principal figures and their interactions recur in each of those series. And indeed they recur in many others as well, as the template of this archetypal story – Joseph Campbell's (1949) *The Hero with a Thousand Faces* – has become a staple of screenwriting manuals and Hollywood machinery, so that you might also have thought the paragraph was in fact about *Spiderman*, or *The Lion King*, or J.J. Abrams's rebooted *Star Trek* or – a female lead at last – *The Hunger Games*. The key thing is what elements are remixed into this story in each case – whether we get it with bickering robots and lightsabres, with boarding school protocol and magic wands, or with cyberpunk couture and *wushu* choreography. Stories are not just adopted, but are also adapted.

I'm not arguing that the *Aeneid* is just the same thing as an internet meme like Foul Bachelorette Frog or 'Fucking magnets, how do they work?' But I am arguing that the remix impulses behind those memes are part of a much older pattern of cultural practices, and that we can locate the *Aeneid* within that pattern too. Such memes are a key part of the social media environment, which makes the telling and retelling of stories, the adoption and adaptation of ideas or jokes, and the sharing and circulation of images to widely dispersed networks of people into simple activities. It does not democratize popular culture exactly, but it lowers the barriers to entry. And such engagement, as Benkler (2006: 275) points out, is likely to make people into sharper readers and viewers of media material.

CTRL + C, CTRL + V

The twentieth century offers four prehistories of twenty-first century social media remix cultures. One of these prehistories would set these contemporary cultures in the context of the remix aesthetics of so much of the arts and popular cultures of the twentieth century (P. Miller 2004, 2008, Chandler and Neumark 2005, Manovich 2009). From T.S. Eliot and his fragments to DJ Shadow and his fragments, from the Cabaret Voltaire in Zurich to the Cabaret Voltaire from Sheffield, high arts and popular cultures were driven by the copy–paste impulse of CTRL + C, CTRL + V.

In art, Cubism, Dada, Surrealism, the Situationists, Pop Art and Fluxus all remixed and reimagined found objects: tickets and menus pasted into collages, bicycle wheels and snow shovels exhibited in galleries, maps and advertisements scribbled upon, soup cans and comic books elevated to high-art icons. To imagine the world anew meant using existing elements of the world that those artists sought to change – it meant making new representations from old ones.

In literature, as we've seen above, the high modernism of Joyce's *Ulysses* saw the narrative structure of Homer's *Odyssey* remixed with a stylized reimagining of Dublin, but this is very far from the only example. A later period of magical realist fiction such as Gabriel García Márquez (*One Hundred Years of Solitude*), Toni Morrison (*Song of Solomon*) or Angela Carter (*The Bloody Chamber*) mashed the conventions and concerns of the modern realist novel with the folk cultures of rural Colombians, African-American slave narratives or pre-modern European fairy tale traditions. Folk narratives that, as Propp (1999) observed, are distinctive in having no individual author: a quality they share with internet memes. Magical realist literature gave those folk narratives a new life by bringing them into new kinds of context, while also opening up fresh possibilities for realist fiction.

In cinema, major developments in editing and narrative all traded in cutting and pasting to offer new meanings from the juxtaposition of images and ideas – this is true of Eisenstein's principles of montage, of Hollywood continuity editing and of the jump cuts of the French New Wave. Cinema is not just the art of the moving image, but is the art of editing, of putting things together in new ways to reveal new possibilities for meaning.

In music, jazz brought collaborative improvisations in which each performance was a one-off remix of a theme. A familiar melody might be set against a different sequence of chords, or its existing chord sequence might be extended or inverted, or the musicians might each bring their own interpretations of a song together to reinvent it for a single moment. This aesthetic of collaborative re-working extends through the cut-and-paste cultures of punk-inspired zines, and the cut-and-paste cultures of hip-hop and electronic dance musics, to find its contemporary digital analogues in the cut-and-paste cultures of YouTube and Tumblr.

These remix aesthetics each involved combining existing ideas and images. Each was held to be radical and difficult when it first appeared, and each became absorbed and made normal – part of the established cultural repertoire of the twentieth century. This was a key legacy of that century to the networked digital century that is now underway. In the twenty-first century, none of this is radical or *avant-garde*, and instead the CTRL + C, CTRL + V impulse is now taken for granted as media and cultural content converges with computers, and networked communications enable its circulation.

This prehistory of contemporary remix aesthetics can be augmented by a second prehistory – that of the development of graphically-enabled personal computers. From Douglas Engelbart's famous 1968 demonstration of innovations – the mouse, windows, hyperlinks – that pointed towards a future in which computers could be used by the non-specialist, through prototypical graphical user interfaces such as Ivan Sutherland's 'Sketchpad' and convergent multimedia devices such as Alan Kay and Adele Goldberg's 'Dynabook' and on to the introduction of the Macintosh in 1984. Each of these – and many cognate – developments offered further resources for the non-specialist individual user to manipulate, edit and remix digital texts of all kinds (Packer & Jordan 2001, Wardrip-Fruin & Montfort 2003). Manovich traces how *copy, cut* and *paste* were among the earliest general commands incorporated into computer operating systems by Xerox and then Apple, noting how powerful it is for the user that they can apply the same set of generic commands across any kind of document or application (Manovich 2013: 212–13). The introduction of web browsers in the early 1990s and the widespread availability of access to the World Wide Web offered users not only limitless access to images and texts, but also the capacity to share and make visible the meanings that they have made from them. The emergence of the Web 2.0 business model (discussed in Chapter 1) in the first decade of the twenty-first century made platforms for the circulation of user-generated content close to ubiquitous. It also simplified and automated practices of creating, editing and sharing ideas, texts and images. If the high arts and popular cultures of the twentieth century had made remix aesthetics a basic element of culture and communication, the digital computer made their production much more accessible.

A third prehistory of the remix aesthetics of social media would trace the cultural habits and expectations developed by the adoption and adaptation of several decades of innovations in consumer electronics and home entertainment, as Henry Jenkins (2003) has pointed out in a discussion that includes photocopiers, videocassette recorders, personal music players, videogames and camcorders. Photocopiers and desktop publishing enabled new forms of subcultural expression such as zines and fan fiction. The videocassette recorder allowed viewers to curate personal libraries of TV shows and films, and to assemble their own edited interpretations of this material. Personal music players, from the transistor radio through the Walkman to the iPod and the smartphone, offered the capacity to customize public and urban spaces with one's private soundtrack. Videogames offered new kinds of immersive engagement and the crucial dimension that one's actions changed the outcome of what was happening on screen. And the ability to create one's own still and moving images offered by devices from the Polaroid to the camcorder, and the ability to edit those images offered by packages from Photoshop to iPhoto, brought the full range of formerly professional image production, editing and manipulation into the home.

And a fourth prehistory of twenty-first century remix cultures would trace the traditions of critical perspectives on the social uses of media and the potentials for different kinds of communication and power relations that could be achieved if 'audiences' became 'producers'. These traditions include such figures as Walter Benjamin (1978) [1934], Bertolt Brecht (1993) [1932], Guy Debord (Debord & Wolman 2009) [1956] and Raoul Vaneigem (1983) [1967], and Hans Magnus Enzensberger (2003) [1970], each of whom called in different ways and different decades for more participatory engagement in the public spaces of mediated communication. In the internet era, such debates continued around variants including radical media (Downing 2001), alternative media (Atton 2002), tactical media (Lovink 2002) or citizens' media (Rodriguez 2001), and much research and argument continues in this sphere (Atton 2015). Perhaps not all of these authors would have been thrilled by doge memes, but the remix cultures environment in which public and personal communication converge offers considerable political potential to reimagine citizenship for a networked environment (a point developed in more detail in Chapter 6).

Each of these prehistories – in the arts, in computing, in consumer electronics, in radical and alternative media – provides a different context for the practices of cut-and-paste circulation that characterize the social media environment, and its characteristic textual form of internet memes.

Don't Worry, We're from the Internet

An internet meme can start anywhere. But more have started on 4chan than anywhere else. 4chan was created in 2003 by Chris Poole, who goes by the username of 'm00t' online. Poole is a fan of Japanese anime, and started 4chan as an English-language version of a Japanese image board, to which people could post without creating an account, or using a persistent identity or contributing to a developing archive (Poole 2010). The default username for posts is *Anonymous*, and although the site does keep logs (Coleman 2014) it maintains no archive, and draws such a volume of traffic that any post or thread will be pushed off the page by new posts very quickly. 4chan is divided into dozens of separate themed boards, from Music or Fashion to Weapons or Pony (for *My Little Pony* adherents). Its central board is *Random*, or /b/. In his 2010 TED talk, Poole said that /b/ saw about a third of the whole site's traffic. How big is that? For a sense of the scale of /b/, when Poole stepped down from running the site in January 2015, he wrote that in its eleven years online 4chan had seen more than 1.7 billion posts by its more than 1.2 million daily visitors (www.4chan.org/news?all#118). /b/ is a very big deal.

As well as such social media essentials as lolcats, 4chan has incubated countless other memes, including the political movements that adopted the default username of *Anonymous*, and that adapted that username across a range of campaigns, splinter groups, actions and controversies from the mid-2000s. Fox News brought Anonymous its first news media attention in 2007 with a report on 4chan as an 'internet hate machine'. This label drew more people to /b/ and reinforced the emerging collective identity of Anonymous (Phillips 2015: 58–60). Activists emerging from 4chan and coordinating through Internet Relay Chat channels used the name Anonymous to troll the Scientology organization in 2008, demonstrating in their hundreds outside Scientology offices around the world, wearing Guy Fawkes masks and waving placards that read 'long cat is long', like some real-life manifestation of the cyberpunk hackers the Panther Moderns of William Gibson's *Neuromancer* and their 'random acts of surreal violence' (Gibson 1984: 80).

Users of the name went on to stage online political actions in support of WikiLeaks in 2010, to foster movements emerging through social media in the Arab Spring of 2011 and to contribute to many other projects and causes, large and small (Coleman 2014). With its 2010 Operation Payback actions against Amazon, Paypal, Mastercard and Visa, in retaliation for those corporations withdrawing their services from WikiLeaks, Anonymous offered the largest and most dramatic examples to date of electronic civil disobedience (Meikle 2008). Electronic civil disobedience is a discourse and a set of practices that dates back to the mid-1990s, and that seeks to align itself with still older traditions of non-violent political action (Critical Art Ensemble 1994, 1995, Wray 1998, Meikle 2002). Operation Payback used the signature electronic civil disobedience tactic of the virtual sit-in or Distributed Denial of Service (DDoS) attack, as thousands of supporters swarmed those sites with automated DDoS tools in an attempt to lock out their other users.

Poole told one interviewer (Krotoski 2010) that the Anonymous movement saw anonymity not as an absence, but as a presence. To be part of Anonymous was not just to withhold one's name, but was to choose this collective identity. In the social media environment in which real names are required by pivotal platforms such as Google and Facebook, electing to use the name Anonymous is a statement about online interaction, about the internet as an open space and about the relationships between individuals and the commercial data-mining platforms of the sharing industry. There are precedents for the use of collective pseudonyms in cultural activism, including the Karen Eliot art project and the use of professional footballer Luther Blissett's name by uncountable artists and activists in the 1990s. There are also other examples of how masks can propose a collective, rather than an individual identity – the balaclavas of the Zapatistas or Pussy Riot, or the ways in which the topless protests of the Femen movement turn their participants from unclothed individuals to collective symbols – all of which are both mediated and intended for mediation (Guertin & Buettner 2014).

The Guy Fawkes mask favoured by Anonymous is itself an internet meme and a complex artefact of remix culture. Its styling comes from the 1980s comic series *V for Vendetta* by Alan Moore and David Lloyd, and draws upon the wider established iconography of Guy Fawkes (for non-UK readers, Guy Fawkes was part of a small group that tried to blow up the Houses of Parliament in 1605. His public execution is invoked every year on 5 November, when his effigy is burned on backyard bonfires. Masks have been part of these effigies for many years). This contemporary Guy Fawkes mask also draws together and remixes many other recognizable intertextual influences. Alan Moore himself identified many of these in a 1983 introductory essay included in the collected graphic novel version of *V for Vendetta*, among them: George Orwell, David Bowie, Max Ernst, *The Prisoner*, Robin Hood and 'the atmosphere of British Second World War films' (Moore 1990: 270). David Lloyd's styling of the Guy Fawkes mask worn by the title character V was replicated in the 2006 film of *V for Vendetta*, for which Time Warner produced masks as promotional items that were licenced for sale (Economist 2014). It was these that were adopted by protesters. Images of groups of Anonymous protesters wearing the Guy Fawkes mask, often in smart business suits, then themselves became a meme, circulating with the captions 'Oh fuck, the internet is here' or 'Don't worry, we're from the internet'.

Anonymous first used the masks in public demonstrations as part of their campaign against Scientology beginning in 2008. It had already been adopted on their home space of 4chan as part of the repertoire of a recurring meme character known as Epic Fail Guy (Phillips 2015: 150). The mask offered protection from being identified by Scientologists, but also brought powerful connotations of insurgency and insurrection through its connection not just with the graphic novel or the film, but with the historical conspirators of the Gunpowder Plot. 'People should not be afraid of their governments', declares the title character of *V for Vendetta* – 'Governments should be afraid of their people'. But, more than that, it also offered a motif that expressed the ideology of anonymity that developed through 4chan and Anonymous.

By 2011, the year of global protests from the Arab Spring to Occupy Wall Street (see Chapter 6), the Guy Fawkes mask could be seen everywhere, showing up in crowds from New York to Athens, from Egypt to Thailand. It was even worn by a group of politicians in the Polish parliament. Since 2012, 5 November each year has seen coordinated global protest events called the Million Mask March in hundreds of cities. The Guy Fawkes mask illustrates how internet memes are adapted into new contexts, including unlikely offline ones (I'm writing this section in a university library that displays a large 'I Can Has Cheezburger?' lolcat in its foyer as part of a message advising that food is not allowed). In an indication of how internet memes are also often commodified by advertisers and other corporate interests, it's worth noting that the mask is trademarked by Time Warner, who get a cut of the sales made to activists. The company that produces the official version told *The New York Times* in 2011 that they were selling more than 100,000 of the masks each year (Bilton 2011). Unlike the use of an internet meme like the 'Double Rainbow' by Vodafone or Subway's referencing of doge grammar, in this case the commercial artefact came before its adoption for use as a meme; however, the activist use of the mask, fuelled by Anonymous, is in this case still generating revenue for one of the world's largest media conglomerates.

Conclusion

The many interventions of Anonymous are serious business, but they also have an important dimension of humour and playfulness. They point to the importance of discourses of *play* for political actions and organization. Brian Sutton-Smith (1997), who anatomized the many different ways in which *play* is used, showed how to speak of *play* can be to speak about development and learning, or about gambling and chance, or about power and conflict. To speak of play can also be to speak about the rituals of festival and celebration, through which community is formed and maintained. And it can also be to speak about imagination, improvisation and creativity. And to speak of play can also be to speak about the development and care of the self, about recreation and self-fulfilment. And play can evoke the carnivalesque and 'historical trickster figures' (Sutton-Smith 1997: 11), from Odysseus to Anonymous.

The uses of internet memes on social media draw upon almost all of these discourses of play (if not, perhaps, that of gambling and chance). Internet users can develop and learn social media literacies through the creation, remixing and sharing of new, unfinished texts and images. They can participate in communities, whether long-term or fleeting, and find pleasures and recreation in these spaces, as well as possible conflicts and contests. Play matters. And humour matters, not least in the kinds of politics that Anonymous has been instrumental in developing. Political humour is, as John Ralston Saul puts it, 'The least controllable use of language and therefore the most threatening to people in power' (Saul

1994: 65). Chinese social media users circulate humorous internet memes as a kind of coded political dissent. Memes can be used to try to circumvent censorship and state surveillance, with political perspectives hidden in plain sight within what seem more trivial or innocuous animal imagery (Mina 2014). Russian authorities have intervened to restrict memes that depict public figures in ways that have 'nothing to do with the celebrity's personality' (BBC Trending 2015).

Anonymous is one example of how some are using the social media environment as a space in which to develop creative political relations with their contemporaries. The projects and operations of Anonymous may seem inchoate or chaotic to some, but they also illustrate processes of communities coming together, developing their own norms and beliefs, and acting upon the shifted experiences and awareness of culture, connection and community that are made possible by widespread adoption and adaptation of networked digital media. The development of Anonymous is an example of what we'll explore further in Chapter 6 as *distributed citizenship*.

Chapter 4

Convergence and the Limits of Citizen Journalism

News is central to an understanding of the media. News is where decisions about how we organize ourselves and each other are proposed, discussed and held up for endorsement or rejection. News is where we hear stories about ourselves and each other, and where we work out how we feel about the decisions and controversies and events of the day. News also confers a particular status on those media organizations that produce it. It allows them to exercise a particular kind of power, of the kind that we discussed in Chapter 2 in relation to Facebook's uses of the word *share* – symbolic power; the power to define reality, to name, to endorse and to persuade. Social media are just one phenomenon made possible by the convergence of content, computing and communications. They are part of a wider emergence of new approaches to presenting public information, one that also includes the rise of data journalism, news aggregators (such as Reddit or Google News), and newsgames and simulations.

Networked digital media enable new convergences of textual forms. Modes of communication that were previously separate – text, image, audio, video, animation – come together within a single platform, bringing new challenges and possibilities for the telling of the news. And it is within this context that the changing roles of both those who produce the news and those who use it need to be understood. This chapter examines developments in news designed for the social media environment as these are influenced by the convergence of *computing* (the cultural form of the database), *communications* (the significance of real-time news) and *content* (who gets to create it and what they get to do with it). These developments include the emergence of platforms such as BuzzFeed and its much-imitated list-based articles, the uses of hashtags on Twitter and the limits of citizen journalism as seen in a case study of Reddit.

All Your Database Are Belong to Us

The convergence of content, computing and communications makes possible new approaches to storytelling for news and public information. These join, if not yet replace, the linear narratives of the print era, and the inverted pyramid structure of the nineteenth century till now. The inverted pyramid is the familiar story form through which the most important details – *who, what, where, when* and, if we're lucky, *why* – come at the start of the story, with each subsequent paragraph offering details and elaboration that are assumed to be steadily less important, enabling the reader to skim through stories without necessarily having to read to the end. It's an enduring plot-structure, which was developed to combine the affordances of telegraphy and print for an emerging mass readership (Pöttker 2003). The inverted pyramid is a convenient formula, which explains its longevity, but one that critics contend leaves readers uninformed (Postman 1985) or turned off by the repetitive structure (Bird & Dardenne 1997).

As all forms of media converge into a networked digital environment, the characteristics and basic affordances of digital information can be exploited to develop new approaches to communicating complex information to twenty-first-century audiences. Among these characteristics and affordances is what Lev Manovich identifies as the *database* as a cultural form. Narrative forms such as the inverted pyramid now contend with database forms, through which users search and navigate (Manovich 2001: 219). Stories are organized around cause-and-effect, and develop from beginning to end; databases, in contrast, are structured collections of separate, discrete items. No item is necessarily any more important than the others, so none necessarily the 'beginning' or the 'end'; rather, the user determines the connections as they make them, through these processes of navigation and search. Choose your own adventure. Manovich argues that these are 'two competing imaginations, two basic creative impulses, two essential responses to the world' (Manovich 2001: 233).

One such adoption of the database as a cultural form for news is the emergence of *data journalism*. Data journalism brings together spreadsheets, graphics and visualizations, data analysis and journalism skills in order to look for new ways of presenting complex information in ways that can engage readers and users (Rogers 2011). One powerful example is a project called #Tracked, created by Danish newspaper *Berlingske* to explore the importance of *metadata* (www.b.dk/sporet). The Edward Snowden revelations (to which we will return in Chapter 5) generated interest in metadata. Metadata is data about data. Your phone's metadata doesn't include a recording or a transcript of your voice calls, but it does include data about those calls – what number you called, when you called and how long you spoke. Your phone is also logging your locations and movements. Other networked digital media transactions also generate this kind of information (your supermarket loyalty card, your work or campus ID card, your public transport card). Governments have responded to the Snowden events by saying that they don't store content, just metadata. But this is not reassuring. Your metadata can build up a very detailed picture of who you are, what you do, where you go, whom you communicate with and how often.

The *Berlingske* #Tracked project recruited two Danish MPs to volunteer their participation and then collected metadata sets on them, which they then analysed and visualized on a dedicated website. The homepage is a picture of each politician at home, surrounded by their laptops, phones, wallets and passports. Clicking on an item in the photograph opens up visualizations based on the data sets that include thousands of emails, phone and text message points, bank account details, web browser histories, online shopping, tax and police records, flight details and Facebook accounts. So clicking on one of the politicians' phones in the picture pulls up a map showing the many different networks to which it has connected, from which a detailed picture of her movements can be extrapolated. Clicking on her purse brings up a video presentation by a data analyst offering a detailed picture of her shopping habits from her financial transaction records. Clicking on her phone invokes a navigable infographic of the 20 people that she texts the most often, and details of just how very often that can be. Using these politicians as examples, this data journalism project shows how much information is available about each of us, and offers a stark illustration of how detailed a portrait can be assembled from metadata.

Another example of the role of the database in the developing news environment is the newsgame. News organizations and games designers alike are experimenting with new forms of convergence, in which videogame engines, mechanics or conventions can be used to allow users to explore issues from the news through new platforms. These can take a range of forms, including documentaries, puzzles, satire and polemics (Bogost *et al.* 2011).

> Unlike stories written for newsprint, or programmes edited for television, videogames are computer software rather than a digitized form of earlier media. Games may sometimes display text, images, sounds or video, but they also do much more than this: games simulate how things work by constructing models that people can interact with. This is a type of experience irreducible to another, earlier medium. (Bogost *et al.* 2011: 84)

The BBC's 2015 newsgame *Syrian Journey*, for example, is a text-based adventure game in which the player has to make a series of decisions about how best to reach safety in trying to escape from Syria to Europe to claim asylum. To Egypt and then risk a hazardous sea crossing? Or to Turkey, and risk being conned by people-traffickers who will take your money and leave you stranded? There are few good options and fewer good outcomes in *Syrian Journey*, which is based upon research with actual asylum seekers undertaken as part of a BBC Arabic project on migration. Some video interviews with those involved are available on the page, below the game, bringing established and experimental modes of news storytelling together in the one frame. Each provides a fresh context for the other, with the video interviewees lending authenticity to the game based on their experiences, and the game offering a simulation of the processes and structures within which asylum seekers must live. Both modes of information also work to personalize and humanize the otherwise abstract processes that are expressed in news headlines whose magnitude often obscures the individual reality of the human cost. Among many other things, the news is 'a representation of authority' (Ericson *et al.* 1989: 3), a textual system through which authorized speakers and sources contend to define the rules of their audience's reality. A videogame is a simulation of a rule-based system (Frasca 2004). To play a game is not so much a matter of following a narrative as it is a matter of learning how to execute the algorithms that govern the system (Manovich 2001, Goffey 2008). To play the game, one has to work out the rules for oneself, and negotiate the environment that they define. So newsgames enable players to explore particular representations of authority, and are a powerful vehicle for exploration of important social issues and concerns.

Such developments can be seen as one line of response to concerns raised over many years by leading news scholar Herbert Gans. In his 1979 book *Deciding What's News*, Gans (1979) discussed the bureaucratic principles and external pressures that structured the selection of news content. Gans was analysing a news environment built around scarcity, in which the management of limited airtime and page-space led to practices of gatekeeping (Shoemaker 1991) and the tacit regime of 'news values', through which certain events are accorded the status of news but the vast majority are not (Galtung & Ruge 1965, Hall 1981). Thirty years later, surveying a news environment built around abundance of information rather than scarcity, but with dwindling audience engagement with established news sources, Gans proposed that journalists would need to adapt to this changing environment. Reporters, he argued: 'will have to learn how complicated events can be described and explained in a more easily understandable fashion; and how connections between events and their contexts can be made intelligibly' (Gans 2009: 23). His argument was that the news needed a degree of popularization. Its tone should be less earnest, its language more everyday; humour should be more prominent at times, and the news should engage more with the ways in which its users talk about it and the uses they make of it in daily conversation and daily life, beyond the ideals of news as a worthy component of a democratic polity.

The convergence of content, computing and communications has seen a number of developments along these lines, including the examples of data journalism and newsgames discussed above. Another such development is the list-based article or *listicle*. Lists are everywhere in the contemporary media environment. A listicle doesn't have a narrative structure, a beginning-middle-and-end, or a cause-and-effect sequence. It is, for better or worse, one response to Gans's call for new forms of news. And it is an example of a cultural database genre developed for the convergent environment of social media, designed to prompt the user to click the *share* button.

Listicles are most often associated with the website BuzzFeed, which has brought us, among so many others, '17 ways you're drinking your tea wrong', '15 hedgehogs with things that look like hedgehogs', and '27 trees that don't give a fuck about you or anything that you do' (it also once ran a piece explaining the Egyptian revolution through *Jurassic Park* gifs). BuzzFeed was founded in 2006 by Jonah Peretti, whose place in internet folklore was already assured as the author of the famous correspondence with Nike about purchasing a customized pair of shoes emblazoned with the word *sweatshop* (Peretti 2001). Peretti had also been involved in setting up *The Huffington Post*. His experiences had made him interested in how content circulates through networks (Peretti 2007), and BuzzFeed emerged from experiments in creating content expressly designed to be circulated and shared (Rowan 2014). Such content, often listicles, is tagged with the derisive label of *clickbait*. BuzzFeed provoked satirical news site *The Onion* to create a spin-off publication *Clickhole* ('because all content deserves to go viral'). Yet BuzzFeed has attracted US$70 million in investment from venture capitalists and has established itself as a major provider of content shared across social media platforms – indeed, the company is built on the model of sharing news content across networks rather than of attracting users to its site (Bell 2015).

The influence of BuzzFeed is plainly visible across the wider news environment. Other platforms have also adopted the listicle. BBC News offers a regular '10 things we didn't know last week' feature. The 2015 election coverage of *The Independent* included '18 general election leaflet mistakes that will make you fear for democracy', and as I write this it is offering '10 of the best freak injuries ever seen in golf'. Two of *The New York Times*'s top ten most-read stories of 2014 were lists. And lists are often turned over to the user to expand: 'Last week we brought you our 10 best fictional bears', said *The Guardian* on 2 May 2014, 'Here we present your thoughts on the bears that should have made the list'.

And Here Are Tomorrow's Headlines ...

Questions of time are always bound up in attempts to define or understand news. Timeliness is at the root of the very word *news*. News can be distinguished from other kinds of information, suggests Roshco, 'by the intimation that it is shared as soon as possible after it is learned' (Roshco 1975: 10). So timeliness, he notes, is of crucial importance in the selection of those events that are to be accorded the status of news. But such temporal dimensions as liveness, immediacy and speed have not always been intrinsic to the news. They only became competitive advantages for news organizations once the electric telegraph was established internationally in the second half of the nineteenth century. The telegraph was the most important development in communication since the printing press, four hundred years before, because it enabled the separation of communication and transportation, with information now able to travel much faster than any human messenger could carry it (Carey 1989). For the news, this meant that faster began to seem better, with news agencies and print organizations competing to get stories out first.

Since the introduction of telegraphy, the news has continued to accelerate, as Hartley (2008: 36–60) observes, with weekly papers joined by daily ones, the evening news programmes joined by live rolling news channels on the CNN template, and static websites joined by up-to-the-second services such as Twitter. In the UK, the BBC News channel has a slot each evening in which guests discuss tomorrow's editions of the national newspapers in a ritual anticipation of the next day's news. The result is a media environment where control of information contends with chaos (McNair 2006), as part of what John Tomlinson describes as 'the condition of immediacy' (Tomlinson 2007: 72) that emerges from a culture that privileges speed. The commercial advantages of being first with a story find their expression in newsroom workplace cultures that some observers have found to equate professionalism with speed. Schlesinger's classic observational research concluded that obsessing about time had become a kind of journalistic fetish (Schlesinger 1987: 105), and the decades since that research have seen the emergence of rolling news and the domestication of the internet, each with fresh imperatives for speed. The need for speed can create tensions between the desire for immediacy on the one hand, and crucial professional values of reliability or accuracy on the other. It can also work against audience understanding of the issues and contexts from which news stories arise, as the endlessly updated moment of *now* places new events in a discontinuous sequence. Details, stories and entire controversies appear as though from nowhere and are replaced without resolution (Bourdieu 1998).

In the social media environment, timeliness takes on a different aspect, as online media are not always subject to the space constraints and scarcity of print or broadcast schedules. So everything can be updated all the time – which is just as well. One index of how the immediacy of the contemporary news environment can tilt more towards chaos than control is the rise of the news genre of the false celebrity death report. Barack Obama, Justin Bieber and Kanye West are just three of the many public figures whose deaths have become trending topics on Twitter, before those mourning them can learn that the initial story was an error or a hoax. In the future, everyone will be dead for fifteen minutes.

Bursting Bubbles

Twitter launched on 21 March 2006, with co-founder Jack Dorsey making the inaugural tweet: 'just setting up my twttr' (Murthy 2013: x). Less than ten years later, Twitter claims to have 288 million monthly active users who send 500 million tweets every day. Twitter illustrates the convergence of public and personal communication, enabling any user to follow any other user and read their tweets (although some users do use the private option to 'protect' their tweets). In principle, Twitter is conversational, again allowing for personal communication to take on a public aspect; this is also a consequence of the portable quality of tweets, which can be easily shared (retweeted) or embedded within web pages or Facebook feeds. The constant updating of Twitter gives the service an immediacy and a sense of liveness that makes it an important part of the overall news environment. But this constant updating also makes it very hard to follow some trending topics or popular hashtags, forcing the user to sample just a selection of passing updates. This sense of immediacy is amplified by mobile use: the company emphasizes that 80% of active Twitter users use it on mobile devices; we'll return to this question of immediacy and speed below.

For news, Twitter can be used for direct reporting or witnessing of events (Allan 2013), or for immediate responses, evaluation and discussion, or for wider commenting and self-expression that may serve to signal the user's personal perspective rather than directly contribute to a debate (Bruns & Burgess 2012). This mix of public and personal, in a real-time environment, attracting the attention of others, is not unique to Twitter, but is shared with many other social media platforms as well – Facebook, Reddit, Instagram or YouTube could all be described with the same emphases. But Twitter is distinct in other ways. The brevity of a tweet gives each a certain urgency, as well as being simple to create (the 140-character limit derives from the 160-character limit of an SMS text message, with the 20-character difference being allocated to one's Twitter username). Its capacity to track and publicize 'trending topics' acts as a kind of social barometer of what is capturing users' attention; this can also become self-reinforcing, as more tweets pile in as a result of the topic trending in the first place (a different sense of the general trend towards monopoly in the social media environment).

Most importantly, the use of the #hashtag makes it possible to aggregate voices, information and commentary around a common theme; those voices may not be in *dialogue* with other voices exactly, but they will be speaking to shared concerns. This makes hashtags a unique mix of the personal and the public, bringing different kinds of users and perspectives into a collective text that can be part performance, part conversation, part mobilization. For example, the #jesuischarlie hashtag that took hold in the days following the mass murder of staff and police at French satirical magazine *Charlie Hebdo* was all of those things. Tags were a feature of the internet before Twitter, and brevity and popularity charts are not innovations either. What is innovative about Twitter is the way that all these simple elements combine into such a complex communication system.

As on other social media platforms, the user identifies a list of contacts with whom she interacts through Twitter. The key element about those contacts in this case, however, is that the relationship can be one-way only – if you want to be someone's friend on Facebook, they have to agree; but if you want to follow someone on Twitter, for the most part you can, and there is no requirement that they follow you back in return. This asymmetry can see Twitter take on a certain broadcasting quality for particularly high-status users who would be unable to follow all their followers in return, even if they wanted to: the Pope has 5.78 million followers, and follows just eight people in return; Taylor Swift has 55.3 million and follows 185; CNN's breaking news feed has more than 25 million followers and follows just 113 back, operating as an additional broadcast feed for its TV broadcast parent.

Twitter allows users to outsource the editorial function of gatekeeping to their own personal networks: 'a person's social circle takes on the role of news editor, deciding whether a story, video or other piece of content is important, interesting or entertaining enough to recommend' (Hermida *et al*. 2012: 821). This is what Bruns (2005) terms gatewatching: the editorial role of selecting what gets published (*gatekeeping*) gives way to the linking and sharing role of drawing attention to what is noteworthy among that which has been published (*gatewatching*). The ability to customize and personalize those whom one follows on Twitter produces a stream of information that is unique to each user, as tweets from politicians or pop stars might rub up against updates or personal messages from one's colleagues or family. It's a personalized information source of a kind that Nicholas Negroponte predicted in 1995 – a kind of newspaper that he called *The Daily Me*, produced in a daily edition of one copy (Negroponte 1995). Some contend that such personalization has a social cost. Eli Pariser describes a 'filter bubble' of solipsism and isolation that each of us risks creating for ourselves through our desires for the familiar:

> In the filter bubble, there's less room for the chance encounters that bring insight and learning. Creativity is often sparked by the collision of ideas from different disciplines and cultures. ... By definition, a world constructed from the familiar is a world in which there's nothing to learn. If personalization is too acute, it could prevent us from coming into contact with the mind-blowing, preconception-shattering experiences and ideas that change how we think about the world and ourselves (Pariser 2011: 15).

Seen from the perspective of its affordances for personalization and customization, then Twitter would be an excellent example of this. But hashtags complicate this picture, and illustrate the complexity of the communication space that Twitter makes possible. In May 2015, for example, the UK staged its first general election in five years. For months beforehand, the most prominent hashtag for this vote was #GE2015. What was striking about this hashtag, and what made it so compelling for those with an active interest in following news and speculation about the campaign, was that it drew contributions from all sides of the debate. It was not dominated by the incumbent Conservative–Liberal Democrat coalition, or by the opposition Labour camp, or by any of the other leading parties (SNP, Green, UKIP). It was not the proprietary domain of any established news organizations (such as the BBC) or individual reporters for newspapers or broadcast media (although some from each of these groups above would no doubt claim that the others did dominate). Instead, it facilitated a kaleidoscope of perspectives on the general election. The result was very far from a filter bubble – rather, following the #GE2015 hashtag throughout the day would expose a user to more diverse perspectives on the campaign than would any preferred newspaper or TV channel. As a user, then, one can aggregate the voices that one wants to hear into a personalized stream, but can also pop that filter bubble through the uses of hashtags.

But there are still real risks to the public sphere that are posed by the emerging roles of social media platforms as key sources of news. For example, Facebook's algorithms determine what content each user sees on their news feed. And this is an increasing part of people's engagement with news – a major international study published in 2015 (Newman *et al.* 2015) found that 41% of online news users across the countries surveyed used Facebook as a source of news (the survey looked at twelve countries, including the US, UK, France, Japan, Germany, Brazil and Australia). A Pew survey of US adults published in July 2015 found that 63% of Twitter users and 63% of Facebook users found those platforms a source of news about public issues and events (Pew Research Center 2015). In May 2015, Facebook began to offer a new feature called Instant Articles through which stories from partner publications (including *The New York Times, The Guardian*, the BBC and BuzzFeed) load directly within the Facebook app rather than linking to the publications' home pages. This gives Facebook a new level of control over what kinds of news content appear in its users' feeds. It also keeps those users within Facebook rather than following a link to the home site of the news organization, with potential risks for those sites' advertising revenue and audience numbers. So as Facebook becomes ever more central to its users' daily lives, its responsibilities change, taking it closer to the role of a publisher than it has so far accepted (Bell 2015). As algorithms replace human gatekeepers in selecting the information that people see, a host of as yet unresolved questions are presented to news organizations, to the social media platforms themselves, and to regulators, each of whom will have to consider how to balance the ethics and responsibilities of news and journalism with the development of viable business models for the social media environment.

Take this example: the murders of US TV journalists Alison Parker and Adam Ward in August 2015 were recorded by their killer, who paused to upload this video to his social media profiles even as he was attempting to escape. News organizations made a range of editorial judgments about how much of this material to show and how to frame it. But many social media users found themselves viewing the raw video as framed by the murderer, because other users shared and retweeted it into their feeds, and the software in their apps automatically played the video without the user needing to click. In this macabre event, algorithms and accountability, editorial judgment and personal communication were all brought into unsettling juxtapositions.

A similar effect surrounded the photos of Alan Kurdi, the three-year-old refugee whose drowned body washed up on a Turkish beach in September 2015 as his family tried to escape the conflict in Syria. The picture of the dead child face-down at the water's edge was a shattering image, and its circulation appeared to directly contribute to significant shifts in both public opinion and government policy in a number of countries. This image also highlighted the questions of accountability in relation to news and social media. Some news organizations, including the BBC, chose not to show that picture, using instead an image of a policeman carrying the child's body; but many thousands of users of Twitter and Facebook made a different choice, sharing and retweeting that distressing photo directly onto the feeds of their friends and followers. The editorial judgment of news organizations now has an altered position in shaping our daily engagement with the news agenda – the personal concerns and judgments of individual users also find public expression, assisted by algorithmic selection that brings those concerns and judgments to their friends' attention, for better or worse.

Check out the Rest of Our Speculation Here

'Big bad wolf boiled alive' reads the newspaper headline. 'Pigs claim they acted in self-defence.' Cut to film of heavily armed police battering down the remaining front door of the Three Little Pigs (*why didn't the wolf try that?*), and arresting them for murder. Comments from social media users drift across the screen as they respond to video reports asking about homeowners' rights to protect their property from wolves. 'This isn't right', tweets one, 'the three little pigs are the victims'. 'The wolf blew down two houses. He got what he deserved' tweets another. While experts and commentators discuss the case in the news and opinion sections, other social media users contribute new leads. 'I knew the wolf', says one, 'there's no way he could've blown down those houses. He had asthma!' Video simulations and animations appear on news sites, casting doubt on an asthmatic wolf's capacity to blow down solid houses. We see the pigs appear in court, under heavy security, and confess to killing the wolf as part of an insurance fraud conspiracy because they were behind on their mortgage payments. The public mood shifts, as the story now becomes a vehicle for an outpouring of anger at the banking sector. The news is now full of stories about mortgage defaults, while social media users share their own personal stories about the struggle to keep up the monthly payments. Rioters in pig masks confront riot police, waving 'Wake up and smell the bacon' placards, before charging the police line. International headlines show protests spreading. 'Riots spark reforms debate' says a final headline.

This is a description of a two-minute video produced by *The Guardian* news organization to promote its vision of multi-platform news in the social media environment. Not just an ad for the paper or its website or its apps, it also acts as a kind of manifesto for a new understanding of news in which users and news organizations collaborate in circulating information and shaping this into stories. *The Guardian* describes it as 'open journalism', but this label has yet to catch on, and the label that has stuck so far is *citizen* journalism. Citizen journalism involves a reimagining of the relationships between audiences and producers of news. Audiences and users are central to the news. We make meanings as well as take them – and make our own media too – although our resources for exercising symbolic power are not on the same scale as those of large media organizations. As media content, computing and communications converge, audiences now not only receive news but also distribute it through sharing ideas and images, information and stories, with self-selected networks of friends, contacts and our own personal audiences.

This opening up of access to public writing raises the existential question of what journalists are for. One answer to this question rests on their self-appointed role as the Fourth Estate. The concept of the Fourth Estate is an ideal role of the press, a democratic role for the news media, but one which is made possible by the commercial nature of that press (Boyce 1978, Schultz 1998, Curran & Seaton 2010). Questions of democracy and questions of industry are both present. It's still common to think of the news media as somehow an independent political institution that represents its audience. Yet now those news media are often part of major global industries, and their interests may be quite different from those of their audiences. Moreover, journalists no longer have a monopoly on writing the news, and this rise of the 'people formerly known as the audience' (Rosen 2006) takes place against a backdrop of a fall in advertising income, of fragmenting audiences, increased competition and under-investment in journalism by news organizations (Harding 2015). As these factors converge, journalists, accustomed to thinking of themselves as the Fourth Estate, the unelected defenders of democracy, have to adjust to finding their continued professional existence questioned every day. How are the cultural roles of journalists changing as new media make possible a redistribution of symbolic power?

One way to answer this question is to look at how news organizations like *The Guardian* have responded to the possibilities of social media forms. A notable development in this respect has been the emergence of live blogs on the websites of established news organizations. Live blogs share the common characteristics of other kinds of blog: short, frequently updated entries, generally with a distinct authorial voice (even when representing an organization) and presented in reverse chronological order so that the most recent update appears first (Rettberg 2014a). Live blogs are increasingly popular, both with news organizations and readers, particularly those logging on from work (Thurman & Walters 2013, Thurman & Newman 2014). *The Guardian* hosts dozens of them each month, including a daily politics live blog, and dedicated series to follow popular TV shows such as *Strictly Come Dancing*. These tend to be run by a journalist in the office, rather than one who is on the scene of the news event they are covering. For live news blogs, this desk-bound curation of incoming updates from other reporters and from social media may lose the aura of credibility that accrues from being present at the scene. But this is compensated by the blogger being able to draw upon and (crucially) *link to* a wider range of sources and perspectives than can most on-site correspondents.

As CNN made liveness an essential element of TV news, Elihu Katz speculated about 'the end of journalism', with the acid insight that news that is endlessly updated is news that 'almost wants to be wrong' (Katz 1992: 9). 'Check out the rest of our speculation here', as *The Guardian* live blog on the launch of Sony's PlayStation 4 console had it in February 2013. Other commentators showed how live coverage of unfolding events could feed back into those events themselves, changing the outcome of the story that they purported to cover, as participants within those very events responded to what they heard in the news (Wark 1994). But live blogging has certain advantages over rolling news channels on television. Where CNN or the BBC have to keep talking and fill the airtime even when there is nothing new to say, live bloggers can pause between posts. Live blogging captures the advantages of speed and immediacy without necessarily having to take on the worst aspects of liveness. Live news blogs, though, do encounter the problem identified by Katz. Some journalist live bloggers have told researchers that this kind of approach to the news has 'lowered the bar to publication in terms of verification' (Thurman & Walters 2013: 93). Just where this bar should be placed is a central question in the social media environment, as the case study of Reddit below explores.

Live blogs offer a substantial role for contributions from the wider social media environment, although users are more likely to be incorporated into the main live blog as quotes from Twitter than they are if they post a comment in the dedicated section below the blog itself, in part because of the risk of astroturf commenters employed by corporations or political parties in the guise of ordinary users (Thurman & Walters 2013). To take just one example of how such live blogs incorporate material from non-professional contributors, on 8 May 2015, *The Guardian* ran a live blog all day to update on the UK general election results and their aftermath. There were 182 posts, with 14,299 comments from readers and 6,324 shares. Those are substantial numbers. Those posts combined contributions from the blogger running the page (who changed several times throughout the day) and links to (and sometimes lengthy extracts from) other articles from journalists and columnists elsewhere on *The Guardian* site. There were also many links to articles from other established news organizations, and lots of pictures, videos and Vines. Embedded tweets figured heavily, but these were almost all tweets made by journalists, politicians and other public figures (including J.K. Rowling). But only two posts linked to content from outside the world of professional media and politics, and both of those were to clickbait novelty items: one to a joke Twitter account in the name of Paddy Ashdown's Hat, a reference to that retired politician's comment on live TV on election night that if a particular prediction were correct, he would eat his hat; the other to the Twitter feed of someone who was 'live stitching' an embroidered map of the UK in colours to depict the vote shares of the various parties. Otherwise, there were no contributions or comments or links to any non-professional media content. These live blogs are a rich mix of images and analysis from a range of media sources both within and without the host news organization, but it is only in the comments that the non-professional can contribute to the discussion. The following case study explores some of the reasons why this might be the case.

Reddit and *findbostonbombers*

At 2.49 pm local time on Monday 15 April 2013, two home-made bombs improvised from pressure cookers were detonated near the finish line of the Boston Marathon – a major annual US public sporting event, which attracts tens of thousands of spectators. Three people were killed in the explosions, including an eight-year-old boy, and hundreds more were injured. For the next four days, under very intense public and media scrutiny, the police and FBI hunted the suspected perpetrators, who were identified on Friday 19 April as brothers Tamerlan (26) and Dzhokhar (19) Tsarnaev. The investigation reached what seemed to be a climax in the shooting of a police officer and the subsequent shooting dead of Tamerlan Tsarnaev in an exchange of gunfire with police in the early hours of Friday 19 April. But with one of the brothers still at large, events then moved to a bizarre plateau when Boston was shut down for the full Friday – the public transport system, businesses, schools, colleges and shops were closed, as people obeyed instructions to stay at home until the eventual apprehension on Friday evening of Dzhokhar Tsarnaev. Many people shared in the manhunt in real-time by following the Boston police department scanner and sharing responses to its updates through social media.

The Boston Marathon bombing and subsequent manhunt took place in an always-on news environment characterized by rolling news channels, push notifications and the non-stop update service that is Twitter. There is a spatial dimension to this environment, characterized above all by the imperative for reporters to be present at a scene. But its dominant dimension is temporal – speed is the perceived cardinal virtue, as news accelerates from telling us what has happened, through telling us what is happening now, to speculating about what might be about to happen next. The Boston events exposed some appalling shortcomings in this established breaking news paradigm, recalling Katz's criticism of rolling news as news that 'almost wants to be wrong' (Katz 1992: 9). Some news organizations reported the story cautiously, with NBC's coverage attracting much acclaim for its accuracy and restraint. But others presented the story in ways which revealed the limitations of a live news approach in which being first counts more than being right.

Very shortly after the bombing, the *New York Post* announced that a Saudi suspect had been 'caught' and was 'under guard' in a Boston hospital, none of which was correct. On Wednesday 17 April, CNN's John King and Wolf Blitzer told their live audience that a suspect had been arrested, King using the phrases 'a dark-skinned male' and 'we got him', and the network repeatedly boosting their own 'exclusive reporting' until investigators stepped in to deny the report as baseless ('it was exclusive', Jon Stewart would later declare on *The Daily Show*, 'because it was completely fucking wrong'). The Associated Press also tweeted at 7.02 pm on that day that a suspect was in custody and expected in court – an error retweeted by thousands of others to an unknowable cumulative audience. The next morning, the *New York Post* came back for another go, running a front-page picture of two entirely innocent individuals with the headline 'BAG MEN: Feds seek these two pictured at Boston Marathon'. The *Post* defended this potentially defamatory labelling by saying the image had been 'distributed' by the FBI – but so had other images of innocent bystanders, to many other media organizations, which did not run them on page one.

If the established news media struggled to cope with this story, it would be heartening to claim that citizen journalists and networked non-professionals had done better. But that wouldn't be true. The Boston bombing case also revealed the limitations of a crowd-sourced citizen journalism in which networked individuals come together on social media platforms to share and make visible ideas. Pierre Lévy's concept of 'collective intelligence' is often invoked in discussions of networked collaboration: Lévy observes that 'No one knows everything, everyone knows something' (Lévy 1997: 13–14). But the limitations of this for real-time citizen journalism are exposed by the Boston bombing case – *sometimes no one knows anything.*

Reddit and the Limits of Citizen Journalism

This section discusses the use of the social media platform Reddit by networks of individuals who attempted to crowd-source the identities of possible bombing suspects by sharing images and speculation. First, it situates these events within the frame of citizen journalism. Second, the case study considers the centrality of sharing to social media and its uses for non-professional journalism and related forms of collaborative information provision. And third, it argues that such uses of social media for citizen journalism reveal the need for an ethics of visibility.

In response to the bombing, thousands of users of social media platforms began sharing photos of crowds of spectators near the marathon finish-line before and after the explosions, in an effort to isolate images of the killers. Images from Flickr were redistributed and edited with graphics programmes to paint red circles around the heads of bystanders who variously had backpacks large enough to have contained a pressure cooker, or who were running away from the explosion, or, in the case of the individual who became known online as Blue Robe Guy, were wearing an oversized fleece; some of these identifications appeared to rest on nothing but crude racial profiling by uninformed amateurs. These edited images were then in turn shared across Facebook, across Twitter and on 4chan, where they were mixed with flakes of information and misinformation shared by users listening to the Boston police radio scanner. Rumours spread that the police had named two suspects over the scanner, one of whom was a university student who had previously been reported as missing (Kang 2013, Madrigal 2013), and who would later be found dead in circumstances entirely unrelated to the marathon bombings. On Thursday 18 April, investigators released pictures of the Tsarnaevs, in part to reduce the impact of misidentifications through social media (Montgomery *et al.* 2013). A central part of this online activity was Reddit.

Reddit is a social media platform, which brands itself as 'the front page of the internet'. One 2013 study by a reputable organization claimed that 6% of all online adults in the US use Reddit (Duggan & Smith 2013). Users can share links, images or text posts to which others can respond by commenting and by offering a single up or down vote; the cumulative score of these votes determines the prominence of each post within the site. As with precursor sites such as Slashdot or Digg, Reddit combines the affordances of user-generated or curated material with community voting on the interest or importance of that material. Anyone can create a free account under any username, and the site discourages the posting of personal information or links to identifiable non-famous individuals such as their Facebook profiles. The platform is divided into thousands of smaller forums or communities called sub-reddits, each moderated by its creator or by other volunteers independent of Reddit the company.

The subreddit *findbostonbombers* was created on 17 April, two days after the bombings, by a redditor using the name 'oops777', who was to later delete that account after giving an interview to the *Atlantic* (Abad-Santos 2013) and participating in a Reddit AMA (Ask Me Anything) Q&A session. By 23 April, the entire forum had been removed from the site, placed behind a page that denies access. However, a substantial sample is still viewable through the Internet Archive's Wayback Machine, which captures 'snapshot' copies of significant web pages for archiving (http://archive.org/web/web.php). For the crucial days of Thursday 18 and Friday 19 April there are three and ten snapshots respectively, each of which offers an archive of the top 25 posts to the subreddit at a given time, along with comments and stats on user numbers. This captures essential dimensions of the subreddit's activity that week, although we should note that some of the content had been deleted by those who had posted it before the archival snapshots could capture it, and that the subreddit's moderators also inter-vened to delete posts which misidentified a missing student as a bombing suspect. There were good reasons for the eventual decision to remove the whole subreddit from public view: some posts appear likely to have been defamatory, others likely to have been distressing to identifiable individuals or to those who know them. So while this chapter quotes some posts from the archived sample of the subreddit, no further usernames are given below.

While contributors to the subreddit at times appeared to imagine they were having a small private discussion, there were actually thousands of people on the forum at any one time (still more than 7,500 shortly before midnight on the Friday, for example, by which time Tamerlan Tsarnaev was already dead and Dzhokhar in custody), and many of those were further distributing material from the forum through other platforms such as Twitter or 4chan; still others, of course, were writing articles about the discussion, which was reported in a large number of established news media outlets, both across the US and around the world, as part of their own coverage of the hunt for the suspected bombers.

The very term *citizen journalism* is at once obvious (journalism is always bound up with citizenship) and shocking (*anyone* can do this now?). It's a term that manages to capture in just two words a whole complex of changing capacities and changing expectations (Allan 2009, Allan & Thorsen 2009, Thorsen & Allan 2014). So the emerging capacities of social media bring new technological affordances for news and journalism, and new kinds of social opportunities and cultural possibilities. They bring altered expectations about voice and participation, feedback and response, access and ubiquity, instantaneity and visibility.

But these are met by the upturned expectations brought by assaults on the business models of the established news industries, as revenues and investment erode, and readership numbers dissolve in the face of new kinds of competition for their attention, and disintegrating trust in journalism. The networked digital media environment is also marked by established news organizations trying to do more with less, and trying to invent, embrace, enhance or rip off newer innovations at the same time as they expect more from less investment and fewer staff.

The result is a complex, convergent media environment built around networked connectivity, and around emerging expectations of news as a networked set of relations rather than a hierarchical one. The news doesn't just talk to us, but we can now talk back; and perhaps more importantly, we are also now all the more likely to talk to each other about what we're hearing. The news – always too important to be left to the news media alone – is now something that its users can *do* as well as watch, listen to or read.

So in what sense was the *findbostonbombers* Reddit activity citizen journalism? After all, the contributors were not writing a news story. They were not collaborating with a particular news organization or outlet. They were not preparing a report for publication. And a substantial number of the comments on many posts were trolling or snark. Indeed, much of the discussion in the forum turned on the question of whether or not it was itself part of the media: recurring themes in the subreddit included not only this question, but also those of the ethical dimensions to public discussion of identifiable people, not least in an environment in which established news media may regard social media interactions as source material.

The subreddit's description states that:

> This is nothing more than one single place for people to compile, analyse, and discuss images, links, and thoughts about the Boston Bombing

and the page explicitly tries to distance the subreddit from journalism:

> IMPORTANT r/findbostonbombers is a *discussion forum*, not a journalistic media outlet. We do not strive, nor pretend, to release journalist-quality content for the sake of informing the public.

But this disclaimer was not an accurate account of how the discussion was being used, even if it were an accurate description of its creator's expectations for the forum. The subreddit's users were responding to and extending a major news story (and in turn themselves became a part of the story). The participants were trying to identify a potential killer and in this were contributing to the story by generating original research – it just turned out to be hopeless, worthless, and to some extent harmful research.

One of the most highly rated posts is one from the day of the subreddit's creation and posted by its creator with the title:

> Media Outlets, please stop making the images of potential suspects go viral, then blaming this small subreddit for it. And read the rules we've imposed before calling us 'vigilantes'.

The post claims:

> Until the media got involved, none of the images were going anywhere but to the FBI.

The rules referred to above are listed prominently in a sidebar:

1   We do not condone vigilante justice.
2   DO NOT POST ANY PERSONAL INFORMATION.
3   Any racism will not be tolerated.
4   Theories are welcome, but make sure you fact check your sources.
5   Remember, we are only a subreddit. We must remember where helping ends and the job of professionals begins.
6   Do not make any images viral. Limit reposting images outside of this sub.
7   Finally keep in mind that most or all of the 'suspects' being discussed are, in all likelihood, innocent people and that they should be treated as innocent until they are proven guilty.

But each of these rules is flouted at every turn, and as the first comment points out in relation to the claim that the images were not going anywhere until 'the media' became involved:

You have to admit, they're actually going everywhere.

And as another adds:

> If you want people to stop reporting on this you should shut it
> down. And you should shut it down because it's a terrible idea.

In contrast, some other commenters defend the subreddit by attacking
the more established news media:

> The media is scared because they are behind us. They want to attack
> our credibility, because we are undermining theirs. Also, we are
> doing what they are doing better, faster, and for free. How can
> CNN expect to make a profit if we will do their job for them better,
> faster, and for free?

But not everyone involved is prepared to accept this distinction between
'the media' and their own large communication platform, 'the front page
of the internet':

> Reddit *is* the media.

And:

> Uh – like it or not, this IS a media outlet

And:

> Reddit: Now no better than CNN.

In response to such criticism, the subreddit's creator weighs in to argue
that:

> If anything we're trying to clear the names of the people who the
> mainstream media just found images of and made go viral.

Some of the longest threads in this subreddit return again and again to
tensions about whether or not what the participants are doing should be
considered journalism, and whether or not the space in which they are
doing it is part of the media. Braun and Gillespie capture something of this
tension in their analysis of the difficulties of integrating the affordances of
social media into the websites of established news organizations:

news organizations now finding that part of their mission includes hosting an unruly user community that does not always honor the norms of journalism; and media platforms and social networks now finding that the user-generated content being shared is often much like news, some of which violates their established content policies. (Braun & Gillespie 2011: 385)

This characterization of an unruly community not honouring the rules of journalism can serve as a very good description of what went on in the Reddit forum. In a networked digital media environment characterized by convergence – of technologies, industries, texts, users, modes of communication – such invisible moments of shared response are made visible to new kinds of networks. A platform such as Reddit allows new kinds of ad hoc, shifting coalitions to come together to share their responses to a news event, with others who the platform makes visible to them and to whom they are made visible in turn. It allows for particular modes of interaction built around *sharing*.

News is social. It is a collaborative process of making meaning from events. 'The first typical reaction of an individual to the news', observed Robert Park as long ago as 1940, 'is likely to be a desire to repeat it to someone' (Park 1967: 42). While Park was writing in a very different news environment, his insight gains renewed force with the daily affordances of networked digital media. Social media platforms enable their users to enter into flows of public communication, and to add a phatic dimension to the public quality of news discourse (V. Miller 2008, Crawford 2011). News is no longer something distributed only by news organizations but is now also redistributed and circulated by its readers, viewers and users, shared and discussed among self-selected networks of friends and contacts. These particular dimensions of sharing should be understood as part of what we think of as citizen journalism. The convergence of the professional and the non-professional is as much about networking and connection, about sharing and its resulting visibility, as it is about public writing.

The *findbostonbombers* forum, and parallel activity elsewhere on Reddit, on Twitter, on Facebook and 4chan, shone a stark light on the contours of mediated sharing in relation to news. At its best, citizen journalism can indeed extend and augment, complement and counterpoint, the practices of the established news media, adding depth, breadth and longevity to discussions otherwise curtailed by the imperatives of news organizations. At its best, citizen journalism is a much needed sharing around of the licence to create non-fiction drama. It can bring both spatial authority (through the actual presence of witnesses; Allan

2013) and temporal authority (through the real-time immediacy made possible by networked digital media).

But as *findbostonbombers* shows, networked collaboration through social media can also be as shoddy and corrosive as the worst of the established news media (for which let the earlier examples from CNN and the *New York Post* serve as metonyms). It can become harder to distinguish signal from noise, and there may not be any necessary extra value in the extra labour involved. So this networked digital news environment does not eliminate the need for journalists. Rather, it gives the Fourth Estate role of the news media a renewed applicability. Professional journalists – acting professionally – can analyse and sift raw material. They can test evidence and redact details that may endanger named individuals. They can offer context to help the reader interpret the material, and can access high-status sources of official information. And they can shape the data into stories, reports and commentaries that make sense of the material for audiences who lack, of course, the time and expertise to process specialized documents and intelligence for themselves – something that was made apparent in the attempts by visitors to the *findbostonbombers* subreddit to undertake DIY forensic work armed only with photos from Flickr and 4chan. There is also the question of accountability – the poor-quality journalism in the examples from CNN and the *New York Post* was produced by reporters who are accountable to their employers, and such employers are accountable to others, including shareholders and (in some countries) regulators; but citizen journalists are not accountable to either professional standards or professional organizations, which may not be something to celebrate. So the paradox of citizen journalism is that rather than rendering professional journalists obsolete, it makes them ever more necessary.

Towards an Ethics of Visibility

In the Boston bombing case, the identification and exposure of named individuals, and the circulation of their photos in defamatory contexts across dispersed media networks, point to the need for an ethics of visibility in the social media environment. Questions of visibility are central to thinking about contemporary developments in networked digital media, not least the many manifestations of citizen journalism. While such questions are most often framed in terms of privacy, this is too narrow a frame through which to view what are a rather larger set of concerns and practices. The case of *findbostonbombers* underscores the fact that we need to think not only about privacy, but also about exposure and display, connection and networking, community and communion. The frame of *visibility* captures more of these than does privacy, and brings with it the need for an *ethics* of visibility in relation to social media, witnessing, sharing and all the other elements that orbit the concept of citizen journalism. Those interactions on such social networks which can be thought of as citizen journalism are not intended to be private in the first place. They're intended to be *shared*. The question is rather with whom we imagine we are sharing, and how the balance between rights and responsibilities is calculated.

The circulation and discussion of misidentified photos, across the networked digital media environment from Reddit to the *New York Post*, highlight the need for a broader and deeper debate about visibility in relation to these converging media platforms. Networked digital media bring with them new kinds of visibility, new opportunities and requirements to monitor and be monitored, to perform and display, and to connect with others who are newly visible to us and to whom we are ourselves in turn made visible. Such affordances are fundamental to the development of the various forms of mediated sharing and collaboration that we class as citizen journalism. But as John Thompson points out, 'mediated visibility is a double-edged sword' (Thompson 2005: 41).

Some contributors to *findbostonbombers* were clearly mindful of the risks of making others visible. As one post notes:

> You can't mark people as terrorism suspects and then get upset that other media pick it up because of your silly rule about it. This is the internet, surprisingly both good and bad information can go viral.

And as another commenter observes:

> everything you are doing here, including all the images and the discussion/interpretation of the details in those images ... is being held on a public forum on a website with billions of pageviews. Everything here is by definition 'going everywhere' and moreover, it's going everywhere instantly via google search and various image/post auto aggregators. years from now all this stuff will still be out there, whether debunked or not. It's completely meaningless to have some sidebar disclaimer if you are going to hold discussions and throw accusations in a place as public as this.

A third points to a particular irony of visibility:

> we bemoan the rise of the surveillance state, but then when something like this happens, everyone's more than happy to post pictures all over the internet, drawing big red circles around anyone carrying a backpack.

One user posted an image of 'Blue Robe Guy', whose key transgression appeared to be wearing a jacket some people didn't like much, under the headline 'Popped up on my facebook newsfeed … this can't happen'; it showed several images of the individual in the blue jacket together with images of a post-explosion backpack and the caption 'Can you identify this man?', which were being circulated across Facebook.

Conclusion

In the context of this kind of activity on this kind of platform, what might an ethics of visibility mean? In individual daily networked digital life, an ethics of visibility would include taking conscious account of the ways in which we make others visible – when we like, when we retweet, when we tag, when we screengrab, when we share. It would include taking conscious account of other people's rights to manage their own visibility as well as our rights to share and comment. It would include asking which invisible audiences are imagined and unimagined in an interaction online, and considering the connections between unsuspecting others that we make each time we link and tag, *like* and *share*, and who we are making visible to whom through these networked interactions.

In collective social life, including news, an ethics of visibility would include a more careful consideration of who and what is valid for exposure. Neither Reddit's Blue Robe Guy nor the *New York Post*'s Bag Men should have been subjected to such intense levels of enforced visibility. While Rupert Murdoch tweeted his support for the *Post*, Reddit the company issued a public apology for what had happened. It addressed their own policies about visibility:

> A few years ago, reddit enacted a policy to not allow personal information on the site. This was because 'let's find out who this is' events frequently result in witch hunts, often incorrectly identifying innocent suspects and disrupting or ruining their lives. We hoped that the crowdsourced search for new information would not spark exactly this type of witch hunt. We were wrong. (erik [hueypriest] 2013)

The apology may have been just an attempt at damage limitation, but it is nonetheless encouraging to see a major social media platform publicly address an ethics of visibility, in an environment in which those very social media platforms themselves so often act in a way that pushes their own users towards ever greater visibility and disclosure for commercial exploitation.

Chapter 5

TMI

In March 2014, Oscars host Ellen DeGeneres posted a group selfie on Twitter during the awards show. Bradley Cooper held the phone, while Meryl Streep, Brad Pitt, Julia Roberts, Kevin Spacey, Jennifer Lawrence and others squeezed into the frame. Helped by DeGeneres encouraging TV viewers to retweet the picture, it was shared more than two million times before the Oscars broadcast ended. Here were A-list performers performing themselves – playing the part of glamorous stars in an impromptu group shot – although the idea was scripted and the phone itself provided by one of the show's major advertisers.

So this group selfie was a particular performance, carefully crafted to appear spontaneous. And in this, it was entirely typical. A selfie is always a performance, both a presentation of oneself and a representation. And it is very often crafted to perform spontaneity. Social media make public and personal communication visible to others within the same frame. Sometimes we choose to make ourselves visible – taking and sharing a selfie, for instance. This is why it's limiting to think of online visibility as just a question of privacy. But visibility is also something that can be imposed on people. In September of that same year, Jennifer Lawrence would again find selfies in which she appeared being shared countless times across social media. But this time, they were nude photos that she had intended for one specific person, instead scaled up for an unimagined and uncountable audience of uninvited viewers.

Selfies are one part of how we present ourselves to others and perform our identities online. But these performances can sometimes take place for unanticipated audiences, as our words and images are shared by others; worse, we may find that we have transgressed the norms of these unimagined audiences. Sometimes, too, material we had never intended to be made public becomes visible. This is the social media environment not of sharing, but of being shared – of doxing and outing, of so-called revenge porn and hacked cloud accounts. And pull back the camera further still and we are all being watched on social media, all our information and data, our messages and images, are being collected, stored and analysed by security agencies around the globe.

This chapter is about how people use social media to make themselves and others visible in new ways. Developments in communication always bring new kinds of visibility to new kinds of public. Social media are only the most recent manifestation of this. The rise of the newspaper helped make possible the modern national consciousness of the 'imagined community', through which the shared stories of a national culture make its common interests and concerns visible in new ways (Anderson 1991). Subsequent innovations in communication also brought changes to the visible. The emergence of the electric telegraph brought global news to light at electric speed (Carey 1989). With photography came new forms of claim to the real, made visible and durable (Evans 1978, Barthes 1981). With broadcasting came the domestication of the public world, and the publicizing of the domestic sphere, through showing each to the other on screen (Meyrowitz 1985) and enabling a new kind of simultaneous, shared attention (Dayan 2009). Live news, made possible by satellite and cable, enabled the mediation of events that unfold before the eyes of viewers and reporters alike (Wark 1994). Media make the invisible visible.

POIDH

At the centre of so much social media activity is the image of the user themselves – the self-taken smartphone photo, the individual *I was here* performance, the *check out my new haircut* announcement, the boast and confession and claim that is the selfie. The selfie is the characteristic image genre of the social media environment. It captures the logic of media convergence – an image (content) taken and viewed upon a computerized device, and shared across telecommunications networks. And it is no coincidence that this form emerged as part of this very particular communication environment. Social media are a move on from the Web 2.0 moment in that they move networked digital communication away from the desktop and laptop screen, and onto mobile devices as well – persistent and pocket-sized, ever-present, always-on.

One way in which those devices have gained or sought competitive edges in the commercial market is through developing their cameras; high-resolution touch screens and built-in photo editing software have also been very important. Phones with both front- and rear-facing cameras have become commonplace. The Sony Ericsson Z1010 included dual cameras for video calls as early as 2003; Apple introduced dual cameras on the iPhone 4 in 2010 for use with its FaceTime video call function.

But as is so often the case, the intended function was not the one that caught people's imagination. Video calls are indeed now common, but they are not yet as common as the shared self-portrait. The front-facing camera turned out to be a technology of the selfie:

> When we take a selfie (or any photograph) with a phone, the phone suggests running it through a filter. After Instagram and apps like Hipstamatic popularised filters, almost every camera or photo sharing app now comes with built-in filters. When you snap a photo on your iPhone, there is a filter icon at the bottom of the screen. When you upload a photo to Instagram, Facebook or Flickr you click through a screen that asks whether you want to filter it, crop it and adorn it. Taken together, filtered selfies are clichés. But for each individual me, seeing ourselves though a filter allows us to see ourselves anew. (Rettberg 2014b: 26)

To make and share a representation of oneself is the most fundamental use to which social media can be put. More so even than the written post, because not everyone is good at expressing themselves in words (as though to confirm this, there is an app called *Snapcat*, designed to allow cats to take and share selfies). The most fundamental form of communication through social media is the image, and the most fundamental form of those images is the selfie. If social media are those that allow anyone, in principle, to say or make things, then what any one of us can make is an image of ourselves, and what those images say is *here I am*. The creation of the selfie is a moment of writing oneself into being in public. It is a performance, a pose, a claim. Me, myself and I. We hold the viewer at arm's length, but invite them in all the same.

The emergence of the selfie as form also connects to the ubiquity of the profile-based social media platform. The rise of the selfie has in part been driven by the interface designs of the major social media firms. On Facebook and Google+, on YouTube and LinkedIn, on Twitter and Spotify, we are asked to provide a profile pic from the moment we register. At every online turn, platform after platform demands that we represent ourselves in their space through a single self-chosen, self-created image.

The selfie is just one point in the long trajectories of both portraiture and photography. From the commissioned portraits of the Renaissance to the *this is me at the Eiffel Tower* arm's-length image that passes from phone to Facebook Timeline in two clicks, both photography and portraiture have become viable for the non-professional. The once elite practice of making portraits is now an everyday DIY activity. We are able to document our presence in real-time – Pics Or It Didn't Happen

(POIDH). We are now all in the business of framing and capturing aspects and moments of ourselves. And as we do so, we may reveal more of ourselves than we realize, much as patrons who paid painters to record their greatness often found that much else had been recorded in the image as well. Just as the greatest portrait painters offer not only a representation of their subject but also an interpretation that may be merciless, so also each of us reveals our senses of self as we frame and share the images we make of ourselves. We not only *give* communication here, but we *give it off* as well (a distinction made by Erving Goffman in 1959). We offer images that say more about us than we may have intended. And moreover, the metadata of that image – the device, the location, the date and time, the IP address from which we share it – are given off too.

In discussions of social media, this increased visibility of personal communication is usually framed around questions of privacy. Social media tools and firms are interrogated for their privacy policies and practices. But privacy is too narrow a frame through which to understand our interactions on social media. After all, a good deal of what people share on social networks isn't intended to be private in the first place – rather, it's intended to be visible, intended to be shared. Across the social media environment, enhanced forms of visibility are not only implicated in surveillance imposed upon us from without, but also in dimensions of performance and display. We present and perform versions of ourselves for self-selected audiences. And there are uses of such performance to connect with others – to network, interact and *share* with others whom we might never have encountered otherwise. This capacity for sharing leads to the affordances of social media for collaboration, networking, and shared creativity and communication. Social media make us visible to others whom we may not have encountered otherwise, and make those others visible to us in turn.

NSFW

Tumblr is a major social media platform. It was bought by Yahoo for US$1.1 billion in 2013, after that firm's other key social media platform, Flickr, had lost significant ground to other photo-sharing spaces, including Facebook. Tumblr's characteristic use is for minimalist short posts – very often images, animated gifs or videos – on a niche overall theme, such as *Hungover Owls, Animals Sucking at Jumping*, or the era-defining *Indifferent Cats in Amateur Porn*. The flexibility of the form opens it up to any kind of use. Barack Obama's team launched an eponymous Tumblr in 2011 as part of his re-election campaign, inviting submissions from supporters; there were more than 100 posts most months until the election was over, with submitted selfies and memes mixed in with professional campaign content. And a significant driver of the Occupy Wall Street movement was the Tumblr *We Are the 99 Percent*, which made very powerful use of the format's standard elements, including UGC images on a single theme, minimal commentary, and the facility for followers to *like* or *share* posts; we'll return to the *We Are the 99 Percent* example in the next chapter.

A Tumblr called *Selfies at Funerals* attracted a lot of attention in late 2013 for its collection of pictures harvested from Instagram and Twitter. In each, someone poses for a selfie and tags it to indicate that they're at a funeral. Journalist Jason Feifer compiled the Tumblr by searching for posts tagged #funeral and #selfie. 'Love my hair today. Hate why I'm dressed up #funeral' posts one young woman. 'Killin the funeral game at pop's funeral', writes one young man, making a V-sign beside some mortuary statuary. After posting 20 of these in October 2013, Feifer was to declare the project over a few weeks later, when Barack Obama was pictured posing for a selfie with the prime ministers of the UK and Denmark at Nelson Mandela's memorial service: 'Obama has taken a funeral selfie', reads the Tumblr's final post, 'so our work here is done'.

Feifer created another Tumblr in February 2014, this time pulling together 27 Instagram posts on the theme *Selfies with Homeless People*. 'Quick selfie with the homeless guy sleeping in the lobby', reads one tweeted picture by a young woman in what looks like a hotel receptionist's uniform. When Feifer found it and shared it on *Selfies with Homeless People*, the woman reblogged this on her own Tumblr and added the note:

> While it was wrong to take a picture with this homeless man, no one knows the context or me. The harassment I'm receiving is far worse than anything I did to this man. The people calling me a 'bitch' or 'cunt' for taking this picture need to look in the fucking mirror and get a life. selfieswithhomelesspeople try doing something productive instead of creeping my twitter. Thanks.

To say 'no one knows the context' is an important point. Feifer's Tumblrs remixed found images into a context that he had devised deliberately to call attention to transgressions against his own ethical standards (see also his earlier *Selfies at Serious Places*, which includes people posting from concentration camps). But what are the ethics of what he himself is doing here?

In an article that he wrote for *The Guardian* about his funeral Tumblr, Feifer noted that the images had 'elicited the web's most natural emotional state – righteous indignation' (Feifer 2013). But this does also rather seem to be the effect that he'd intended. After all, bereavement, grief and funeral etiquette are not simple things for anyone to negotiate, and it is not hard to imagine that some of those photos that Feifer aggregated to his Tumblr are moments from much more complicated processes for those who shared the original selfies. For example, they may have been trying to find ways of signalling to their friends that they were dealing with loss, while not feeling able to be fully open about that in a part-public space like Instagram or Twitter. It is a simple thing to provoke righteous indignation on social media, as Feifer has shown with each of his Tumblr projects. And this underlines the need for an ethics of visibility. Sharing a person's image in order to shame that person for the way they chose to present themselves in that image is itself a dubious choice. It's an action that claims the moral superiority of upholding standards that are transgressed by the people in whichever picture one posts next. The young hotel receptionist (whom I'm deliberately not identifying by name here) is right to point out that nobody knows the context of her image. It's an example of the common phenomenon of people using social media as part of a performance of self for one kind of imagined audience, only to find themselves pushed onto a different stage in a different theatre.

I'm taking this language of *performance, theatre* and *stage* from Goffman's 1959 book *The Presentation of Self in Everyday Life*. It's a book about how people interact in social situations: how we offer each other certain kinds of cues and indications about how we would like to be seen; how we choose to present different aspects of ourselves to different people in different situations; how we *perform* different parts of our identities to try to fit the roles in which our daily lives cast us – work, family, friendships. It's also a book about how we may perhaps inadvertently reveal aspects of our identities that don't fit a particular performance – sometimes communication is something we *give*; but at other times it's something we *give off*. Like other kinds of theatre, our daily lives have onstage and backstage areas ('front region' and 'back region', in Goffman's terms), in which we either adopt the part or let the mask slip. Daily life, in this analysis, is an endless process of improvised performance, through which we negotiate both our sense of self and our sense of those others with whom we share the day's stages, by slipping in and out of our various roles. It's also an endless process of theatre-going, in which we respond to the performances that are both given and given off by other people.

In his book *No Sense of Place*, Joshua Meyrowitz (1985) adapts Goffman's theatrical discourse in an analysis of how television complicates the presentation of self. He adds to Goffman's argument a consideration both of electronic media and of changes in social relationships. Meyrowitz explores how TV brings together aspects of public and domestic life, breaking down established ways of presentation between women and men, between adults and children, and between politicians and citizens. Each is able to perceive through TV not just the performances that are being given, but also the inadvertent impressions that are being given off. Television, Meyrowitz observes, is 'a secret-exposing machine' (Meyrowitz 1995: 42). It collapses the distinctions between different contexts in which people may wish to play different roles.

Social media make it even harder to maintain distinctions between the different contexts of our daily lives – recall Mark Zuckerberg's argument from Chapter 2 that 'you have one identity'. We might prefer to show ourselves to our boss in a different way than to that person we met on that holiday, and we might not want our kids or our parents to see either of those sides of ourselves. We might play one part with our elderly neighbour and another with our oldest friend. But on Facebook, all of those people may be on our list of friends, and all might see aspects of our identity that we might not have chosen to show them in offline contexts. Social media make these different aspects of ourselves visible to those from whom we might otherwise have withheld them. Social media enable the walls that we build between different parts of our world to come down. Our different social contexts collapse into one.

A number of scholars have explored the implications of these collapsed contexts. Michael Wesch examined how YouTubers address the invisible audience beyond their webcams. Wesch contrasts the *to whom it may concern* address of a personal vlog with the ways in which we interact in specific daily situations. In a café or a classroom or an office, we can each assess the context in which we're interacting and how to present ourselves to those we are with. But whom are we with when we talk to a webcam and post the recording on YouTube?

> The problem is not lack of context. It is context collapse: an infinite number of contexts collapsing upon one another into that single moment of recording. The images, actions, and words captured by the lens at any moment can be transported to anywhere on the planet and preserved (the performer must assume) for all time. The little glass lens becomes the gateway to a black hole sucking all of time and space – virtually all possible contexts – in on itself. (Wesch 2009: 23)

How should users negotiate these collapsed contexts? Livingstone (2008) found young people trying to balance using social media platforms to display aspects of themselves while also using them for connection with others: two approaches that may not always be easy to effect at the same time. Marwick and boyd's research on Twitter users (Marwick & boyd 2011) identified a range of strategies through which people imagine their preferred audience for their tweets while at the same time acknowledging the difficulties of knowing just who that audience for any given tweet actually is. Such strategies might include avoiding writing about certain kinds of subjects, or trying various kinds of concealment, such as using multiple accounts. They might also include versions of steganography, or hiding the real meaning of a message within plain sight as part of something more innocuous, so that the meaning is clear only to those already in the know (boyd 2014). And maintaining a sense of authenticity while practising self-censorship can get to be demanding. 'Anxiety', as Sherry Turkle observes, 'is part of the new connectivity' (Turkle 2011: 242). What is at stake here, argues Carolyn Marvin, is 'social trust itself, the fragile conviction that our shared world is manageable and safe' (Marvin 2013: 155).

Alice Marwick draws on her ethnographic study of the tech start-up scene in San Francisco to argue that awareness of the existence of unknowable audiences and collapsed contexts leads to people crafting an online presentation of self that is not NSFW, but rather SFW – safe for work. And so in presenting ourselves in public as though to a room full of colleagues, we become complicit in the entrepreneurial, market-focused worldview of the social media companies themselves:

> Web 2.0 is a neoliberal technology of subjectivity that teaches users how to succeed in postmodern American consumer capitalism. Social media not only demonstrates the lessons of white-collar business success by rewarding flexibility, entrepreneurialism, and risk-taking; it also provides a blueprint of how to prosper in a society where status is predicated on the cultural logic of celebrity, according to which the highest value is given to mediation, visibility, and attention. That is, the technical affordances of social media reward with higher social status the uses of behaviors and self-presentation strategies that make people look. (Marwick 2013a: 14)

These market-focused business models and their entrepreneurial discourse also frame our understanding of privacy and visibility online. Nissenbaum (2011) argues that we too often tend to frame this in terms of notice-and-consent or transparency-and-choice. That is, when we sign up for Facebook, we are supposed to read the Terms and Conditions and the Privacy Policy, and we then give our informed consent to these in proceeding. This assumes, she points out, that we each have a full and complete under-standing of all the relevant facts and potential consequences at the moment we accept the terms. But we might not; we might not understand the complex legalese of the document. The fact that these terms and policies change frequently, and that what we consented to may no longer be the sub-stance of these documents by the time we have become regular users of the service, also complicates things further. Moreover, this approach also assumes that privacy is a matter of control and a matter of choice. To frame our relationships online just through these kinds of *contract* also limits our understanding of the horizons of the internet to a purely commercial set of transactions. This reduces considerations of privacy to:

> a matter of protecting *consumers* online and protecting *commercial* information: that is, protecting personal information in commercial online transactions. (Nissenbaum 2011: 41, original emphasis)

But the success of Wikipedia or of the BBC online point to the possibilities of a more public service approach. These seem exceptions, in an online environment dominated by commercial organizations. But commerce should not necessarily mean that a firm can get away with anything it wants and justify this by appeals to market logic. Many other profes-sional arenas (education, law, health) manage to combine a commercial basis with professional standards and ethical tenets that offer a service without necessarily seeking to exploit their users or elevate the com-mercial dimension above all other considerations. The social media environment should be no different.

So Nissenbaum argues for a different approach to constraining the use of our personal information online. She describes this as contextual integrity, arguing that digital media are not entirely separate from other aspects of our social worlds in which well-developed ethical norms might apply. We all recognize that we need to offer personal information to our doctor, and that she might have to share it with a specialist; but we'd be unhappy if she sold it to the *Daily Mail*, because the norms and the integrity of that context would have been broken. The context determines our expectations about how and why our personal details can be used.

In applying this argument to the internet, Nissenbaum offers the example of using a search engine: this is a process of research, she suggests, so should be governed by similar principles to offline research, as this is the relevant context. So Google shouldn't be able to exploit the search histories of our personal profiles for advertising, in the same way that the library doesn't sell our search histories on its catalogues to supermarkets. In other cases (she offers the example of a political website that invites citizens to post comments), there may be no obvious offline precursor. But this does not mean that the political website is licensed to grab all the personal information it can get, because this may discourage the very democratic debate that the site exists to foster, as users move to self-censor themselves, aware that their data is being captured. So the social context should govern the approach to handling people's personal information, rather than the profit concerns of commercial digital networks. Informed consent remains important (as we will see at the start of Chapter 6) and there is scope for profitable business models as well; but these need not be on the take-it-or-leave-it Terms and Conditions that currently govern most of our engagement with social media, and which have enabled the largest social media firms to become an elite oligopoly. Contextual integrity is a model with some force to it, but it leaves a daily challenge for all users of social media: how do we negotiate and balance contextual integrity in an environment where contexts collapse? And how do we respond to contexts in which our mediated visibility is not always under our own control?

In September 2014, actor Emma Watson gave a speech in New York about gender inequality to launch a UN campaign called 'HeForShe'. The campaign was to encourage men and boys to stand up for gender equality, and Watson, so far best known for playing Hermione in the *Harry Potter* films, was speaking this time in her capacity as United Nations Women Goodwill Ambassador. 'I think it is right that I should be able to make decisions about my own body', she said in the speech; 'I think it is right that socially I am afforded the same respect as men. But sadly I can say that there is no one country in the world where all women can expect to receive these rights' (Watson 2014). As though to underline the truth of that last sentence, a website at EmmaYouAreNext. com appeared soon afterwards. It showed Emma Watson's face beside a countdown clock and the 4chan logo, and a caption reading 'Never forget. The biggest to come thus far'.

The words *you are next* encouraged many people to think that Watson was about to become the latest celebrity to have their private nude selfies shared on 4chan. The *never forget* caption seemed to anchor the 4chan logo, as it nodded towards the Anonymous credo – *We do not forgive. We do not forget. Expect us.* And 4chan was very much in the news that week. Only days earlier, that site had precipitated an enormous leak event that became known as the #Fappening. Dozens of female celebrities found caches of their most intimate personal photos made public on social media, including Rihanna, Kirsten Dunst, Avril Lavigne and Jennifer Lawrence. Many of the images are believed to have been found on the victims' iCloud accounts.

Lawrence became the focal point of this media event, as its highest profile victim – both an Oscar winner and the star of an action franchise – and her lawyers did what they could to discourage other websites from allowing reposts of the images. But making them invisible was impossible. By 3 September 2014, more than 135,000 Reddit users had subscribed to updates from one subreddit at reddit.com/r/TheFappening alone. The top-rated post had been upvoted more than 3,200 times and had drawn more than 330 comments. The information sidebar on the page also offered a link to a list of around sixty sites where users could find the stolen images or repost copies that they were keen to share, from high-profile picture platforms like Instagram and Flickr, to file-sharing locker sites like Mega and Zippyshare, and on to UGC porn sites like YouPorn. Add to that the usual enormous daily traffic to 4chan's /b/ board on which the pictures first emerged, and the frantic reposting of images, albums and the entire haul to torrent sites and to Google Drives, and the scale of their distribution made the stolen images one of the biggest internet events of the year.

From here, the images crossed over to other forms of media. Celebrity blogger Perez Hilton posted some of the unedited Lawrence versions on his site, later taking them down and apologizing. Some major news organizations republished some of Lawrence's stolen nudes with token redactions, although their use of her face, her posed body and the caption identifying the photo as an illicitly sourced, personal sexting image put those publications into essentially the same game as those sharing the unedited versions on Reddit. Meanwhile, as the images were reappearing and disappearing from Reddit, Imgur, Photobucket, YouTube and The Pirate Bay, trolls on 4chan started a hoax #LeakforJLaw hashtag, trying to create fresh victims by getting other women to post their own naked selfies on social media in solidarity with the celebrity victims. The Emma Watson countdown turned out to be a hoax too, with a social media marketing firm called Rantic claiming responsibility for it. The firm's statement (Rantic 2014) said that the hoax 'didn't exactly have a definite purpose' – but as Rantic's business is selling fake followers to those who want to beef up their presence on Instagram, Twitter or Facebook ('Buy Fans Now!'), unflattering conclusions about their motives are there to be drawn.

The subreddit at /r/TheFappening was closed down within days. But as with the *findbostonbombers* subreddit discussed in Chapter 4, archived copies of its content can be found at the Internet Archive's Wayback Machine. This archiving in itself illustrates some of the characteristics of sharing images on social media. In danah boyd's analysis (boyd 2011), what we share online is persistent, replicable, scalable and searchable.

It's persistent, in that even the most ephemeral of online moments will pass through many servers, many networks and many devices, on which traces and copies may remain. It's replicable, in that computers are copying machines and reproducing any file is not just what those machines are built to do, but also a routine daily practice for many millions of net users who save things they like. It's scalable, in that any online interaction can in principle be scaled up and shared with a huge unknown and unknowable audience (ask Jennifer Lawrence). And it's searchable, in that every online interaction becomes part of networked databases that others can explore: including some whose entire purpose is archiving and organizing digital information, such as Google, or the Internet Archive and its Wayback Machine.

If we want an example that crystallizes the contemporary social media environment, then the #Fappening is it. It illustrates the convergence of personal communication (private nude photos taken for one's lover) with public media (those images were suddenly on the fastest-growing page ever added to the website that calls itself 'the front page of the internet'). At the centre of the event are selfies, smartphone images shared from one device to another, and then from those devices into networks of unknowable others. These images were taken from Apple's iCloud accounts and other online spaces, implicating the consumer services of the major tech firms that drive the social media environment. It's an event that orbits the multiple connotations of *sharing* that spin off from social media. And it's an event that underlines the crucial importance of questions of *visibility*, and of their ethics.

Young women are most often the victims of such campaigns of enforced visibility. Ess (2014) describes the case of Amanda Todd, who shared a topless photo of herself through a webcam at the age of twelve, and who was then relentlessly pursued by a stalker who continued to send those images to her friends, teachers and parents for three years until she committed suicide. Blogger Adrian Chen (2011) describes the case of Angie Varona, a fourteen-year-old girl whose Photobucket account was hacked, and whose images were shared millions of times, drawing their own dedicated subreddit forums through which she became a sexualized pin-up while still legally a child.

Reddit is a particular vortex for such enforced visibility: one high-profile moderator, who went by the handle Violentacrez, ran hundreds of subreddits including /r/jailbait and /r/creepshots, which specialized in sharing sexualized images of women taken in public without their awareness (Chen 2012). When Gawker outed Violentacrez as a middle-aged Texas office worker named Michael Brutsch, its reporter came under fire for having exposed Brutsch's real identity – for having made him visible.

To my mind, in this case, identifying the user of the Violentacrez handle was a solid and ethical choice because his own anonymity gave him part of the power over others that he used to enforce their visibility on a forum like /r/creepshots. But not everyone agrees – many of the biggest subreddits banned Gawker links in solidarity with Brutsch.

Journalist Jon Ronson's 2015 book *So You've Been Publicly Shamed* works through a terrible catalogue of misadventures, as one individual after another transgresses their unimagined audience's codes and is made to feel that audience's rage. The young woman, for instance, who tweeted 'Going to Africa. Hope I don't get AIDS. Just kidding. I'm white!' and found herself the number one global trending topic on Twitter, losing her job as well as getting doxed, trolled and receiving rape and death threats. Or the other young woman who posed for an inappropriate picture at a military cemetery as an in-joke with a friend, which led to her losing her job as well as getting doxed, trolled and receiving rape and death threats. The emergence of such mob shamings, Ronson writes, is as though Twitter users were 'soldiers in a war on other people's flaws, and there had suddenly been an escalation in hostilities' (Ronson 2015: 86).

This pattern of young women in particular encountering visibility as a weapon is one that recurs across social media. For example, it's central to the #GamerGate controversy that began in 2014. #GamerGate is a bewildering warzone of extreme online misogyny mixed in with arguments about ethics in the videogame industry. Its first epicentre was the release of the online non-linear narrative game 'Depression Quest' by indie game author Zoe Quinn. Allegations that her game had received a favourable review by a former lover rapidly spiralled into an ongoing conflagration in which Quinn experienced the enforced visibility of being doxed and having intimate photos circulated online, as well as receiving rape and death threats. As #GamerGate developed, others found themselves caught up in the same, now very familiar cycle of doxing/trolling/threats: game developer Brianna Wu was forced, like Quinn, to flee her home, while feminist critic Anita Sarkeesian had to cancel speaking appearances because of death threats (Stuart 2014).

The use of visibility as a weapon is also central to the phenomenon of involuntary porn – more commonly called revenge porn – through which intimate photos from consensual contexts are posted without their subjects' consent on online forums such as the now closed website *Is Anyone Up?*. The label 'revenge porn' is a problem because it suggests a general motive which may not always be present in every case – and indeed, worse, it implies a justification. So Anne Burns's (2015) term 'involuntary porn' is better. The label of 'involuntary porn' focuses on the perspective of the victim rather than that of the perpetrator (although it does beg the question of to what extent actors in professional porn are doing so on a voluntary basis). Users of *Is Anyone Up?*, and of those sites that replaced it, typically posted intimate images alongside screenshots that identified the victim. So a photograph that had been shared with a partner or an ex would be posted beside a screengrab of the front-page of the victim's Facebook Timeline. The framing of the Emma Watson hoax, in its juxtaposition with her UN address on women's rights, showed how this kind of enforced pornographic visibility is an attempt to discipline women by mediating their sexuality. It represents one extreme of the convergence of public and personal that characterizes social media. There is, however, also a further level of enforced visibility, as revealed by Edward Snowden.

PRISM

Google's browser Chrome offers a private browsing mode called Incognito. An Incognito session doesn't retain cookies or your search or browser history. Up until 2013, launching an Incognito window would bring up a message from Google that explained what the feature protected its user from and what it didn't. This message advised the user to 'be wary' of a number of threats, including: 'websites that collect or share information about you', 'people standing behind you' and 'surveillance by secret agents'. People standing behind you are beyond the scope of this book, but Google itself is one of the world's most successful websites when it comes to collecting or sharing information about you. And it was to be revealed in June 2013, that the threat of surveillance by secret agents was no joke (or else a bad one), as Google became one of the leading companies to be implicated in the security revelations made possible by Edward Snowden.

A prism is a transparent optical technology that separates and screens light into colours – a technology of visibility. PRISM is also an intelligence code-name for a data-gathering programme run by the US National Security Agency (NSA) – a very different kind of technology of visibility. PRISM was created in 2007, under the second George W. Bush administration, and continued under Barack Obama. The programme collects information directly from several of the world's leading social media and computing firms: Facebook, Google, Microsoft, Apple and Yahoo among them. Its access to Google also covers YouTube, and its access to Microsoft also covers Skype. Recall also that Yahoo owns both Tumblr and Flickr, and that Facebook owns both Instagram and WhatsApp, and the full spectrum of leading social media platforms can be seen to be refracted through the prism of the NSA. PRISM is a quite different pro-position from a system through which those firms might be asked to turn over specific details about an individual user through a court order: instead, PRISM involves the NSA having direct access to the servers of those companies.

The programme first came to light as part of the revelations facilitated by Edward Snowden (Gellman & Poitras 2013). Snowden, twenty-nine at the time, was a former CIA analyst employed by security contractors Booz Allen Hamilton, for whom he was working on developing NSA infrastructure. His relatively senior position gave him access privileges to a very wide range of systems and files, many of which he collected and copied, creating an archive which he went on to share with *The Guardian* reporters Glenn Greenwald and Ewen MacAskill, the documentary film-maker Laura Poitras and others. Snowden's motivations remain fascinating and, to some extent, enigmatic. Interviewed in Poitras's (2014) film *Citizenfour* he says: 'It all comes down to state power against the people's ability to meaningfully oppose that power. And I'm sitting there every day getting paid to design methods to amplify that state power.'

The Guardian's first story on PRISM (Greenwald & MacAskill 2013a) included several slides from an internal NSA training presentation. The list of company names appears beside a second bulleted list:

What Will You Receive in Collection (Surveillance and Stored Comms)? It varies by provider. In general:

- Email
- Chat – video, voice
- Videos
- Photos
- Stored data
- VoIP
- File transfers
- Video Conferencing
- Notifications of target activity – logins, etc
- Online Social Networking details
- Special Requests

So social media users' messages, search histories, videos, photos, online activity and connections are all covered by PRISM. The NSA could access stored messages and communication, or could monitor activity in real-time. PRISM collects not just metadata but the actual content of communications. Microsoft had been part of the programme since as far back as 2007, with Yahoo joining in 2008, Google and Facebook in 2009 and Apple in 2012.

Some of the most prominent social media firms have declared their fierce opposition to surveillance programmes such as PRISM; the irony that those firms' own business models are built on surveilling their users and using algorithms to build up models of those users' behaviour should not go unnoticed. Some have denied their involvement in PRISM. Reporting of the programme has been marked throughout by ambiguity and contradictory claims about the relationships between these social media and technology firms and the security agencies: about the extent to which there may have been direct collusion, about whether the PRISM programme may have operated without the knowledge of the technology firms, about whether the leaked documents accurately described the operation of the system, and about whether the firms would be legally able to discuss it with the news media. Surveying these arguments, Greenwald notes:

> the Internet companies' denials were phrased in evasive and legalistic fashion, often obfuscating more than clarifying. For instance, Facebook claimed not to provide 'direct access,' while Google denied having created a 'back door' for the NSA. But as Chris Soghoian, the ACLU's tech expert, told *Foreign Policy*, these were highly technical terms of art denoting very specific means to get at information. The companies ultimately did not deny that they had worked with the NSA to set up a system through which the agency could directly access their customers' data. (Greenwald 2014: 109)

What is not in any doubt is that the system exists. In September 2014 (Timberg 2014), Yahoo clarified much of this ambiguity when it revealed that it had been coerced into participating in the PRISM programme by the threat in 2008 of an ongoing daily fine of US$250,000. Far from being unaware of PRISM, Yahoo had in fact opposed it in court, but was legally unable to discuss this at the time of the initial Snowden revelations. A classified appeal court ruling against Yahoo, forcing them to comply with the surveillance programme, was subsequently instrumental in bringing other firms within PRISM (Timberg 2014). Microsoft, in contrast, was reported to have collaborated closely with the NSA to help the agency circumvent its encryption on its email and storage systems, and to provide it with fuller access to Skype (Greenwald *et al.* 2013).

PRISM quickly proved to be just one of a huge range of related secret surveillance systems revealed by Snowden. Among the other most important ones is BOUNDLESS INFORMANT. This is a data visualization and analysis tool used by the NSA to process the material it collects. *The Guardian* reported its existence on 8 June 2013, publishing an image produced by the tool that showed a colour-coded world map (Greenwald & MacAskill 2013b). That image revealed that 97 billion communications had been collected in one particular thirty-day period in 2013, including 3 billion from inside the US, where the NSA is not allowed to operate. The significance of this tool is that it shows the communications intercepted by the NSA are not just collected in some indiscriminate fashion to be discarded, but are indeed being analysed.

Another system, XKEYSCORE, vacuums up data from the fibre-optic cables that are the backbone infrastructure of global communication networks, storing both data and metadata including web searches, emails and passwords, as well as pictures taken by webcams and logged keystrokes (Marquis-Boire *et al.* 2015). NSA analysts can run searches and queries from their desks, choosing to track activity attached to a particular email account or a particular device; the system exploits the persistence of browser cookies, which were originally developed for online businesses to recognize their customers. It also exploits vulnerabilities in smartphone apps and even crash reports sent by machines to Microsoft as unencrypted data that provide full details of a user's hardware and software configurations. The website *The Intercept*, bankrolled by eBay founder Pierre Omidyar as a vehicle for Greenwald, Poitras and others to continue writing about the Snowden documents, reports that XKEY-SCORE has been central to activities including getting access to US Secretary General Ban Ki-moon's meeting notes in advance of talks with Barack Obama, and hacking the world's largest SIM card manufacturer in order to access millions of encryption keys destined for use in mobile phones (Marquis-Boire *et al.* 2015).

Other programmes among many include TEMPORA, run by the UK's GCHQ intelligence centre, which taps internet data directly from fibre-optic cables and shares it with the NSA, and EGOTISTICAL GIRAFFE (no, really): a programme that exploited vulnerabilities in outdated web browsers to allow intelligence agencies to track users of the Tor anonymous internet network, whose unique selling point is its supposed anonymity. GCHQ was reported in 2014 to have operated a programme called OPTIC NERVE that intercepted and collected millions of still images from webcam chats on Yahoo, regardless of whether or not the participants were targets of any particular surveillance; one GCHQ document on this programme was quoted as saying that: 'it would appear that a surprising number of people use webcam conversations to show intimate parts of their body to the other person' (Ackerman & Ball 2014).

In his book about working with Snowden to reveal the story, Glenn Greenwald sums up this bewildering profusion of acronyms and bizarre code-names, of secret systems and covert agreements like this:

> Taken in its entirety, the Snowden archive led to an ultimately simple conclusion: the US government had built a system that has as its goal the complete elimination of electronic privacy worldwide. Far from hyperbole, that is the literal, explicitly stated aim of the surveillance state: to collect, store, monitor, and analyze all electronic communication by all people around the globe. The agency is devoted to one overarching mission: to prevent the slightest piece of electronic communication from evading its systemic grasp. (Greenwald 2014: 94)

The classic concept for analysing state surveillance has long been the Panopticon, originally devised by Jeremy Bentham in the eighteenth century and given fresh currency in the 1970s by Michel Foucault. The Panopticon offers a model of power based on visibility. In Bentham's original vision (Bentham 2002), it described a model of prison architecture in which cells encircled a central guard tower from which any prisoner could be observed at any time. Never knowing whether they were actually being watched at any given moment, the prisoners would have to behave at all times as though they were. They would internalize the work of their own surveillance, adjusting their behaviour to accommodate a possible observer. 'Visibility', observed Foucault (1977: 200), 'is a trap'. The same principle of permanent potential visibility animated George Orwell's fictional telescreen in *Nineteen Eighty-Four*. Foucault extended Bentham's model in a wider analysis of institutions including the school, the factory and the hospital: in each of these we internalize our own surveillance, monitoring ourselves, in 'a machine in which everyone is caught' (Foucault 1980: 156).

Almost 200 years after his death, the theorist of the Panopticon himself remains caught in the machines of contemporary systems of surveillance: Bentham's preserved physical remains are mounted and on display to passers-by in a glass case at University College London. A webcam above his head records and shares online the reactions of visitors to the campus as they look at, and frequently photograph, his body, sometimes including Bentham's corpse as background in the inevitable selfies (watch at http://blogs.ucl.ac.uk/panopticam). This seems a punishment as apt and grotesque as anything from Dante.

But Bentham's Panoptic model of surveillance is quite different from that deployed in a system like PRISM. The Panopticon depends on those caught up within it *knowing* that they are being watched, while the

NSA's systems instead depend on our *not* knowing. Rather than changing our behaviour to accommodate the possibilities of being observed, the NSA's systems aim to capture and record our unadjusted behaviour. The surveillance of the enclosed institutions of modernity – the prison, the factory, the school – gives way to the surveillance of dispersed databases, of electronic communications through networks (Deleuze 1992).

The Snowden revelations continue to unfold and reverberate, and have had consequences for governments and security agencies, for the news media, for social media firms, for their users and of course for Snowden himself. Governments and their security agencies have suffered some reverses as a result of the Snowden revelations. Chief among these is the new visibility of their covert activities: their invisible surveillance programmes that made visible the private communications of many millions of people have now themselves been made visible; and moreover, we should note that those programmes were made visible by long-established publications of the Fourth Estate, not by social media. The revelations have also been damaging for the US abroad. German Chancellor Angela Merkel, French President François Hollande and Brazilian President Dilma Rousseff are just three of the world leaders to have complained to the White House about the interception of their personal communications (although of those three, only Merkel received an apology).

The Snowden files have also damaged the reputations of the security agencies involved and have triggered a number of legal processes which seem likely to take years to unfold (and which will demand entire books in their own right). At the time of writing, the US Congress has recently passed into law the USA Freedom Act, which removes the NSA's capacity to collect its citizens' telephone records in bulk; this is not about prohibiting targeted surveillance of specific individuals suspected of possible illegal behaviour, but about prohibiting the indiscriminate mass surveillance of all users of telecommunication systems. In the UK, in contrast, the independent Anderson report has left open the capacity for the security services to continue to engage in such bulk surveillance, and the Cameron government looks likely to legislate to enable them to do so. Indeed, at the time of writing, it proposes to go further and ban all encrypted communications, in an ironic response to the massacre at the offices of French satirical magazine *Charlie Hebdo*: free speech, on this proposal, must be protected by banning private speech.

The consequences for the news media involved have also been complex. On the one hand, the work of Greenwald, Poitras, MacAskill, *The Guardian*'s then-editor Alan Rusbridger and others is a first-class example of the Fourth Estate ideal of the news media in action. It involved real personal risk, and also risks to *The Guardian*, in order to expose illegal activity at the heart of state institutions and security agencies. It showed an independent news organization holding state power up to public scrutiny: work that was recognized with a Pulitzer prize for the news teams at *The Guardian* and *The Washington Post*, an Emmy for *The Guardian*'s interactive multimedia work on the story, and an Oscar for the documentary feature *Citizenfour*, directed by Poitras, which records the initial meetings over eight days in the Hong Kong hotel room between Snowden and his chosen media voices. On the other hand, though, not all the news media responded to discussing these revelations in the same spirit, in some cases perhaps because of the commercial imperative not to give too much attention to a competitor's scoop. Others, including US TV networks, failed to engage with the evidence of state wrongdoing and turned instead to the question of whether Snowden or the journalists themselves were committing crimes, perhaps treason.

Snowden, interviewed in *Citizenfour*, says that he chose to involve journalists as he had no direct experience with the news media himself, and did not want to make the decisions about how to present the material. He sought to remove his own judgment in the hope that the public interest would be better served. There is a clear parallel with WikiLeaks, who began by trying to circulate their own versions of leaked material with the 'Collateral Murder' video of April 2010, but quickly saw the advantages of working instead with established news organizations that could bring not only human resources and editorial judgment, but also a degree of protected status and reputational clout (Meikle 2012).

On the other hand, the Snowden affair has set the relationships between government and news media in a new light. The UK government pressed *The Guardian* to physically destroy hard drives containing copies of the Snowden documents. Cabinet secretary Jeremy Heywood, sent as Prime Minister David Cameron's personal envoy, told Rusbridger that: 'A lot of people in government think you should be closed down' (Harding 2014). *Guardian* staff filmed as hard drives were destroyed with drills and angle grinders, under the supervision of GCHQ staff, despite *The Guardian* being open about having other copies in overseas locations. As though to underline the symbolic nature of this procedure, the wrecked hard drives were later to appear as an exhibit in a V&A museum show. Even if this was a symbolic or pseudo-event (in Boorstin's 1961 terms, one that takes place for no other reason than to be reported), its implications for the autonomy of the news media and the viability of their Fourth Estate role are not good.

The Snowden revelations also brought considerable embarrassment for the social media and tech firms themselves. Some, including Facebook and Apple, have since moved to implement strong encryption within their messaging and notification systems (the Electronic Frontier Foundation's 'Encrypt the Web' campaign lobbies large services to implement encryption on users' data and keeps track of which firms have adopted which security measures: find updates at www.eff.org/encrypt-the-web-report). But the paradox remains that the basic social media business model of personalized advertising itself demands surveillance in some ways as egregious as that of the NSA.

Ethan Zuckerman (2014), who was involved in creating the pop-up online ad in the 1990s, has argued that advertising as a business model for the web makes surveillance inevitable. In a pre-web environment, most advertising was unverified: TV advertisers, for instance, had no way to be sure whether the viewers, to whom they were paying to get access, actually watched the commercials or not. This led both advertisers and TV networks into a cycle of developments designed to better target their audience (Ang 1991). Online advertising, in contrast, is verifiable: the act of looking at an ad in itself becomes visible. To refine this system involves ever more closely targeting individuals and building up profiles of their interests, activities, preferences and habits. What's more, the content that we are offered itself becomes tailored to those interests and preferences, from clickbait listicles to personalized news feeds, in an upwards spiral of surveillance (Zuckerman 2014).

As digital information, data and metadata proliferate, it becomes possible to move away from targeting subjects for surveillance, and simply collect everything, hang on to it, and then make use of it for analysis as and when it becomes needed. And as Andrejevic points out, the technical capacity to collect and store limitless data escalates the need to collect and store still more data: 'There is no logical endpoint to the amount of data required ... no clear point at which marketers or the police can draw the line and say no more information is needed' (Andrejevic 2012: 94).

It remains to be seen where users will draw the line with this spiral, and what limits users will ultimately demand. A principle such as the so-called Right To Be Forgotten offers one benchmark, with its provision for individuals within Europe to request that Google make certain links about them invisible in search results. This is about cases where an individual's past life is casting a digital shadow over their present: a long-ago bankruptcy that now interferes with their capacity to find employment, for example, or an involuntary porn listing appearing in search results for the person's name. So it is not about targeted advertising and the surveillance practices that enable it. But the Right To Be Forgotten does establish an important precedent about how long the traces of our digital footprints should be kept on record, and whether we are able to resist their persistent visibility.

From workplace performance management to the recording of everyday financial transactions, from policing to espionage, from CCTV to international travel, from popular entertainment to social media, one must at all times and in myriad ways submit to inspection, recording and scrutiny. And yet, as leading surveillance scholars note, these regimes of surveillance attract surprisingly little resistance (Lyon *et al.* 2012). For the most part, many people seem either happy or resigned to acquiesce in the exchange of personal visibility for claims of security or for access to services.

It remains too early to tell whether Snowden has galvanized change for significant numbers of users of social media. Some reports have found that some people are changing their information security practices since the revelations. A Pew survey in the US released in March 2015 found that 30% of adult respondents had responded to the Snowden revelations by taking at least one step to protect their personal information from the government: changing privacy settings, avoiding or deleting certain apps, or using social media less and speaking in person more (Shelton *et al.* 2015). In the UK, Ofcom surveys have tracked UK citizens' perceptions of internet security since 2005, and have found that the percentage of users who feel comfortable with giving out personal information online, such as mobile numbers, email addresses or credit card details, continues to fall (Ofcom 2015b), although there is no direct suggestion of a link to the Snowden revelations. Internet users may turn to services that offer greater anonymity and privacy than their more familiar counterparts, such as the anonymous search tools DuckDuckGo and Disconnect.me, and the anonymous browser Tor (although, paradoxically, the very use of Tor in itself may attract the attention of security agencies). But for a different kind of evidence about how social media users have responded to the Snowden revelations, we might also note that Facebook's annual reports claim that by the end of 2013, the year that saw the start of the Snowden events, the service had enjoyed an increase in user numbers of 16% on the year before, and by the end of 2014, an increase of 13% on that previous year. And on Monday 24 August 2015, for the first time, one billion people used Facebook on the same day.

Finally, there are the consequences for Snowden himself. From the beginning, he was clear that he did not want to become the story. Interviewed in *Citizenfour*, he tells Greenwald: 'I feel the modern media has a big focus on personalities and I'm a little concerned that the more we focus on [his personal story] the more they're gonna use that as a distraction ... I'm not the story here.' This too is in part a question of visibility. On the one hand, Snowden told Greenwald (2014) that he wanted to be identified as the source of the material; that he felt an obligation to explain why he was doing this and to what end. In other words, that he had to be visible. But at the same time, making himself visible as the source would also reframe the story as one about him personally. It is a very difficult thing to use the possibilities of visibility offered by the media without facing some kind of consequence as a result.

Two years on from his surfacing, his personal name recognition is probably a good deal higher with the general public than that of, say, XKEYSCORE. His central role in the story, in its documentary film version *Citizenfour*, and in the forthcoming feature film version directed by Oliver Stone all make it difficult for him to recede into the background as the events continue to unfold. The Bourne-film-style drama surrounding his departure from Hong Kong to Russia reached bizarre depths, with a planeload of international reporters mistakenly heading to Cuba in the belief that Snowden was on the plane with them; a Twitter account in the name of 'Snowden's seat' tweeted throughout the flight ('I feel empty'). At the same time, another plane carrying Bolivian President Evo Morales home from Russia was forced to make an unscheduled stop in Vienna after other European countries refused to allow it through their airspace in case Snowden was on board. The news brought the bizarre spectacle of the US warning Russia not to let a US citizen leave Russia. At the time of writing, the US continues to rule out any amnesty for Snowden, and he remains in Russia at the pleasure of Vladimir Putin. On 29 September 2015, Snowden joined Twitter. Within 24 hours, he had a million followers, but followed only one other user himself – the NSA.

TL;DR?

In March 2014, many thousands of women joined the #nomakeupselfie moment, sharing pictures of themselves without make-up to promote cancer research (some men joined in by sharing selfies of themselves *in* make-up). This campaign proposed that people share a kind of backstage image, in which the public performance of the made-up self was briefly suspended and some more authentic self was somehow revealed. But many people also shared tips on which photo filters, which camera angles and which kinds of lighting to use in order to present this authentic face in the most advantageously staged way, turning the #nomakeupselfie into a new kind of performance. Such campaigns as #nomakeupselfie highlight the complex uses of social media for performance, self-presentation and the public mediation of the personal.

Social media bring real pleasures and real opportunities for self-expression and personal connection. They allow us to make ourselves visible to others and to share experiences of being connected with others who are made visible to us in turn. But social media platforms are, among many other things, vast surveillance and monitoring mechanisms. Participatory culture on networked databases is also participatory surveillance. We watch each other and perform for those who watch us. And these performances are also staged for unknowable audiences – all of our activity is also watched by the algorithms that run the platform, recording what we say and look at, and who looks at us in turn. And governments and security agencies watch those algorithms too. At the point of capture, a particular presentation of self stops being a performance and takes on a different kind of status – that of authentic evidence. The ways in which we choose to present ourselves in social media posts, the individuals with whom we interact on a particular network, the links we choose to click on and read: all shift from being subjective experiences to becoming *data* that can be used to define us in fixed ways.

Chapter 6

Distributed Citizenship

In January 2012, a small team of researchers from Facebook and Cornell University conducted an experiment on some of Facebook's users. On 689,003 of its users, to be exact. For a week, the researchers manipulated what those users saw in their news feeds when they logged in to Facebook. The idea was to measure whether exposing the selected users to more 'negative' content left those users more likely to post 'negative' content themselves. Could Facebook alter its users' moods? The researchers tweaked some of those users' news feeds to reduce the number of posts from their friends featuring 'positive content' – the good news that their friends had wanted to share with them, the new job announcements and new baby pictures, the party details, the status updates that contained happy-sounding words. By the end of the week, the posts made by those users who had had their flow of this stuff reduced had themselves become less positive. The experiment, later published as Kramer *et al.* (2014), claimed to show that, as a result: 'emotional states can be transferred to others via emotional contagion, leading people to experience the same emotions without their awareness' (pp. 87–88). That use of 'without their awareness' is a revealing choice of words. Because none of these users had given permission, far less informed consent; none of them had been offered the choice to opt out; and none of them was to know that they had been part of this study designed to manipulate their emotions. Almost 700,000 people had been unknowingly conscripted into an experiment designed to see if the researchers could make them feel bad.

For some critics this was a story about research ethics (I write this a year after the story broke, and an active discussion about this dimension continues online in a dedicated group page hosted on, you guessed it, Facebook). It was a story that crystallized anxieties about the ethics of using so-called Big Data for research (boyd & Crawford 2012). For others it was a story about corporate responsibility and the black-box nature of Facebook's hidden algorithms. As Nicholas Carr (2014) points out: 'If the Post Office had ever disclosed that it was reading everyone's mail and choosing which letters to deliver and which not to, people would have been apoplectic, yet that is essentially what Facebook has been doing'. In fact, this is how the news feed has always operated. Facebook curates the flow of information seen by each individual user, rather than passing on every last post. If the average adult user of Facebook has 338 friends (Smith 2014; probably more by the time you read this), then most will not have the time or inclination to read through everything posted, shared, commented upon or liked by each of those friends on a given day. It would be overwhelming. So Facebook makes selections for what appears in our news feeds, based on what it thinks we most want to see. But the problem is that, as users, we don't know how it does this, and nor do we have any meaningful ways to make those selections for ourselves (assigning some people to a 'Close Friends' list is a crude and inflexible option). The curation of one's news feed is a top-down, take-it-or-leave-it proposition managed by Facebook, not by the user. And the 'emotional contagion' project – which came to light only because its researchers opted to publish their findings in an academic journal in 2014 – lifts the lid on just what we may be giving up in allowing Facebook to make these choices on our behalf.

This secret manipulation of people's emotions through algorithms is a stark insight into the power relationships between social media platforms and their users (Gillespie 2014). Facebook did this, without asking those users, because it could. Any new information that can be gleaned about how to push users' buttons to keep them using the network and building its database seems to provide it with a good enough justification. And as for those of us who may be conscripted into such experiments without our knowledge? Those of us who may log into Facebook on a bad day, looking for some kind of moment of pleasure or communion or validation, only to have those invisibly re-routed as part of a Facebook project designed to try to make us feel sad that week? Here are the early signs of the consequences of bringing the personal and the public together in a proprietary commercial space that runs on algorithms. It's not that we are reduced to our data. It's worse than that. It's that we are reduced to *their* data.

The Facebook/Cornell experiment created a lot of bad press for all involved. The gist of much of the news reporting and op-ed commentary was that Facebook should treat its customers with more respect and consideration. But as we saw in Chapter 2, Facebook's users are not its customers. Facebook's users are the raw material for the data products that the company sells to its actual customers – advertisers, brands and marketers. So this chapter argues that we need to rethink our relationships with social media firms, and our position within the contemporary internet environment. We need to move away from asserting our sovereign rights as customers of firms that don't see us that way in the first place. Instead, we should rethink our relationships in terms of *citizenship*.

In his book *Cultural Citizenship*, Toby Miller suggests that 'We are in a crisis of belonging' (Miller 2007: 1). Miller's book is mainly concerned with television, but its year of publication coincided with the mainstream consolidation of social media platforms, most notably Facebook. Almost a decade later, we could restate the claim of a crisis of belonging, but this time in relation to social media. This time, the crisis is that we are obliged to belong to commercial data-mining networks, even as we may know that they do not operate in our best interests. The ubiquity of Facebook, of Google, of Twitter, keeps us there because our friends are there, our families are there, our colleagues, our peers, our neighbours are there. The contemporary cultural crisis of belonging is that belonging has become obligatory. But in what sense do we belong to Facebook? Only in the sense that it owns our ideas and images, our address books and personal histories, our public statements and our private secrets. So how should we respond? One line of response is to reconsider our uses of social media in terms of a different sense of belonging – that of citizenship. This chapter offers a new way of thinking about the relationships between citizenship, activism and social media.

To be a citizen, James Carey once observed 'is to assume a relation in space to one's contemporaries' (Carey 1989: 4). His concern was to connect certain conceptions of communication with the problems of establishing and maintaining a democracy on the scale of the US. Carey distinguished between two fundamental ways of conceiving of communication. On the one hand, there is what he termed the *transmission* view of communication, through which messages are sent across space for the purposes of controlling territory; and on the other, there is what he called the *ritual* view of communication, understood as a symbolic process of maintaining community through time. In the social media environment, the centralized production and one-way distribution of the transmission model blurs with the ritual model's personal communication and the sharing of networked individuals. Meanings are not just transmitted through networks, but rather they circulate, with each new moment of sharing sparking a fresh association in a fresh context. The making of meanings is distributed.

This chapter proposes the concept of *distributed* citizenship – to assume a creative political relation within networks with one's contemporaries. Relations of distributed citizenship are not defined by or restricted to a particular geographical location or polity, but are defined rather by shared meanings and collaborative creativity and action within and through networked digital media. Distributed citizenship is a political possibility of the social media environment, but it needs a rethink of the commercial terms demanded of us as users and that we as users are prepared to accept. It can exist not within a given space, but within networks – it is a form of citizenship that can develop within what Castells terms the space of flows, which he defines as 'the technological and organizational possibility of practicing simultaneity without contiguity' (Castells 2009: 34). Distributed citizenship describes a set of potentials made possible by social media, and by the altered experiences and awareness of culture, connection and community that result from their widespread adoption and adaptation.

To recap on key points from this book's first two chapters, social media are networked database platforms that combine public with personal communication. For the most part, these are commercial operations that grow by having their users contribute content; this builds the database that those platforms can exploit for advertising and marketing. Social media are those that allow any user, in principle: to say and make things; to share the things that they or others have said and made; and to make that saying, making and sharing visible to others in new kinds of contexts. So social media can be understood by analysing their uses and affordances in terms of *creativity* (saying and making), *sharing* and *visibility*. The focus in this chapter is on the first of these – creativity – and in particular on the forms of collaboration that Tim Berners-Lee has termed *intercreativity* (Berners-Lee 1989: 182–3). The chapter begins by briefly reviewing some key modern formulations of citizenship and media, before developing the concept of distributed citizenship in relation to networks, responsibility and spatiality. It then goes on to apply this to four key examples of distributed citizenship projects: the global #Occupy movement; the fleeting *Kony 2012* phenomenon; cryptocurrencies, typified by Bitcoin; and the diaspora* social media platform.

From Civil to DIY Citizenship

In an influential essay originally published in 1950, T.H. Marshall distinguished between three dimensions of citizenship, which he termed the civil, political and social. By *civil*, he referred to Enlightenment rights such as personal liberty, freedom of speech and of religion, and rights of property and the law. By *political*, he referred to the rights to vote and participate in the mechanisms, processes and institutions of government, from national parliament to local council. And by *social*, he referred to those rights bound up most closely with the twentieth-century expansion of education, welfare and health services:

> from the right to a modicum of economic welfare and security to the right to share in the full in the social heritage and to live the life of a civilised being according to the standards prevailing in the society. (Marshall 1992: 8)

The development of citizenship in Marshall's analysis was coterminous with the development of capitalism, but citizenship, as he observed, is a system of equality whereas capitalism is one of inequality. 'Citizenship', Marshall (1992): 18) wrote, 'is a status bestowed on those who are full members of a community'. Critics of Marshall (such as Smith 2002) have pointed out that the eighteenth- to twentieth-century narrative of progress he presents is not without its own inequalities, with some social groups – indigenous peoples, for instance – gaining access to civil, political and social citizenship on very different timelines to that of Marshall's schema.

So an important addition to this three-part model was the concept of *cultural* citizenship (Hartley 1999, Miller 2002). Citizenship, argues Hartley, is 'a term of *association* among *strangers*' (Hartley 2012: 133), and is to be understood as 'a *relational identity*, inconstant, dynamic, and evolving', rather than as a universal constant condition (p. 135). To this end, Hartley (1999, 2012) extends Marshall's three-part schema to include cultural citizenship. Cultural citizenship describes the recognitions of differences demanded by the identity politics of the late twentieth century. For Miller, it is about 'the maintenance and development of cultural lineage via education, custom, language, and religion, and the positive acknowledgement of difference in and by the mainstream' (Miller 2002: 231). It is made possible by broadcast media and the way that television 'gathers populations' (Hartley 1999: 158). Hartley expands on this:

> Television ... is no respecter of differences among its audiences; it *gathers populations* which may otherwise display few connections among themselves and positions them as its audience 'indifferently', according to all viewers the same 'rights' and promoting among them a sense of common identity *as* television audiences. At one and the same time, then, people can experience political differences based on territory, ethnicity, law and heritage between one another, but also, simultaneously and conversely, they can enjoy undifferentiated 'identity' with others based on television audiencehood. (Hartley 1999: 158)

Television made possible new ways of thinking about the public world of the social and private sphere of the home (Meyrowitz 1985), and new styles in which to imagine community (Anderson 1991). It made possible new calendars of shared national moments and events, and a new conception of a *general* public (Scannell & Cardiff 1991). And it also contributed to making possible new kinds of recognitions of difference, or *identity* politics (Castells 2004). But while television is still a dominant medium, its hold on our attention is now complemented by other media, making possible other ways of thinking about how we organize ourselves and each other.

So following on from cultural citizenship and its politics of shared identity, Hartley also proposes *DIY* (do it yourself) citizenship. This is 'the practice of putting together an identity from the available choices, patterns and opportunities on offer' (Hartley 1999: 178). DIY citizenship is about consumption and choice; it is a postmodern bricolage of fashions, gestures, practices and ideas, and is again very much bound up with television.

> Whether it's a full 'fitted' identity, expensive, integrated and in a recognizable off-the-shelf style, or an identity more creatively put together from bits and pieces bought, found or purloined separately, is a matter of individual difference. The point is, 'citizenship' is no longer simply a matter of a social contract between state and subject, no longer even a matter of acculturation to the heritage of a given community; DIY citizenship is a choice people can make for themselves. Further, they can change a given identity, or move into or out of a repertoire of identities. (Hartley 1999: 178)

But as Turner points out, the 'repertoire of identities' that are made available through such contemporary genres as reality TV, and its annual contestants' 'journey' towards a new public self, are quite constrained and limited. Hartley's use of the term DIY also means that his concept of DIY citizenship has been taken up by participants in design, craft and makers movements, and by theorists and practitioners of critical making (Ratto & Boler 2014). While some of this work is fascinating (such as Mann 2014), it is a quite different sense of DIY from Hartley's original usage, which was again concerned with television. And neither makers movements nor television can quite help us to understand social media.

Each of Hartley's new forms of televised citizenship, he notes, is 'increasingly reliant on *communication* and less on *the state*' (Hartley 2012: 147). But in the social media environment, large corporate entities such as Google and Facebook are sovereign. The unwritten social contract gives way to the unread Terms of Service agreement – man is born free, and everywhere he is on Facebook. So if the granting of rights has been ceded from states to Silicon Valley corporations, then for whom is this a good outcome? So this chapter instead proposes a model rooted in the contemporary social media environment – distributed citizenship.

Distributed Citizenship

What, then, is distributed citizenship? Distributed citizenship describes taking up a creative political relation with one's contemporaries within social media networks. It is more concerned with the exercise of rights and responsibilities than with choice and consumption. Its key terms are creativity, sharing and visibility. It is self-reflexive citizenship, which is as yet more concerned with winning and securing its rights than with exercising them. It is not a description of a condition that has as yet been fully realized; rather, it is an aspiration. In this, it is no different from the other key conceptions of citizenship above – civil, political, social, cultural – not all of which have yet been obtained by everyone who could enjoy their benefits, and which remain aspirations for many people around the world. In what senses is this citizenship *distributed*? It is distributed in three ways – in terms of networks, in terms of responsibility and in terms of spatiality.

First, it is distributed in the same sense as a distributed computer network – one with multiple points of connection and contact, with deliberate redundancy of connectivity, and with fewer hubs and points of centralized control than in other forms of network topology. The internet was conceived as a distributed network, but contemporary developments by firms such as Facebook, Apple and Google reimagine the internet as at best *decentralized* (with certain key hubs dominating traffic, interactions, attention and revenue), or at worst *centralized* (with all communication flowing through Facebook's servers to be data-mined and monetized). So in relation to networks, distributed citizenship describes an environment in which the infrastructure of participation, rights and responsibilities is not concentrated in centralized spaces or in decentralized hubs, but is rather distributed widely across the network.

Second, it is distributed in terms of *responsibility*. The language and interface of social network spaces put each individual at the centre. Each platform is built around our profile, our personal timeline, our individual history, CV and address book. Yet our interactions with others on these platforms do not take place in our individual space, but are distributed. You craft a status update that represents you to your chosen network in the way that you most prefer; but I comment on your post, and my comment becomes a part of your self-presentation too, in ways which may work against your intended performance. What are the ethics of this? I then share your post with my own chosen networks, taking it out of the context for which you had shaped it, and repositioning your words within a new context of my own preference. What are the ethics of that? Such interactions are not the individual presentations or performances of autonomous selves, but are rather collaborations between distributed users. Our profiles are *co-constructed* with others in our networks (Trottier & Lyon 2012, Ellison & boyd 2013). Even though certain high-status users may have greater concentrations of attention than others, those collaborations are nonetheless distributed across networks.

Distributed citizenship involves each of us reassessing our responsibilities towards others in our networks. The Snowden revelations show that government security agencies and Silicon Valley corporations alike share an interest in harvesting and archiving what we say, feel, think and do through networked digital media. So the responsibility for developing an ethics of distributed citizenship has to start with the users of those networks. We now know for certain that we can't trust Facebook or the NSA to look out for us. Instead, we have to look out for ourselves and each other. This is not an argument for self-censorship, or that we should internalize the work of our own surveillance, but rather that we rethink our interactions on these networks as not personal or self-directed communication, but rather as *distributed* communication. We need to develop technologies of the selfie, as Foucault almost said. We do not only have rights to speak, share and to make ourselves and our interactions visible, but we also have responsibilities to those with whom we speak, with whom we share, and whose interactions with us we make visible in social media networks.

And third, it is distributed in *spatial* terms. Distributed citizenship is not bound to a particular state – and far less to the *city* from which the word *citizen* derives. Instead it is an aspect of a world characterized by increasing mobility, as flows of tourists, students, asylum seekers, business people and migrants intersect with flows of ideas, finance, technologies and images (Appadurai 1996, Urry 2007, Bellamy 2008). This is not to argue that the state has lost its salience. Far from it – look across Europe today, and the continued salience of the state is fundamental to situations as diverse as the Ukraine crisis, the vicissitudes of the Euro, or the Scottish independence referendum of 2014. The state is not going anywhere. But questions of ideas and property, of voice and participation, of creativity, sharing and visibility, are increasingly the domain of communicative environments which are largely under the control of enormous US media and technology corporations. So as networks such as Facebook expand still further into further non-western, non-northern territories, then questions of voice and governance, of sharing and visibility – questions of *ethics* and distributed citizenship – will become more pressing. If citizenship, in Marshall's terms, describes the status of one who is a full member of a community, equal in terms of both the rights and the responsibilities of that community, then it does not necessarily have to be a condition restricted to nations or states.

Intercreativity

These three aspects of distributed citizenship are each bound up with the creativity, sharing and visibility of users and uses of social media. A very useful concept here is intercreativity, as defined by World Wide Web creator Tim Berners-Lee:

> We ought to be able not only to find any kind of document on the Web, but also to create any kind of document, easily. We should be able not only to follow links, but to create them between all sorts of media. We should be able not only to interact with other people, but to create with other people. *Intercreativity* is the process of making things or solving problems together. If *interactivity* is not just sitting there passively in front of a display screen, then *intercreativity* is not just sitting there in front of something 'interactive.' (Berners-Lee 1999: 182–3)

Berners-Lee identifies here the crucial element of collaborative online creativity. Intercreativity is intrinsic to social media, through their capacity to connect people who are made visible to each other through digital networks. So it ought to be central to any attempt to use social media for political or cultural activism.

We can identify four dimensions of such intercreative online activism. First, textual intercreativity, through which existing media images and narratives are reimagined and reworked into entirely new texts or into hybrid subversions of their component images. Second, tactical intercreativity, as activists develop online variations of established protest gestures and campaign tactics. Third, strategic intercreativity, which builds upon the traditions and conventions of alternative media. And fourth, network intercreativity, whose participants work to build new media network models, including those which link open source software to experimental online publishing practices. The following sections offer examples of each of these dimensions of intercreativity: textual (#Occupy), tactical (*Kony 2012*), strategic (Bitcoin) and network (diaspora*). Each of these examples is, of course, a complex, multi-faceted phenomenon, and this chapter is not suggesting that any of them can be reduced to the single aspect of each that is isolated here just as an example for discussion.

Intercreative Texts – #Occupy

On 17 September 2011, activists began to occupy Zuccotti Park in Manhattan, under the banner of Occupy Wall Street. In a matter of weeks, this occupation became a movement that spread to hundreds of cities across the US and to scores of countries around the world. Where did #Occupy come from? The financial crisis from 2008 on and the subsequent blunted hopes for the Obama presidency were two factors in its development. They had engendered a context in which many people felt ripped off and aggrieved – Christian Fuchs's survey of more than 420 #Occupy activists found their motivations to include opposition to injustice and inequality, financial and political corruption, and austerity policies, among other things (Fuchs 2014c: 50–61). But many of those same people had also already experienced collective mobilization around one common cause (*yes we can*) or another, and had also experienced the ways in which this could take place in and through online networks as well as physical places. And the wave of popular uprisings of early 2011, from Tunisia to Cairo's Tahrir Square, and across Europe from Iceland to Greece to Spain offered magnetic examples (Castells 2012).

One important impetus came from the Canadian culture jamming organization Adbusters, discussed in Chapter 3. Adbusters posted a 500-word call on their website, titled '#OCCUPYWALLSTREET: A shift in revolutionary tactics', on 13 July 2011. 'Are you ready for a Tahrir moment?' it began. 'On Sept 17, flood into lower Manhattan, set up tents, kitchens, peaceful barricades and occupy Wall Street.' It's worth quoting at length to give something of its tone, as well as to note the call for a specific goal, right at the start of the movement:

> Alright you 90,000 redeemers, rebels and radicals out there,
>   A worldwide shift in revolutionary tactics is underway right now that bodes well for the future. ... The beauty of this new formula, and what makes this novel tactic exciting, is its pragmatic simplicity: we talk to each other in various physical gatherings and virtual people's assemblies ... we zero in on what our one demand will be, a demand that awakens the imagination and, if achieved, would propel us toward the radical democracy of the future ... and then we go out and seize a square of singular symbolic significance and put our asses on the line to make it happen.

The time has come to deploy this emerging stratagem against the greatest corrupter of our democracy: Wall Street, the financial Gomorrah of America.

On September 17, we want to see 20,000 people flood into lower Manhattan, set up tents, kitchens, peaceful barricades and occupy Wall Street for a few months. Once there, we shall incessantly repeat one simple demand in a plurality of voices.

Tahrir succeeded in large part because the people of Egypt made a straightforward ultimatum – that Mubarak must go – over and over again until they won. Following this model, what is our equally uncomplicated demand?

The most exciting candidate that we've heard so far is one that gets at the core of why the American political establishment is currently unworthy of being called a democracy: we demand that Barack Obama ordain a Presidential Commission tasked with ending the influence money has over our representatives in Washington. It's time for DEMOCRACY NOT CORPORATOCRACY, we're doomed without it. (Adbusters 2011)

The #Occupy movement, from Zuccotti Park in lower Manhattan to Quito, Berlin and Melbourne, from Seoul to Abuja, was, of course, a movement that highlighted the importance of shared public and urban spaces. But it was also a movement built around both creating and challenging symbols and abstractions. *Wall Street*, as McKenzie Wark points out, is a metonym for the US financial system, an abstraction, which is not confined to the particular physical street itself – but then the actual occupation wasn't really of Wall Street either (Wark 2012). Both the established narrative of Wall Street as a locus of power and the counter-narrative of #Occupy could make meanings from this abstraction. Activists occupied key strategic sites and used these as bases for discussion and education, for organization and demonstration. So while the physical occupations were crucial, it was also a movement which challenged established stories and offered new ones of its own. In particular, #Occupy brought forth stories that made inspired use of the social media logic of the convergence of the personal and the public. It was a movement in which particular kinds of intercreative text were central in distributing its core ideas and its most effective simple messages.

One such text was, of course, the key term *Occupy*, with or without its #hashtag. It's worth noting that Adbusters' original call for action not only named the movement in the title of its blog post, but actually named it with a hashtag. The word *occupy* proved limitlessly adaptable – from the germinal Occupy Wall Street, to the humorous Occupy Sesame Street, later reworked as a pointed response to US presidential candidate Mitt Romney's criticism of that show's public broadcaster, and on into space: 'One star controls 99% of Earth's visible light resources – #Occupythesun'. The image of the occupying citizenry, rather than the occupying army, resonated in different ways in many different contexts. It variously echoed civil rights movements, anti-war activism, labour movements, women's suffrage, the ouster of governments (Eastern Europe in 1989) or thwarted student movements (China in 1989). The idea of *occupy* connected with multiple histories and trajectories of protest and non-violent civil disobedience, and this gave it both legitimacy and an easily grasped familiarity.

The unheeded call to occupy the sun also played on the other key intercreative text of the movement – the slogan *we are the 99 percent*, which spread across social media platforms and from them to other forms of media as well. The simplicity of the idea that 1% of the population control its wealth made it easy to both adopt and adapt in new contexts as it circulated through networks of ideas and association. Such shared personal expression as part of a wider political movement but with relatively little coordinated organization is an example of what Bennett and Segerberg (2012) call connective action. Many hundreds of images of individuals holding up statements of their own circumstances and self-identifying as the 99% are collected at the original eponymous Tumblr blog (http://wearethe99percent.tumblr.com/archive). They demonstrate how each contributor was able to take the idea and adapt it to their own circumstances and subjectivity.

A young man holds this text in front of his face:

> I am 22 years old. One year ago, I broke my ankle during a hiking accident. I was unemployed and uninsured, it left me with $28,000 medical debt … My medical debt destroyed my credit, I can't get a job or any sort of loan. Even jobs do credit checks which limits where I can work … I am the 99%.

A boy aged about seven holds up this text for the camera:

> My Mom is a single parent and unemployed. We live day to day struggling to get by. She is in major debt due to school loans and taxes. We ARE the 99%!!!

An older man holds up his story:

> We are an older couple living off social security, this was earned by paying into the system for 40+ years. Now Congress wants to save money by cutting our benefits … We are the 99%.

And a younger woman shares hers:

> Single mom, grad student, unemployed, and I paid more tax last year than GE [General Electric corporation]. I am the 99 Percent. Occupy Wall Street, Sept. 17.

This Tumblr became a space for shared personal storytelling and for public manifestations of support – support for others sharing their stories and support for the occupation and its participants. Each individual story, captured in the same genre of written text held up for the camera by its teller – selfies, for the most part, although the subjects were not always identifiable – illustrated the social media logic of the convergence of personal and public communication, as each personal story took on a public quality as part of a larger political narrative.

In this sense, the statement *Occupy + place*, the hashtag #Occupy, and the slogan *We are the 99 percent* are all internet memes in the sense explored in Chapter 3. Each was a shared, rule-based representation of online interactions that was not only adopted but also adapted by others. Gerbaudo (2012) highlights the differences between the initial professional Occupy imagery created by Adbusters and the subsequent personal stories of *We are the 99 percent*. Adbusters is a sophisticated design house, with decades of experience in creating images for campaigns and for its glossy magazine. Its initial imagery, above all the iconic picture of the ballerina atop the Wall Street bull statue, draws on this expertise, and situates the call to action in a context that reaches back to the anti-capitalist carnivals of Reclaim the Streets and the anti-globalization movements of the late 1990s and early years of this century (Jordan 1998, McKay 1998, Meikle 2002). In contrast, the aesthetics of *We are the 99 percent* are those of the selfie and of the hand-drawn note. Their very amateurism speaks to the personal expression being shared. But there is also an important dimension that these approaches have in common. Each of these inter-creative texts has a powerful and simple theme that makes it easy to translate into new contexts – Occupy Nigeria, Occupy Berlin – and each can circulate from point to point within distributed networks of users and contexts.

Intercreative Tactics – *Kony 2012*

On 5 March 2012, the thirty-minute video *Kony 2012* was uploaded to YouTube. Within its first week online, the film had been viewed 100 million times. *Kony 2012* is an activist campaign film, built around the affordances of social media for sharing and visibility. The film achieved an unexpected, indeed unprecedented level of awareness within days. A Pew survey in the days after the film's release found that almost 60% of young adults in the US knew about the video (Rainie et al. 2012). *Kony 2012* was made by Invisible Children, a US non-profit organization founded in 2004 to generate and coordinate public support and action to stop the activities of Joseph Kony, the leader of a paramilitary organization called the Lord's Resistance Army (LRA). Kony had been indicted by the International Criminal Court (ICC) in The Hague in July 2005 on multiple counts of crimes against humanity and war crimes.

The film's project was to 'make Kony famous'. In a bizarre inversion of the cultural logic of media celebrity, the campaign aimed to turn Joseph Kony into a celebrity in order to maximize public awareness and so put pressure on the US to pursue his capture. This publicity campaign was built around the affordances offered by social media for the circulation and sharing of ideas and images, of emotions and opinions. The film presents Invisible Children's earlier campaigning and lobbying efforts through a *mise-en-scène* built around the visual repertoire of social media, with images of the growth of their campaign's Facebook presence used as a key visual indicator of momentum, and archive footage of earlier campaign events introduced within the film through embedded video links on their Facebook page. *Kony 2012* begins with a ninety-second montage of images and clips, moving from shots of the Earth seen from space, to images illustrating social media: fragments of YouTube videos show a child being rescued from the Haitian earthquake, a young woman in an audiology clinic hearing her own voice for the first time, images of Twitter and Facebook from the Arab Spring, a child learning to ride a bike, grand-parents and grandchildren sharing a video chat and images of cursors clicking on 'share' buttons. Director Jason Russell's voiceover begins:

> Right now, there are more people on Facebook than there were on the planet two hundred years ago. Humanity's greatest desire is to belong and connect. And now we see each other, we hear each other, we share what we love and it reminds us what we all have in common. And this connection is changing the way the world works. Governments are trying to keep up and older generations are concerned. The game has new rules.

In a problematic move, the film makes heavy use of Jason Russell's five-year-old son Gavin as the viewer's proxy. Russell explains the issues about Kony and his organization to the viewer by explaining them to a small child, which can come across as patronizing, and is a strange shift of attention away from the actual child victims of the LRA. Luis Moreno

Ocampo, prosecutor for the International Criminal Court in The Hague, is then interviewed on-camera to set Kony in an appropriate international juridical context. Kony, we are told, was the first man indicted by the ICC, in July 2005, for crimes against humanity. Both Ocampo and Gavin are then shown saying the solution is to 'stop' Kony. 'Here's the biggest problem', Russell tells his son. 'You want to know what it is? Nobody knows who he is.' Gavin demurs – he knows who Kony is; he can see him in the picture his Dad gave him. Russell disagrees with him: 'He's not famous. He's invisible. *Joseph Kony is invisible.*'

The solution, Russell says in voiceover, is to make Kony visible. There could be no more stark example of how central questions of visibility are in the social media environment, than this most widely seen social media text that is built and framed around such questions, from the name of its producers to its tactics and strategy. Visibility was the entire project. It was also, to some extent, the undoing of the project, as the greater than anticipated sharing of the film saw the campaign move away from Invisible Children's control. Indeed, Invisible Children was to announce in December 2014 that it was winding up its activities because it could no longer secure the funding to continue its work.

As well as the 100 million views, references to the film swamped Facebook and Twitter, and were picked up by the major established news media around the world. The enormous attention drawn by the film was a prime example of what Wark terms the 'weird global media event':

> Something of significance that appears to happen in a particular place, but which actually takes place along the vectors which connect that place to a world. The world called into being by the event is not global in the sense of universal, but rather it invokes *a* world. Its weirdness stems from some unexpected novelty in where and how it happens. (Wark 2012: 208)

Kony 2012 illustrates this particular kind of media phenomenon very well. It was a *media* event, in that it did not take place in a physical space but rather played out through networks of digital connections. It was a *global* media event, in that it captured the news agenda around the world: from the BBC and *The Guardian* to a front-page story in *The New York Times*; to Australia, where the film was broadcast in full on a major national TV network; and across Africa, where it provoked much controversy and outrage. And it was a *weird* global media event in that its unpredictable novelty and its unexpected circulation made it resistant to normal news frames and narratives. Its weirdness was sealed, and the campaign perhaps fatally derailed, when the film's director and on-screen narrator Jason Russell performed a very public breakdown two weeks after its release, being filmed naked and pounding the streets with his fists in rush-hour traffic in San Diego – video of which also spread rapidly across the net. Mediated visibility, as we saw in Chapter 5, has its consequences.

The *Kony 2012* campaign's 'Cover the Night' event, for which supporters around the world were urged to plaster their town with Kony posters, stickers and graffiti, could have been a challenge to its supporters to create, collaborate upon and share the most novel, surprising and powerful responses they could imagine. But instead of an appeal for supporters to create their own textual, tactical, strategic and network approaches, the film presents a repertoire of products available for purchase – posters, stickers, yard signs and a bracelet with a unique ID number that gives access on the campaign website to 'the mission to make Kony famous'. 'Everything you need', explains Russell, 'is in a box called the Action Kit'. The film does not mention that this box cost US$30.

The *Kony 2012* campaign illustrates the importance and centrality of the visible in relation to social media. As we saw in Chapter 5, social media bring with them new kinds of visibility, new opportunities and requirements to monitor and be monitored, to perform and display, and to connect with others who are newly visible to us and to whom we are ourselves in turn made visible. The case of *Kony 2012* is a spectacular invocation of a nascent distributed citizenship, but it also points to the possibilities, the limitations and the dangers of a politics of enforced visibility or radical transparency. And it also suggests that the use of a consumption model of social media activism is not necessarily going to translate into widespread action. 'Buy our action kit' is not a proposition that is best suited to an environment in which mediation is not something we are subject to, but also something that we *do*. A media politics, an internet activism, of intercreativity, of collaboration and collaborative making, and of collaborative creativity and sharing, is one better suited to the environment in which public media and personal communication converge, and in which the potential of that convergence is realized by people not only sharing links but creating together.

Intercreative Strategies – Bitcoin

Bitcoin is, at the time of writing in 2015, the best-known cryptocurrency. Cryptocurrencies are experimental media for financial transactions, through which *coins*, or unique digital identifiers, are *mined*, or released by expending very high levels of computer processing power on cracking complex maths problems. The finite number of such identifiers, and the metaphorical labour needed to find them, create the scarcity from which the coins derive their value. These cryptocurrency principles have been remixed into many variants such as Sexcoin, Scotcoin or the Kanye-West-themed Coinye. In February 2014, the Jamaican national bobsleigh team made it to the Winter Olympics in Sochi, Russia, after supporters raised US$30,000 in donations made through the doge-based cryptocurrency Dogecoin (*much coin, very currency, wow*). Such remixes indicate that Bitcoin itself is, among many other things, an internet meme.

But Bitcoin is also a distributed, collaborative creative attempt to develop not just a new currency or medium of exchange, but an entirely new kind of financial system – one that is independent from both the established global banking infrastructure and the national governments that underpin much of it. Where the #Occupy movement called for reform of financial structures, Bitcoin actually enacts one. In this, Bitcoin is an activist strategy that aims at consolidating an alternative way of doing things that had previously seemed settled. At the same time, it is important to recognize that mining Bitcoins is also a fairly elite practice, requiring sophisticated understandings of maths and cryptography. It demands ever higher levels of processing power from the increasingly dedicated, custom-built, computer mining rigs required to release new blocks of Bitcoins. Nonetheless, Bitcoin and other cryptocurrencies are a provocation to established social and financial conventions – a provocation that is distributed in terms of networks, responsibility and spatiality.

A technology can be understood as a way of imposing order on a social situation, of resolving a debate or of closing down contending possibilities. Technology, in Bruno Latour's (1991) phrase, is 'society made durable'. As Langdon Winner argues: 'specific features in the design or arrangement of a device or system could provide a convenient means of establishing patterns of power and authority in a given setting' (Winner 1986: 38). So for this reason, we need to ask who benefits from any particular proposed technological solution. What is the problem that it is supposed to solve? And what social consequences are implied or invoked in the way it reaches its solution? So if we are to understand the contribution that Bitcoin could make to the development of distributed citizenship, we need to ask what problem it proposes to solve and how it is to go about this.

Bitcoin is a system for making digital transactions or payments on a peer-to-peer basis, without the need for a third party such as a bank to guarantee the transaction. It is, as its mysterious author Satoshi Nakamoto puts it in the original proposal, 'a system for electronic transactions without relying on trust' (Nakamoto 2008: 8). Bitcoin tries to solve the problem of 'double-spending'. A peer exchange of digital 'coins' could be repeated by either party in the exchange without some way of validating that neither is ripping off the other by exchanging already spent coins. The Bitcoin system relies on 'proof-of-work' to ensure authenticity and single-spending. The computer processing power that has been expended in releasing the encrypted coin becomes encoded into that coin, as does every subsequent transaction in which it's involved.

But as David Golumbia (2015) argues, the problems that Bitcoin sets out to solve reveal the system as one that embodies and actually encodes certain strands of libertarian anti-government thinking. It proposes a solution to the existence of banks, and by extension to the existence of taxes and the governments that manage them. But it's a system built upon refining a technical problem in peer-to-peer transactions (double-spending), not upon a political analysis of the financial system. The banks, which caused the global crisis of 2008 onwards, are in dire need of such an analysis, but Bitcoin is instead a technical fix to a technical problem. It also unwittingly shows the importance of regulation, and of the system of trust that it seeks to undermine. Because without the regulatory oversight made possible by government, Bitcoin is 'particularly prone to the kinds of hoarding, dumping, derivation, and manipulation that characterize all instruments that lack central bank control' (Golumbia 2015: 123).

A thick seam of libertarian attitudes has always run through internet cultures. These were given their most indelible expression in John Perry Barlow's 'Declaration of the Independence of Cyberspace' in 1996. This text (Barlow 1996), which addressed governments as a technology of the past, and told them they were unwelcome in the 'new home of mind' that was the internet, has been a central root of some of the most enduring misapprehensions about the internet (among these, the still persistent error that the internet is somehow unregulated). It articulates a world-view in which, as Ronald Reagan put it, government is the problem. It's simultaneously nostalgic and futurist.

In a counter-move to such libertarian positions, Terranova and Fumagalli (2015) ask whether other values can be encoded into alternative cryptocurrencies, rejecting the in-built politics of Bitcoin itself:

> Bitcoin encodes the core values of the libertarian cypherpunk society: a rejection of state control and of the dominion of large corporations; the endorsement of anonymity or at least pseudonymity; the deployment of a peer-to-peer architecture with no central control; and a distrust of subjective relations which aims at minimizing the human and social element by means of objective mechanisms.
> (Terranova & Fumagalli 2015: 154)

They describe a proposed cryptocurrency called Commoncoin that would reject the proof-of-work element of Bitcoin and its commitment to the established financial regime of scarcity. Instead, Commoncoin would develop cooperation-based approaches to establishing value. Instead of money earned and money spent, it would record contributions made and taken from the network, so putting the emphasis on the commons rather than on the individual. Commoncoin would draw upon the affordances of social media (they mention 'social plugins, tagging, comment boxes', p. 156) in order for its users to develop and express different values to those of the existing financial system. Whether or not the Commoncoin system ever gets off the ground, it points to the experiments and explorations being undertaken to develop intercreative strategies that enable a redistribution of rights and responsibilities. And Bitcoin itself also underscores the fact that while distributed citizenship is both possible and emerging, there is no reason to assume that there need be anything progressive about it.

Intercreative Networks – diaspora*

The distributed social media platform diaspora* styles itself as 'the online social world where you are in control'. The diaspora* network comprises separately run and maintained servers, each of which is a node called a *pod*, and each of which runs the free Diaspora software (diaspora* with a lowercase d and an asterisk is the name of the social media platform; Diaspora with a capital D and no asterisk is the name of its software). Anyone with the resources to run a pod is able to start one, and the users of that pod can connect with others across the whole diaspora* network. The network is also marked by a rejection of advertising, and by its use of open source principles of development and design. Specifically, it uses the Free Software model originated by Richard Stallman in 1985 (Stallman 2003), through which users are free to modify and improve the code, but are not allowed to make a proprietary modification or version (it's free as in free speech rather than free beer, as the saying goes). The Diaspora software system has adopted some common conventions from other social media, such as the use of hashtags and the ability to *like* (or in this case <3) a post. And it has initiated others, so that Google+'s *circles* function can be seen as derived from diaspora*'s *aspects*, through which users can stream posts to custom lists or subsets of all their contacts – posting something only for relatives or only for work colleagues, for instance (see http://wiki.diasporafoundation.org/FAQ_for_users).

The diaspora* project began in 2010 as an attempt to create a social media tool that operated in a different way to commercial data-mining networks such as Facebook. Instead of yielding their personal data to Facebook's servers, users of diaspora* would keep their data on their own machines or on those of trusted contacts. Instead of Facebook's proprietary code and algorithms, diaspora* would be open source, allowing its users not only to see how it worked, but also to improve it if they could see a useful hack of its code. It would be an example of what Benkler (2006) calls *peer production* in action. There would be no advertising, no ever-changing privacy policy. A Kickstarter drive to raise US$10,000 to build the software instead raised US$200,000. Even Mark Zuckerberg told *Wired* that he'd donated money to the diaspora* cause (Nussbaum 2010, Singel 2010).

But all this attention raised expectations. Initial versions of the software were scrappy. The big social media firms kept moving, even as the four students behind diaspora* tried to get started. The *circles* function of Google+ came out in 2011, occupying much of the ground that diaspora* had tried to stake out with its own *aspects*. Ilya Zhitomirskiy, one of the four diaspora* founders, killed himself in November 2011 (Liu 2012). The following year, the remaining founders stepped back and turned the project over to its community to keep developing it. As of July 2015, diaspora* continued to develop, with a major new software release appearing in May 2015. The fleeting moment of excitement around the launch of the similarly advertising-averse social media tool Ello in 2014 may have reinvigorated the diaspora* development community, as Ello at first appeared a potential competitor.

The website of the foundation that runs both the diaspora* network and the Diaspora software that underpins it lists three key principles: decentralization, freedom and privacy (https://diasporafoundation.org). The first of these is in practice closer to distributed than decentralized, given the absence of any major hubs, and the fact that the software allows anyone to run their own server and connect it to the whole network. Because the network is distributed across these pods, with none more central than others, the structure ensures the network's continued independence. The second principle, freedom, in particular relates to diaspora*'s encouragement of pseudonymous user names, in marked contrast to the insistence on real names by Facebook and Google, which demand a consistent identity for the data-mining purposes of their business models. As to the third principle, privacy, the system is designed so that each user not only owns and is responsible for their own data and content, but is also able to choose who sees what they do with that content.

It has been possible to join diaspora* since November 2010, and yet at the time of writing in July 2015, the project had managed to build only a relatively small number of users. User numbers for each pod can only be estimated, as the information is not all public, but one pod's own statistics suggest a total of something below 400,000 individual user accounts across the network, with many of those likely to be inactive (https:// diasp.eu/stats.html). For comparison, Facebook's March 2015 quarterly report to shareholders claims 1.44 billion monthly active users, of whom 936 million were active on the site on a daily basis. The database business model of the large commercial social media firms means that those who have developed the largest databases become hard to compete with or supplant.

Michael Seemann (2015) compares diaspora* with WhatsApp. The success of the latter, he argues, was built on pre-existing social networks – each user's address book. To create an account, the user allows the app to access the list of contacts on their phone. A new user opening WhatsApp then immediately sees a list of people whom they already know who also use WhatsApp and whom they can contact on the service. All of those address books, writes Seemann, were *already* a distributed social network; WhatsApp just adds a layer of software on top to make users within that network visible to each other. But the privacy focus of diaspora* makes it actively hard to find other users with whom you might want to communicate. The solution, Seemann argues, is to keep the data open so that others can also use it, in an analogous way to that in which Google indexes the web but doesn't prevent other search engines from also searching the web. Neither WhatsApp nor diaspora* has done this.

Metcalfe's Law, which observes that a communications network rises dramatically in value the more users or devices it connects, is the source of the network effects that keep people tied to the largest networks. At a certain point, a network can become mandatory, in the way that internet access and telephone connectivity have become essentials in daily life rather than just nice things to have. If everyone else is on Facebook, it's harder to switch to diaspora* or any other competitor. It may have taken a user years to develop their network on Facebook to the point where they can use it to connect with people from all parts of their life. The difficulties of switching to a new network and trying to persuade your Facebook friends to come with you are substantial. Network effects are very powerful and the corresponding lock-in and switching costs very real (although network effects can also be built very quickly in the contemporary media environment – consider Facebook's decision to purchase WhatsApp and Instagram rather than compete with them as a recognition of the network effects that those platforms had already established).

Yet diaspora* proves that it's possible to build a non-commercial, non-proprietary social media network, on a distributed model. That it hasn't yet succeeded does not show that such a network cannot succeed.

Other tools are also contending to create distributed or federated social media platforms (at the time of writing, examples would include Friendica, Crabgrass, Maidsafe, Lorea and others). Theirs is an important mission, and an important example of emergent distributed citizenship. Their role should be seen in the light of what Tim Berners-Lee warned of in 2010. Writing in *Scientific American*, twenty years after he had activated the very first website, Berners-Lee observed that social media platforms had exploited the open standards of the web to build their success, but were now subverting that openness in building centralized networks: 'Once you enter your data into one of these services, you cannot easily use them on another site. Each site is a silo, walled off from the others' (Berners-Lee 2010: 82). The more such silos develop, and the more that the very largest and most visited websites adopt the silo approach, the less universal the web then becomes, and the harder it becomes for future innovators to make use of that same openness that had allowed the silo sites to achieve dominance. The web is too important and too valuable to let a handful of firms remake it in their own image.

Conclusion

Each of the example projects above has its limitations and, of course, its critics. The #Occupy movement was widely – if not accurately – criticized both for lacking clear objectives and for failing to achieve them. The *Kony 2012* campaign peaked too soon and fell victim to its own success, as the unexpected scale of its circulation and celebrity brought its own creators the same visibility and scrutiny to which they had set out to subject Joseph Kony, and distracted supporters from the project's intended climactic day of action. Bitcoin and other cryptocurrencies are not yet widely accepted, are subject to volatility and insecurity and are in some measure tainted by associations of illegality and criminality from their early adopters such as the now-closed Silk Road website. And diaspora* has so far failed to achieve a critical mass of users.

Yet each of these projects also shows the contours of a nascent form of citizenship – a distributed citizenship characterized by creativity, sharing and visibility; by emerging senses of communicative ethics; and by distribution in terms of networks, responsibility and spatiality. The #Occupy movement was an archetypal distributed network, with multiple points of connectivity and no central oversight or control hubs. In its physical gatherings, it emphasized anti-hierarchical and distributed patterns of participation within meetings, and the movement was adopted and adapted across the planet. The *Kony 2012* campaign sought to devolve action and participation to distributed networks of mainly school- and college-age supporters, although it undermined this in its emphasis on their using its pre-packed US$30 'action kit' of stickers and stencils and posters: a tension between centrality and distribution, which worked to the disadvantage of the centre. In its call to individuals around the world to recognize their responsibility to join in combating a particular local issue, it invoked a specifically distributed citizenship. Bitcoin and other cryptocurrencies are distributed projects in which users, advocates and investors come together in shifting coalitions of practice. They suggest a set of social relations in which value is established on different terms to those of the established financial system. And the diaspora* platform comprises a global network of distributed servers, each running a common software system, and each connected to all the others, yet each autonomous and independent – distributed not only in terms of network topology or physical spatiality, but also in the dimensions of ethics and responsibility which it sets out to reclaim from the depredations of Silicon Valley. Each of these examples sketches the contours of an emerging form of citizenship for the social media environment – one characterized not in cultural terms of who we are, but in networked media terms of what we do.

Conclusion

Social media have captured the attention and imagination of many millions of people. They have also captured those people's personal information and turned their daily lives into commercial data. This book has tried to navigate between these two poles, acknowledging the pleasures and excitements of social media while scrutinizing their problems. We've never before had a situation where a fifth of the planet is using the same connected database to present themselves and observe each other. It is quite beautiful, quite disturbing and quite dangerous.

This book has argued throughout that a defining characteristic of the contemporary media environment is the convergence of content, computing and communications. All forms of content become digital, the computer becomes the default way of experiencing that content, and both that content and those experiences can be circulated across networks of all sizes. Media industries both old and new develop ways of exploiting the possibilities of this convergence. Social media are one kind of media industry built on those possibilities. Their technological foundations and affordances, their business models and the characteristic ways in which audiences have come to both adopt and adapt them are made possible by convergence.

As we've seen throughout the preceding chapters, the key element of social media is the convergence of public and personal communication. This challenges much of what we know about both. Much of our understanding of the various systems of public communication and their technological, economic, cultural and textual forms still assumes the broadcast paradigm of the twentieth century. It still assumes empowered producers of meanings, distributing these to dispersed but simultaneous audiences. It still assumes that meanings are made for sale, and that they are intended to be public. It assumes that media industries produce and circulate texts (ideas and images, stories and songs) to audiences who can hear but can't speak, who can read but not write. It assumes that successful communication can be measured by bulk – the bigger the audience, the more important the meaning. It assumes that the user at home is invisible to everyone else involved. And it assumes that the public quality of shared communication brings with it certain kinds of responsibilities for producers and regulators – responsibilities shaped by questions of standards and taste, of risk and harm, of cultural expectations being defined and met (if not necessarily challenged). Debates about censorship and access, about the limits of the acceptable in scarce public speech, about the licensing and accreditation of voices and producers, all derive from this public quality of media. All of these assumptions about media are challenged by their convergence with forms of personal communication.

What we think we know about personal communication will also need to be rethought, as this converges with forms of public media. The give and take of meanings, the attempts to exert influence or achieve communion, the routines and cues, the unexpected pleasures or hurts of one-to-one communication, the experiences of friendship and love (and hate) – all of these can now be made visible to others, reframing the selves that we wish to perform for audiences who may have preferred a different kind of show. This may not just change how we are understood, but also how we present ourselves. If our selves are a series of performances, then the very selves that we choose to perform – the act we act – may change. The risks of sending the wrong message to the wrong receiver are so high: not the risks of clicking on the wrong email address, but of making a performance on the wrong stage. It may involve the emergence of those Safe For Work personae discussed by Marwick (2013a); or it may involve the emergence of more spaces of privileged anonymity such as 4chan, or of systems of supposedly ephemeral engagement such as Snapchat.

Social media firms that have emerged to exploit the possibilities of convergence have tended to show less interest in creating content of their own. Someone else will always do that. They are instead computing companies, software enterprises, who find new ways to network people and information – from Google's project of 'organizing the world's information', to Apple's subversion of the content industries with its iTunes Store, to Spotify's subversion of the very idea of a store. Social media represent a new way of doing and making media, in which content is shared and circulated through media companies rather than written and produced by them. This is in a certain sense parasitic. It is also one way in which arguments about social media and unpaid labour are inaccurate, in that users of social media platforms are not being conscripted to work unpaid on producing TV dramas or feature films.

One warning about this new sharing industry is sounded by the ways it chooses to present and withhold aspects of its commercial identity, as we saw in Chapter 2. The car industry is generally pretty open that its project is making and selling cars for profit. But the sharing industry is generally less open that its project is making and selling data about its users. Instead, it obfuscates and dodges, ducking behind motherhood mission statements of global connection and of a life made more fulfilling by sharing.

News in the convergent spaces of social media will demand a reconsideration of accountability and authority. Who is accountable to whom? What kinds of authority count? The Fourth Estate ideal of the news media as democracy's unelected protectors was already hard to sustain in the late twentieth century, with many leading news organizations then part of colossal communication conglomerates whose profit motives and ways of operating were incompatible with a watchdog role. This has been underscored in the twenty-first century, as the phone hacking scandal of the UK tabloid press has revealed not only the distance that press maintains from the Fourth Estate ideal, but also the ways in which digital communication can open up users to surveillance by predatory organizations (on this scandal and its aftermath, see Fenton 2012 and Barnett 2013).

As more and more news is experienced through social media platforms – platforms whose operators have in some cases established themselves as voracious competitors for market share and users' attention, and whose identity, practices and self-presentation leave no room for a Fourth Estate role, then who is accountable for public debate and for the provision of information about matters of public importance and concern? Facebook's feeds are governed by algorithms that are weighted to prompt the user to share more personal information in order that this can be sold to advertisers. This mechanism of coaxing the user to respond in order to better package that user for sale is not compatible with one of providing information as a public service. Accountability is a problem for the established news industries as well, but this doesn't let the social media industry off that hook.

Authority also shifts in the social media environment. One of the biggest problems with the established news has been its reliance on high-status authorities as sources of information. This leads to news that can best be characterized as 'negative, detached, technical, and official' (Schudson 1995: 9). In a networked digital environment, new kinds of authority emerge – the temporal authority of being first to share (crucial since the telegraph, but now a more widely distributed capacity), and the spatial authority of being physically present at an event. Neither of these necessarily implies judgment or insight, and neither necessarily implies accuracy or authenticity. New kinds of participant in the news environment also claim the authority to speak. Citizen journalism is a rightful redistribution of the licence to tell non-fiction stories in public. But it is one that also creates a new need for professional journalists to complement – and at times to correct – the contributions of the non-professional.

The discussion of internet memes in Chapter 3 showed how ideas can be moved from one context to another through social media, gaining interpretations, but perhaps losing something too in the process. Memes are an important index of how people communicate on social media. An internet meme may have no single originator, but be used by a great many people to express ideas through processes of shared interpretation and remix. An internet meme is a collaborative process of making and sharing meanings across networks. And as we saw in Chapter 6, internet memes from Adbusters to *We are the 99 percent* had an important role in the development of the #Occupy movement. The ways in which we create and share ideas and images through social media will be central to developing any new forms of citizenship that can emerge from digital media networks. As social media become ever more embedded within everyday life, the ways in which users and other media organizations adopt and adapt them will change. As we become more literate and experienced in this media environment, we will develop coping strategies. These will be forms of social media literacy.

Social Media Literacy

What does it mean to be *literate* in the twenty-first century? And what is the role of a university education in the humanities and social sciences in developing literacy? After all, one purpose of such an education has long been the development both of the learner's literacy, and of their capacity to continue to extend that literacy beyond their degree. I expect that this is an issue that connects in some way with anyone likely to read this book. For writers of academic books, it's standard to invoke an address to some *general reader*, but I'm actually pretty certain that most people reading this book are instead reading it in one university capacity or another, whether as researchers, as students or as teachers.

Arguments for literacy can be civic – it enables people to participate in political and social processes, including voting. Or they can be economic – it enables people to work in a range of professions and vocations. Or they can be personal – it enables people to develop their capacity for lifelong learning and for cultural participation (Livingtone *et al.* 2008). But in the twenty-first century, with the increased embedding of networked digital media in every aspect of civic, economic and personal life, literacy has to be understood as wider than reading printed texts and producing written words. Questions of *media* literacy and *information* literacy have become more important. And the rise of social media brings both of these together.

The importance of media literacy can be seen in the roles of certain institutions. In the UK, for example, communications regulator Ofcom has a statutory obligation to promote media literacy under the Communications Act of 2003 (Ofcom n.d.), and the BBC has an important media literacy strategy to help it meet the specific public service obligations of its current charter (BBC 2013). But how are new forms of literacy being developed or addressed within university education? It's clear from the literature that academic and policy debates about media literacy have most often been focused at the level of primary and secondary school curricula. But, as with more established forms of literacy, there is scope for media and information literacy to be developed to higher levels in tertiary education. It's not 'patronising' to talk of teaching media literacy, as David Gauntlett (2011b) suggests. If we're *not* teaching media literacy in the many, many media courses at many, many universities around the world, then what is it that we are actually teaching? And if we *are* teaching this, then what is it that we think media literacy means?

When we study the networked digital communications environment of the twenty-first century, we need to reassess our understandings of what kinds of skills it requires. *Media literacy* has been pursued in media degree courses since the 1970s, as well as being a part of related courses in journalism or film. Part of these disciplines' offer to students has rested on the development of forms of critical literacy that enable them to interpret complex multimodal texts and to engage with questions of ideology and power. Another, and quite different, part of their offer has rested on training in vocational craft skills within a pre-industry pathway. These two kinds of emphasis can be understood as *reading* and *writing*, broadly defined. So media students are taught to *read* media through approaches including semiotics, discourse analysis and genre study, or through the articulation of media texts, audiences, industries or technologies with various kinds of critical and cultural theory. And they are also – although not always on the same courses or to the same ratios – taught to *write* media, through training in production techniques and in the craft skills of particular communication industries. This may be on a professional scale, with training accredited by a particular industry body, or it may be on an educational scale, with such production work intended to complement the *reading* work done elsewhere in the course.

Both the *reading* and the *writing* approaches to media education were developed in and for a particular communications environment – the twentieth-century mass media paradigm. This was built around what we can call the broadcast model of centralized production of texts, distributed in a one-way pattern to disparate and largely simultaneous audiences of various sizes. It was part of an environment built around various kinds of *scarcity*, including scarcity of expertise. A very prominent literacy discourse within this model is what we might call the protective perspective, designed for such a media environment. Potter's textbook *Media Literacy*, for example, advises students to 'Beware of factors that increase mindlessness' (Potter 1998: 369). Defence against such dark arts is needed: 'Advertisers rely on this to get their message into your subconscious without your defense mechanisms being aroused' (p. 369). From this perspective, media literacy is a style of self-defence, which enables even small individuals to overcome larger and more powerful opponents through the dexterous application of their reading of the Frankfurt School or their awareness of genre.

Information literacy, in contrast, is about enabling learners to cope with *abundance* – to navigate, retrieve and evaluate information from an ever-increasing range of sources. It includes skills in search and retrieval, the ability to identify sources and authorities, to check facts and evaluate accuracy and relevance (what Rheingold 2012: 77–109 lists in his taxonomy of information literacy as 'crap detection'). Where concepts of media literacy have their roots in English and Sociology, information literacy has developed in Library Science and IT (Marcum 2002, Hobbs 2006). In practice, like everything else in the media environment (Meikle & Young 2012), these approaches are now converging.

The emerging social media environment is characterized by both continuity and transformation. *Continuity*, in that established industries and systems of communication remain central to the fabric of the everyday life of many millions of people. Broadcast television, for instance, still commands three hours and forty minutes of the average UK adult's day (Ofcom 2015a: 39). *Transformation*, in that modes of production and distribution, textual systems and cultural habits, business models and regulatory approaches are all in flux as cultural expression becomes not only digital but also networked. UK adults report spending over two hours a day engaged in multiple simultaneous media and communication use – watching TV while talking on the phone, for instance – as part of a total of the more than eleven daily hours of communication activity that are crammed into just nine multi-tasked hours each day (Ofcom 2014: 44).

The challenges of these continuities and transformations for university media education have been acknowledged for some years, but often seem to have been met by sticking a module on digital media onto an existing degree course. The real challenge is to re-think the fundamentals of media literacy. It's not enough just to add in some additional elements of *reading* different kinds of digital media (as in, for example, the common undergraduate dissertation topic of gender stereotypes in videogames) or of *writing* for digital media (as in, for instance, a module on web production and design). Rather, the widespread adoption and adaptation of networked digital media both enable and demand new kinds of media literacy, and the addition of new dimensions to both reading and writing. They demand *social media literacy*.

But aren't people just literate users of social media already? Of course, the everyday uses of Facebook and YouTube, of Instagram and Twitter, have become second nature to many hundreds of millions of people. *But there is more to literacy than everyday use.* We should not accept the assumption that people who grow up surrounded by digital media are natively literate in their uses and possibilities (Buckingham 2003). This generational fantasy of the 'digital native' is useless because it elides questions of literacy. For example, when Ofcom published its annual report on the UK communications sectors in August 2014, one key finding was reported in a very misleading way in the media as saying that 'the average six-year-old child understands more about digital technology than a 45-year-old adult' (Garside 2014). But the research had actually tested whether both children and adults had *heard of* particular digital products and services, not whether they in any way understood them.

Whenever we hear similar stories about 'digital natives' (and this one was quite typical), we should recall that earlier generations grew up surrounded by books, but some people still became more literate than others. Literacy involves a very broad spectrum of skills, each of which can be developed to very different levels. So just as older generations were taught to read and write but achieved and made use of different elements of that spectrum and to different levels within the headings *read* (the headlines) and *write* (*The Waste Land*), so too there are a range of aptitudes, competencies and potentials that not everyone is able to manifest through social media. I am still haunted by what one of my undergraduate students wrote in a class blog in December 2013: 'I seem to find that most of my time I am finding the answers to my questions on Ask Yahoo. They aren't always right but they are usually the easiest way to get the answer'.

Social media literacy is about both media literacy and information literacy skills in the context of the ongoing practical and conceptual convergence of content, computing and communications, and the resulting networked digital media environment in which public and personal communication are combined. Social media literacy is *not* just about learning how to use specific proprietary software or devices. So it is not about training 'better' users for Facebook or YouTube. Nor is it the same thing as educational technology skills. So we're not talking here about how to use PowerPoint or Excel to pass a class. And it is not just about protecting people from the risks of social media, or warning them not to put their home address on Facebook or their naked photos on iCloud (although yes, those are both lessons that need to be learned as well).

One map of the components of social media literacy might look like this:

1   *Access, interpret* and *evaluate*: These are skills broadly concerned with *reading* in networked digital environments. They are about being able to find and understand ideas. They include skills of navigating and of making meanings. And they require an understanding of the roles of software, of algorithms and of databases, in shaping the social media environment.

2   *Remix, organize and create*: These are skills broadly concerned with *writing* in networked digital environments. They are multimodal – making an image, remixing a song, writing a blog. The inclusion of *organize* is about managing created material for oneself and for others – tags and hashtags, playlists and channels, and the social media impulse of curation.

3   *Collaborate* and *share*: These are skills that are broadly concerned with *interacting* with others. Most of the uses of *share* explored in Chapter 2 apply here, from publishing to publicizing, from communicating to communing; I exclude the sense of *share* that is a euphemism for *sell*. They are skills that bring together the personal and the public; skills that put the *social* in social media.

I offer this book as one small contribution to the development of social media literacy. Social media literacy matters for the same complex set of reasons as are advanced for other kinds of literacy. So it matters for civic reasons, because it enables people to better engage in debates and issues of public significance; to make and contribute to political decisions; and to contribute and belong to a range of communities (including but not limited to local physical ones). It matters for economic reasons, because it offers skills that are fundamental to the contemporary creative industries sector (and that may enable its workers to renegotiate its problematic approach to intellectual property). And above all, it matters for personal reasons. Social media literacy enables people to be creative in a range of ways; to share and collaborate and hence be social and sociable within networks. And it enables people to better balance the excitements and pleasures of digital networks with the risks of·mediated visibility in a social media environment where the personal and the public converge.

References

Abad-Santos, A. (2013) 'Reddit's "Find Boston Bombers" Founder Says "It Was a Disaster" but "Incredible"', *The Atlantic Wire*, 22 April, <www.thewire.com/national/2013/04/reddit-find-boston-bombers-founder-interview/64455>, accessed 24 July 2015.

Ackerman, S. and Ball, J. (2014) 'Optic Nerve: Millions of Yahoo Webcam Images Intercepted by GCHQ', *The Guardian*, 28 February, <www.theguardian.com/world/2014/feb/27/gchq-nsa-webcam-images-internet-yahoo>, accessed 24 July 2015.

Adbusters (2011) '#OCCUPYWALLSTREET: A Shift in Revolutionary Tactics', 13 July, <www.adbusters.org/blogs/adbusters-blog/occupywallstreet.html>, accessed 24 July 2015.

Allan, S. (2009) 'Histories of Citizen Journalism' in S. Allan and E. Thorsen (eds) *Citizen Journalism: Global Perspectives*, New York: Peter Lang, pp. 17–31.

Allan, S. (2013) *Citizen Witnessing*, Cambridge: Polity.

Allan, S. and Thorsen, E. (eds) (2009) *Citizen Journalism: Global Perspectives*, New York: Peter Lang.

Allen, M. (2013) 'What Was Web 2.0? Versions as the Dominant Mode of Internet History', *New Media & Society*, vol. 15, no. 2, pp. 260–275.

Alt, E. (2009) 'If Homer's Odyssey Was Written on Twitter', Holy Taco, 5 April, <www.holytaco.com/if-homers-odyssey-was-written-twitter>, accessed 24 July 2015.

Anderson, B. (1991) *Imagined Communities* (revised edition), London: Verso.

Andrejevic, M. (2012) 'Ubiquitous Surveillance' in K. Ball, K.D. Haggerty and D. Lyon (eds) *The Routledge Handbook of Surveillance Studies*, London: Routledge, pp. 91–98.

Ang, I. (1991) *Desperately Seeking the Audience*, London: Routledge.

Appadurai, A. (1996) *Modernity at Large: Cultural Dimensions of Globalization*, Minneapolis, MN: University of Minnesota Press.

Arvidsson, A. (2006) '"Quality Singles": Internet Dating and the Work of Fantasy', *New Media & Society*, vol. 8, no. 4, pp. 671–690.

Arvidsson, A. and Colleoni, E. (2012) 'Value in Informational Capitalism and on the Internet', *The Information Society*, vol. 28, no. 3, pp. 135–150.

Atton, C. (2002) *Alternative Media*, London: Sage.

Atton, C. (ed.) (2015) *The Routledge Companion to Alternative and Community Media*, London: Routledge.

Barbrook, R. and Cameron, A. (1995) 'The Californian Ideology', <www.hrc.wmin.ac.uk/theory-californianideology-main.html>, accessed 24 July 2015.

Barlow, J.P. (1996) 'A Cyberspace Independence Declaration', Electronic Frontier Foundation <https://projects.eff.org/~barlow/Declaration-Final.html>, accessed 24 July 2015.

Barnett, S. (2013) 'Leveson Past, Present and Future: The Politics of Press Regulation', *The Political Quarterly*, vol. 84, no. 3, pp. 353–361.

Barthes, R. (1981) *Camera Lucida: Reflections on Photography*, London: Vintage.

Baym, N.K. (2010) *Personal Connections in the Digital Age*, Cambridge: Polity.

Baym, N.K. (2011) 'Social Networks 2.0' in M. Consalvo and C. Ess (eds) *The Handbook of Internet Studies*, Malden, MA: Blackwell, pp. 384–405.

BBC (British Broadcasting Corporation) (2013) *BBC Media Literacy Strategy*, <www.bbc.co.uk/learning/overview/about/assets/bbc_media_literacy_strategy_may2013.pdf>, accessed 24 July 2015.

BBC Trending (2015) 'Russia's (Non) War on Memes', *BBC News*, 16 April, <www.bbc.co.uk/news/blogs-trending-32302645>, accessed 24 July 2015.

Bell, E. (2015) 'The Rise of Mobile and Social News – And What it Means for Journalism' in N. Newman with D.A. Levy and R.K. Nielsen (eds) *Reuters Institute Digital News Report 2015: Tracking the Future of News*, Oxford: Reuters Institute for the Study of Journalism, pp. 88–91.

Bellamy, R. (2008) *Citizenship*, Oxford: Oxford University Press.

Benjamin, W. (1978) [1934] 'The Author as Producer' in *Reflections*, New York: Harcourt Brace Jovanovich, pp. 220–238.

Benkler, Y. (2006) *The Wealth of Networks*, New Haven, CT: Yale University Press.

Benkler, Y. (2012) 'Sharing Nicely: On Shareable Goods and the Emergence of Sharing as a Modality of Economic Production' in M. Mandiberg (ed.) *The Social Media Reader*, New York: New York University Press, pp. 17–23.

Bennett, W.L. and Segerberg, A. (2012) 'The Logic of Connective Action', *Information, Communication & Society*, vol. 15, no. 5, pp. 739–768.

Bentham, J. (2002) 'The Penitentiary Panopticon or Inspection House' in T.Y. Levin, U. Frohne and P. Weibel (eds) *CTRL [Space]*, Cambridge, MA: MIT Press, pp. 114–119.

Bercovici, J. (2010) 'Who Coined "Social Media"? Web Pioneers Compete for Credit', *Forbes*, 9 December, <www.forbes.com/sites/jeffbercovici/2010/12/09/who-coined-social-media-web-pioneers-compete-for-credit>, accessed 24 July 2015.

Berners-Lee, T. (1999) *Weaving the Web*, London: Orion Business Books.

Berners-Lee, T. (2010) 'Long Live the Web', *Scientific American*, December, pp. 80–85.

Bilton, N. (2011) 'Masked Protesters Aid Time Warner's Bottom Line', *New York Times*, 28 August, <www.nytimes.com/2011/08/29/technology/masked-anonymous-protesters-aid-time-warners-profits.html>, accessed 24 July 2015.

Bird, S.E. and Dardenne, R.W. (1997) [1988] 'Myth, Chronicle and Story: Exploring the Narrative Qualities of News' in D. Berkowitz (ed.) *Social Meanings of News*, Thousand Oaks, CA: Sage, pp. 333–350.

Blackmore, S. (1999) *The Meme Machine*, Oxford: Oxford University Press.

Bogost, I., Ferrari, S. and Schweizer, B. (2011) 'Newsgames: An Introduction' in G. Meikle and G. Redden (eds) *News Online: Transformations and Continuities*, Basingstoke: Palgrave Macmillan, pp. 84–98.

Bolaño, C.R.S. and Vieira, E.S. (2015) 'The Political Economy of the Internet: Social Networking Sites and a Reply to Fuchs', *Television & New Media*, vol. 16, no. 1, pp. 52–61.

Boorstin, D. (1992) [1961] *The Image*, New York: Vintage.

Bourdieu, P. (1991) *Language and Symbolic Power*, Cambridge: Polity.

Bourdieu, P. (1998) *On Television*, New York: The New Press.

Boyce, G. (1978) 'The Fourth Estate: The Reappraisal of a Concept' in G. Boyce, J. Curran and P. Wingate (eds) *Newspaper History: From the Seventeenth Century to the Present Day*, London: Constable, pp. 19–40.

boyd, d. (2006) 'Friends, Friendsters, and MySpace Top 8: Writing Community Into Being on Social Network Sites', *First Monday*, vol. 11, no. 12, <http://firstmonday.org/htbin/cgiwrap/bin/ojs/index.php/fm/article/view/1418/1336>, accessed 24 July 2015.

boyd, d. (2008) 'Facebook's Privacy Trainwreck: Exposure, Invasion and Social Convergence', *Convergence*, vol. 14, no. 1, pp. 13–20.

boyd, d. (2011) 'Social Network Sites as Networked Publics: Affordances, Dynamics, and Implications' in Z. Papacharissi (ed.) *A Networked Self: Identity, Community, and Culture on Social Network Sites*, London: Routledge, pp. 39–58.

boyd, d. (2014) *It's Complicated: The Social Lives of Networked Teens*, New Haven, CT: Yale University Press.

boyd, d. and Ellison, N.B. (2008) 'Social Network Sites: Definition, History, and Scholarship', *Journal of Computer-Mediated Communication*, vol. 13, no. 1, pp. 210–230.

boyd, d. and Crawford, K. (2012) 'Critical Questions for Big Data: Provocations for a Cultural, Technological, and Scholarly Phenomenon', *Information, Communication & Society*, vol. 15, no. 5, pp. 662–679.

Braun, J. and Gillespie, T. (2011) 'Hosting the Public Discourse, Hosting the Public', *Journalism Practice*, vol. 5, no. 4, pp. 383–398.

Brautigan, R. (1970) [1967] *The Pill Versus the Springhill Mining Disaster*, London: Jonathan Cape.

Brecht, B. (1993) [1932] 'The Radio as an Apparatus of Communication' in N. Strauss (ed.) *Radiotext(e)*, New York: Semiotext(e), pp. 15–17.

Bruns, A. (2005) *Gatewatching: Collaborative Online News Production*, New York: Peter Lang.

Bruns, A. (2011) 'News Produsage in a Pro-Am Mediasphere: Why Citizen Journalism Matters' in G. Meikle and G. Redden (eds) *News Online: Transformations and Continuities*, Basingstoke: Palgrave Macmillan, pp. 132–147.

Bruns, A. and Burgess, J. (2012) 'Researching News Discussion on Twitter', *Journalism Studies*, vol. 13, nos. 5–6, pp. 801–814.

Bucher, T. (2013) 'The Friendship Assemblage: Investigating Programmed Sociality on Facebook', *Television & New Media*, vol. 14, no. 6, pp. 479–493.

Buckingham, D. (2003) *Media Education: Literacy, Learning and Contemporary Culture*, Cambridge: Polity.

Burgess, J. (2013) 'YouTube and the Formalisation of Amateur Media' in D. Hunter, R. Lobato, M. Richardson and J. Thomas (eds) *Amateur Media: Social, Cultural and Legal Perspectives*, New York: Routledge, pp. 53–58.

Burgess, J. and Green, J. (2009) *YouTube*, Cambridge: Polity.

Burns, A. (2015) 'In Full View: Involuntary Porn and the Postfeminist Rhetoric of Choice' in C. Nally and A. Smith (eds) *Twenty-First Century Feminism: Forming and Performing Femininity*, Basingstoke: Palgrave Macmillan, pp. 93–118.

Campbell, J. (1949) *The Hero with a Thousand Faces*, London: Paladin.

Carey, J. (1989) *Communication as Culture*, New York: Routledge.

Carr, N. (2014) 'The Manipulators: Facebook's Social Engineering Project', *Los Angeles Review of Books*, 14 September, <http://lareviewofbooks.org/essay/manipulators-facebooks-social-engineering-project>, accessed 24 July 2015.

Castells, M. (1998) *End of Millennium*, Oxford: Blackwell.

Castells, M. (2001) *The Internet Galaxy*, Oxford: Oxford University Press.

Castells, M. (2004) *The Power of Identity* (second edition), Oxford: Blackwell.

Castells, M. (2009) *Communication Power*, Oxford: Oxford University Press.

Castells, M. (2012) *Networks of Outrage and Hope*, Cambridge: Polity.

Chandler, A. and Neumark, N. (eds) (2005) *At a Distance: Precursors to Art and Activism on the Internet*, Cambridge, MA: MIT Press.

Chen, A. (2011) 'How a 14-Year-Old Girl Became an Unwilling Internet Pin-Up', Gawker, 23 September <http://gawker.com/5843355/how-a-14-year-old-girl-became-an-unwilling-internet-pin-up>, accessed 24 July 2015.

Chen, A. (2012) 'Unmasking Reddit's Violentacrez, the Biggest Troll on the Web', Gawker, 12 October <http://gawker.com/5950981/unmasking-reddits-violentacrez-the-biggest-troll-on-the-web>, accessed 24 July 2015.

Cheung, C. (2007) 'Identity Construction and Self-Presentation on Personal Homepages: Emancipatory Potentials and Reality Constraints' in D. Bell and B.M. Kennedy (eds) *The Cybercultures Reader* (second edition), London: Routledge, pp. 273–285.

Coleman, G. (2014) *Hacker, Hoaxer, Whistleblower, Spy: The Many Faces of Anonymous*, London: Verso.

Connery, B.A. (1997) 'IMHO: Authority and Egalitarian Rhetoric in the Virtual Coffeehouse' in D. Porter (ed.) *Internet Culture*, London: Routledge, pp. 161–179.

Crawford, K. (2011) 'News to Me: Twitter and the Personal Networking of News' in G. Meikle and G. Redden (eds) *News Online: Transformations and Continuities*, Basingstoke: Palgrave Macmillan, pp. 115–131.

Crawford, K. (2012) 'Four Ways of Listening with an iPhone' in L. Hjorth, J. Burgess and I. Richardson (eds) *Studying Mobile Media: Cultural Technologies, Mobile Communication, and the iPhone*, New York: Routledge, pp. 213–228.

Critical Art Ensemble (1994) *The Electronic Disturbance*, New York: Autonomedia.

Critical Art Ensemble (1995) *Electronic Civil Disobedience and Other Unpopular Ideas*, New York: Autonomedia.

Curran, J. and Seaton, J. (2010) *Power without Responsibility: The Press, Broadcasting, and New Media in Britain* (seventh edition), London: Routledge.

David, M. (2010) *Peer to Peer and the Music Industry: The Criminalization of Sharing*, London: Sage.

Dawkins, R. (1976) *The Selfish Gene*, Oxford: Oxford University Press.

Dayan, D. (2009) 'Sharing and Showing: Television as Monstration', *Annals of the American Academy of Political and Social Science*, September, vol. 625, pp. 19–31.

Debord, G. and Wolman, G. (2009) [1956] 'Directions for the Use of Détournement' in D. Evans (ed.) *Appropriation*, London: Whitechapel Gallery, pp. 35–39.

Deleuze, G. (1992) 'Postscript on the Societies of Control', *October*, no. 59, pp. 3–7.

Delwiche, A. and Henderson, J.J. (2013) 'Introduction: What Is Participatory Culture?' in A. Delwiche and J.J. Henderson (eds) *The Participatory Cultures Handbook*, New York: Routledge, pp. 3–9.

DCMS (Department for Culture, Media and Sport [UK]) (2001) *Creative Industries: Mapping Document 2001*, London: Department for Culture, Media and Sport.

Dery, M. (1993) *Culture Jamming: Hacking, Slashing and Sniping in the Empire of Signs*, Westfield, NJ: Open Magazine Pamphlet Series no. 25.

Dery, M. (1996) *Escape Velocity: Cyberculture at the End of the Century*, New York: Grove Press.

Deuze, M. (2007) *Media Work*, Cambridge: Polity.

Douglas, N. (2014) 'It's Supposed to Look Like Shit: The Internet Ugly Aesthetic', *Journal of Visual Culture*, vol. 13, no. 3, pp. 314–339.

Downey, G.J. (2014) 'Making Media Work: Time, Space, Identity, and Labor in the Analysis of Information and Communication Infrastructures' in T. Gillespie, P.J. Boczkowski and K.A. Foot (eds) *Media Technologies*, Cambridge, MA: MIT Press, pp. 141–165.

Downing, J. with Ford, T.V., Gil, G. and Stein, L. (2001) *Radical Media: Rebellious Communication and Social Movements*, Thousand Oaks, CA: Sage.

Duggan, M. and Smith, A. (2013) '6% of Online Adults are Reddit Users', Pew Internet Project, 3 July, <www.pewinternet.org/2013/07/03/6-of-online-adults-are-reddit-users>, accessed 24 July 2015.

Duncombe, S. (1997) *Notes from Underground: Zines and the Politics of Alternative Culture*, London: Verso.

Economist (2014) 'How Guy Fawkes Became the Face of Post-Modern Protest', 4 November, <www.economist.com/blogs/economist-explains/2014/11/economist-explains-3>, accessed 24 July 2015.

Eggers, D. (2014) *The Circle*, London: Hamish Hamilton.

Ellison, N.B. and boyd, d.m. (2013) 'Sociality through Social Network Sites' in W.H. Dutton (ed.) *The Oxford Handbook of Internet Studies*, Oxford: Oxford University Press, pp. 151–172.

Elmer, G. (2002) 'Consumption in the Network Age: Solicitation, Automation, and Networking', *Convergence*, vol. 8, no. 1, pp. 86–99.

Enzensberger, H.M. (2003) [1970] 'Constituents of a Theory of the Media' in N. Wardrip-Fruin and N. Montfort (eds) *The New Media Reader*, Cambridge, MA: MIT Press, pp. 261–275.

Ericson, R.V., Baranek, P.M. and Chan, J.B.L. (1989) *Negotiating Control: A Study of News Sources*, Milton Keynes: Open University Press.

erik [hueypriest] (2013) 'Reflections on the Recent Boston Crisis', blog.reddit, 22 April, <www.redditblog.com/2013/04/reflections-on-recent-boston-crisis.html>, accessed 24 July 2015.

Ess, C. (2014) *Digital Media Ethics*, second edition, Cambridge: Polity.

Esteves, V. and Meikle, G. (2015) 'LOOK @ THIS FUKKEN DOGE' in C. Atton (ed.) *The Routledge Companion to Alternative and Community Media*, London: Routledge, pp. 561–570.

Evans, H. (1978) *Pictures on a Page*, London: Pimlico.

Facebook, Inc. (2013) *Annual Report 2012*, <http://investor.fb.com/annuals.cfm>, accessed 24 July 2015.

Facebook, Inc. (2015) *Form 10-K (Annual Report)*, 29 January, <http://investor.fb.com/financials.cfm>, accessed 24 July 2015.

Fairclough, N. (1995) *Critical Discourse Analysis*, London: Longman.

Fairclough, N. (2003) *Analysing Discourse: Textual Analysis for Social Research*, London: Routledge.

Feifer, J. (2013) 'Obama's Funeral Selfie Is a Fitting End to My Tumblr – Selfies at Funerals', *The Guardian*, 11 December, <www.theguardian.com/commentisfree/2013/dec/11/obama-funeral-selfie-tumblr-mandela-teens>, accessed 24 July 2015.

Fenton, N. (2012) 'Telling Tales: Press, Politics, Power, and the Public Interest', *Television & New Media*, vol. 13, no. 1, pp. 3–6.

Fiske, J. (1990) *Introduction to Communication Studies* (second edition), London: Routledge.

Foucault, M. (1977) *Discipline and Punish*, Harmondsworth: Penguin.

Foucault, M. (1980) 'The Eye of Power' in C. Gordon (ed.) *Power/Knowledge: Selected Interviews and Other Writings 1972–1977*, Brighton: Harvester Press, pp. 146–165.

Fowler, R. (1991) *Language in the News*, London: Routledge.

Frasca, G. (2004) 'Videogames of the Oppressed: Critical Thinking, Education, Tolerance, and Other Trivial Issues' in P. Harrigan and N. Wardrip-Fruin (eds) *First Person: New Media as Story, Performance, and Game*, Cambridge, MA: MIT Press, pp. 85–94.

Fuchs, C. (2011) 'An Alternative View of Privacy on Facebook', *Information*, vol. 2, no. 1, pp. 140–165.

Fuchs, C. (2014a) *Digital Labour and Karl Marx*, London: Routledge.

Fuchs, C. (2014b) *Social Media: A Critical Introduction*, London: Sage.

Fuchs, C. (2014c) *OccupyMedia! The Occupy Movement and Social Media in Crisis Capitalism*, Winchester: Zero Books.

Fuchs, C. (2015a) 'Baidu, Weibo and Renren: The Global Political Economy of Social Media in China', *Asian Journal of Communication*, DOI:10.1080/01292986.2015.1041537.

Fuchs, C. (2015b) 'Against Divisiveness: Digital Workers of the World Unite! A Rejoinder to César Bolaño', *Television & New Media*, vol. 16, no. 1, pp. 62–71.

Galtung, J. and Ruge, M.H. (1965) 'The Structure of Foreign News', *Journal of Peace Research*, vol. 2, no. 1, pp. 64–91.

Gans, H.J. (1979) *Deciding What's News*, New York: Pantheon.

Gans, H.J. (2009) 'Can Popularization Help the News Media?' in B. Zelizer (ed.) *The Changing Faces of Journalism: Tabloidization, Technology and Truthiness*, New York: Routledge, pp. 17–28.

Garrett, P. and Bell, A. (eds) (1998) *Approaches to Media Discourse*, Oxford: Blackwell.

Garside, J. (2014) 'Ofcom: Six-year-olds Understand Digital Technology Better than Adults', *The Guardian*, 7 August, <www.theguardian.com/technology/2014/aug/07/ofcom-children-digital-technology-better-than-adults>, accessed 24 July 2015.

Gauntlett, D. (2011a) *Making is Connecting*, Cambridge: Polity.

Gauntlett, D. (2011b) *Media Studies 2.0, and Other Battles around the Future of Media Research*, self-published Kindle e-book.

Gellman, B. and Poitras, L. (2013) 'U.S., British Intelligence Mining Data from Nine U.S. Internet Companies in Broad Secret Program', *Washington Post*, 7 June, <www.washingtonpost.com/investigations/us-intelligence-mining-data-from-nine-us-internet-companies-in-broad-secret-program/2013/06/06/3a0c0da8-cebf-11e2-8845-d970ccb04497_story.html>, accessed 24 July 2015.

Gerbaudo, P. (2012) *Tweets and the Streets: Social Media and Contemporary Activism*, Pluto: London.

Gibson, W. (1984) *Neuromancer*, London: HarperCollins.

Gibson, W. (1986) 'Burning Chrome', collected in (1995) *Burning Chrome and Other Stories*, London: HarperCollins.

Gillespie, T. (2010) '"The Politics of "Platforms"', *New Media & Society*, vol. 12, no. 3, pp. 347–364.

Gillespie, T. (2014) 'The Relevance of Algorithms' in T. Gillespie, P.J. Boczkowski and K.A. Foot (eds) *Media Technologies*, Cambridge, MA: MIT Press, pp. 167–193.

Godwin, M. (1994) 'Meme, Counter-meme', *Wired*, 2.10, <http://archive.wired.com/wired/archive/2.10/godwin.if.html>, accessed 24 July 2015.

Goffey, A. (2008) 'Algorithm' in M. Fuller (ed.) *Software Studies: A Lexicon*, Cambridge, MA: MIT Press, pp. 15–20.

Goffman, E. (1959) *The Presentation of Self in Everyday Life*, London: Penguin.

Goggin, G. (2006) *Cell Phone Culture*, New York: Routledge.

Goggin, G. (2011) *Global Mobile Media*, New York: Routledge.

Goggin, G. (2012) 'The iPhone and Communication' in L. Hjorth, J. Burgess and I. Richardson (eds) *Studying Mobile Media: Cultural Technologies, Mobile Communication, and the iPhone*, New York: Routledge, pp. 11–27.

Goggin, G. (2014) 'Facebook's Mobile Career', *New Media & Society*, vol. 16, no. 7, pp. 1068–1086.

Goggin, G. and Hjorth, L. (eds) (2014) *The Routledge Companion to Mobile Media*, London: Routledge.

Goldsmith, B. (2014) 'The Smartphone App Economy and App Ecosystems' in G. Goggin and L. Hjorth (eds) *The Routledge Companion to Mobile Media*, New York: Routledge, pp. 171–180.

Golumbia, D. (2015) 'Bitcoin as Politics: Distributed Right-Wing Extremism' in G. Lovink, N. Tkacz and P. de Vries (eds) *MoneyLab Reader: An Intervention in Digital Economy*, Amsterdam: Institute of Network Cultures, pp. 118–131.

Green, J. and Jenkins, H. (2011) 'Spreadable Media: How Audiences Create Value and Meaning in a Networked Economy' in V. Nightingale (ed.) *The Handbook of Media Audiences*, Malden, MA: Blackwell, pp. 109–127.

Green, N. and Haddon, L. (2009) *Mobile Communications*, Oxford: Berg.

Greenwald, G. (2014) *No Place to Hide: Edward Snowden, the NSA, and the U.S. Surveillance State*, New York: Metropolitan Books.

Greenwald, G. and MacAskill, E. (2013a) 'NSA Prism Program Taps in to User Data of Apple, Google and Others', *The Guardian*, 7 June, <www.theguardian. com/world/2013/jun/06/us-tech-giants-nsa-data>, accessed 24 July 2015.

Greenwald, G. and MacAskill, E. (2013b) 'Boundless Informant: The NSA's Secret Tool to Track Global Surveillance Data', *The Guardian*, 11 June, <www.the-guardian.com/world/2013/jun/08/nsa-boundless-informant-global-datamining>, accessed 24 July 2015.

Greenwald, G., MacAskill, E., Poitras, L., Ackerman, S. and Rushe, D. (2013) 'Microsoft Handed the NSA Access to Encrypted Messages', *The Guardian*, 12 July, <www.theguardian.com/world/2013/jul/11/microsoft-nsa-collaboration-user-data>, accessed 24 July 2015.

Gregg, M. (2011) *Work's Intimacy*, Cambridge: Polity.

Grossman, L. (2006) 'You – Yes, You – Are TIME's Person of the Year', *Time*, 25 December, <http://content.time.com/time/magazine/article/0,9171,1570810,00. html>, accessed 24 July 2015.

Guertin, C. and Buettner, A. (2014) 'Introduction: "We Are the Uninvited"', *Convergence*, vol. 20, no. 4, pp. 377–386.

Hall, S. (1981) 'The Determinations of News Photographs' in S. Cohen and J. Young (eds) *The Manufacture of News* (revised edition), London: Constable, pp. 226–243.

Hansen, A. and Machin, D. (2013) *Media and Communication Research Methods: An Introduction*, Basingstoke: Palgrave Macmillan.

Harding, J. (2015) 'Future of News', BBC, 28 January, <www.bbc.co.uk/news/ magazine-30933261>, accessed 24 July 2015.

Harding, L. (2014) 'Footage Released of Guardian Editors Destroying Snowden Hard Drives', *The Guardian*, 31 January, <www.theguardian.com/uk-news/2014/

jan/31/footage-released-guardian-editors-snowden-hard-drives-gchq>, accessed 24 July 2015.

Hartley, J. (1999) *Uses of Television*, London: Routledge.

Hartley, J. (2000) 'Communicative Democracy in a Redactional Society: The Future of Journalism Studies', *Journalism: Theory, Practice and Criticism*, vol. 1, no. 1, pp. 39–48.

Hartley, J. (2008) *Television Truths*, Malden, MA: Blackwell.

Hartley, J. (2009) *Uses of Digital Literacy*, St. Lucia: University of Queensland Press.

Hartley, J. (2012) *Digital Futures for Cultural and Media Studies*, Oxford: Wiley-Blackwell.

Hartley, J., Potts, J., Cunningham, S., Flew, T., Keane, M. and Banks, J. (2013) *Key Concepts in Creative Industries*, London: Sage.

Hartley, J. (ed.) (2005) *Creative Industries*, Malden, MA: Blackwell.

Hermida, A., Fletcher, F., Korell, D. and Logan, D. (2012) 'Share, Like, Recommend', *Journalism Studies*, vol. 13, nos. 5–6, pp. 815–824.

Hindman, M. (2009) *The Myth of Digital Democracy*, Princeton, New Jersey: Princeton University Press.

Hinton, S. and Hjorth, L. (2013) *Understanding Social Media*, London: Sage.

Hjorth, L. (2012) 'iPersonal: A Case Study of the Politics of the Personal' in L. Hjorth, J. Burgess and I. Richardson (eds) *Studying Mobile Media: Cultural Technologies, Mobile Communication, and the iPhone*, New York: Routledge, pp. 190–212.

Hjorth, L., Burgess, J. and Richardson, I. (2012) 'Studying the Mobile: Locating the Field' in L. Hjorth, J. Burgess and I. Richardson (eds) *Studying Mobile Media: Cultural Technologies, Mobile Communication, and the iPhone*, New York: Routledge, pp. 1–7.

Hjorth, L., Wilken, R. and Gu, K. (2012) 'Ambient Intimacy: A Case Study of the iPhone, Presence and Location-based Social Media in Shanghai, China' in L. Hjorth, J. Burgess and I. Richardson (eds) *Studying Mobile Media: Cultural Technologies, Mobile Communication, and the iPhone*, New York: Routledge, pp. 43–62.

Hjorth, L. and Arnold, M. (2013) *Online@AsiaPacific: Mobile, Social and Locative Media in the Asia-Pacific*, New York: Routledge.

Hjorth, L. and Khoo, O. (eds) (2015) *The Routledge Handbook of New Media in Asia*, New York: Routledge.

Hobbs, R. (2006) 'Multiple Visions of Multimedia Literacy: Emerging Areas of Synthesis' in M.C. McKenna, L.D. Labbo, R.D. Kieffer and D. Reinking (eds) *International Handbook of Literacy and Technology, Volume II*, Mahwah, NJ: Lawrence Erlbaum Associates, pp. 15–28.

Hodge, R. and Kress, G. (1993) *Language as Ideology*, London: Routledge.

ITU (International Telecommunication Union) (2015) 'The World in 2015: ICT Facts and Figures' <www.itu.int/en/ITU-D/Statistics/Documents/facts/ICTFacts Figures2015.pdf>, accessed 24 July 2015.

Jäger, S. (2001) 'Discourse and Knowledge: Theoretical and Methodological Aspects of a Critical Discourse and Dispositive Analysis' in R. Wodak and M. Meyer (eds) *Methods of Critical Discourse Analysis*, London: Sage, pp. 32–62.

Jenkins, H. (2003) 'Quentin Tarantino's Star Wars? Digital Cinema, Media Convergence, and Participatory Culture,' in D. Thorburn and H. Jenkins (eds) *Rethinking Media Change*, Cambridge, MA: MIT Press, pp. 281–312.

Jenkins, H. (2008) [2006] *Convergence Culture* (updated edition), New York: New York University Press.

Jenkins, H. (2009) 'What Happened before YouTube' in J. Burgess and J. Green *YouTube*, Cambridge: Polity, pp. 109–125.

Jenkins, H., Green, J. and Ford, S. (2013) *Spreadable Media*, New York: New York University Press.

John, N.A. (2013) 'Sharing and Web 2.0: The Emergence of a Keyword', *New Media & Society*, vol. 15, no. 2, pp. 167–182.

Jordan, J. (1998) 'The Art of Necessity: The Subversive Imagination of Anti-Road Protest and Reclaim the Streets' in G. McKay (ed.) *DiY Culture: Party & Protest in Nineties Britain*, London: Verso, pp. 129–151.

Joyce, D. (2005) 'An Unsuspected Future in Broadcasting: Negativland' in A. Chandler and N. Neumark (eds) *At a Distance: Precursors to Art and Activism on the Internet*, Cambridge, MA: MIT Press, pp. 176–189.

Kang, C. (2015) 'The Real Reasons Why Youtube's 5 Biggest Stars Became Millionaires', *Washington Post*, 23 July, <www.washingtonpost.com/blogs/the-switch/wp/2015/07/23/how-these-5-youtube-stars-became-millionaires-and-why-you-wont-be-joining-them-anytime-soon>, accessed 24 July 2015.

Kang, J.C. (2013) 'Should Reddit Be Blamed for the Spreading of a Smear?', *New York Times*, 25 July, <www.nytimes.com/2013/07/28/magazine/should-reddit-be-blamed-for-the-spreading-of-a-smear.html>, accessed 24 July 2015.

Katz, E. (1992) 'The End of Journalism? Notes on Watching the War', *Journal of Communication*, vol. 42, no. 3, pp. 5–13.

Kennedy, J. (2013) 'Rhetorics of Sharing: Data, Imagination, and Desire' in G. Lovink and M. Rasch (eds) *Unlike Us Reader: Social Media Monopolies and their Alternatives*, Amsterdam: Institute of Network Cultures, pp. 127–136.

Kirkpatrick, D. (2010) *The Facebook Effect*, New York: Simon & Schuster.

Kramer, A.D.I., Guillory, J.E. and Hancock, J.T. (2014) 'Experimental Evidence of Massive-Scale Emotional Contagion through Social Networks', *Proceedings of the National Academy of Sciences*, vol. 111, no. 24, pp. 8788–8790.

Kress, G. and Van Leeuwen, T. (2001) *Multimodal Discourse*, London: Arnold.

Krotoski, A. (2010) 'Meet the Cyber Radicals Using the Net to Change the World', *Observer*, 28 November, 'New Review' section, pp. 8–11.

Lambert, A. (2013) *Intimacy and Friendship on Facebook*, Basingstoke: Palgrave Macmillan.

Lanier, J. (2010) *You Are Not a Gadget*, New York: Vintage.

Lasn, K. (1999) *Culture Jam*, New York: Eagle Brook.

Latour, B. (1991) 'Technology Is Society Made Durable' in J. Law (ed.) *A Sociology of Monsters: Essays on Power, Technology and Domination*, London: Routledge, pp. 103–131.

Latour, B. (2005) *Reassembling the Social: An Introduction to Actor-Network-Theory*, Oxford: Oxford University Press.

Leadbeater, C. (2008) *We-Think*, London: Profile.

Leiner, B.M., Cerf, V.G., Clark, D.D., Kahn, R.E., Kleinrock, L., Lynch, D.C., Postel, J., Roberts, L.G. and Wolff, S. (2000) 'A Brief History of the Internet', Internet Society, <www.internetsociety.org/internet/what-internet/history-internet/brief-history-internet>, accessed 24 July 2015.

Lessig, L. (2006) '(Re)creativity: How Creativity Lives' in H. Porsdam (ed.) *Copyright And Other Fairy Tales: Hans Christian Andersen and the Commodification of Creativity*, Cheltenham: Edward Elgar Publishing, pp. 15–22.

Lessig, L. (2008) *Remix*, London: Bloomsbury Academic.

Lévy, P. (1997) *Collective Intelligence*, Cambridge, MA: Perseus Books.

Levy, S. (2013) 'Mark Zuckerberg on Facebook Home, Money, and the Future of Communication', *Wired*, 4 April, <www.wired.com/2013/04/Facebookqa>, accessed 24 July 2015.

Licklider, J.C.R. and Taylor, R.W. (1999) [1968] 'The Computer as a Communication Device' in P.A. Mayer (ed.) *Computer Media and Communication: A Reader*, Oxford: Oxford University Press, pp. 97–100.

Licoppe, C. (2004) '"Connected Presence": The Emergence of a New Repertoire for Managing Social Relationships in a Changing Communication Technoscape', *Environment and Planning D: Society and Space*, vol. 22, no. 1, pp. 135–156.

Lindsay, R. and Yung, R. (2013) 'Adding What You're Doing to Status Updates', 10 April, <http://newsroom.fb.com/news/2013/04/adding-what-youre-doing-to-status-updates>, accessed 24 July 2015.

Ling, R. and Donner, J. (2009) *Mobile Communication*, Cambridge: Polity.

Liu, A. (2012) 'What Happened to the Facebook Killer? It's Complicated', *Motherboard*, 2 October, <http://motherboard.vice.com/blog/what-happened-to-the-facebook-killer-it-s-complicated>, accessed 24 July 2015.

Livingstone, S. (2008) 'Taking Risky Opportunities in Youthful Content Creation: Teenagers' Use of Social Networking Sites for Intimacy, Privacy and Self-expression', *New Media & Society*, vol. 10, no. 3, pp. 393–411.

Livingstone, S., van Couvering, E. and Thumim, N. (2008) 'Converging Traditions of Research on Media and Information Literacies' in J. Coiro, M. Knobel, C. Lankshear and D.J. Leu (eds) *Handbook of Research on New Literacies*, New York: Lawrence Erlbaum Associates, pp. 103–132.

Lobato, R., Thomas, J. and Hunter, D. (2013) 'Histories of User-Generated Content: Between Formal and Informal Media Economies' in D. Hunter, R. Lobato, M. Richardson and J. Thomas (eds) *Amateur Media: Social, Cultural and Legal Perspectives*, New York: Routledge, pp. 3–17.

Lovink, G. (2002) *Dark Fiber: Tracking Critical Internet Culture*. Cambridge, MA: MIT Press.

Lovink, G. (2008) *Zero Comments*, London: Routledge.

Lovink, G. (2011) *Networks without a Cause*, Cambridge: Polity.

Lyon, D., Haggerty, K.D. and Ball, K. (2012) 'Introducing Surveillance Studies' in K. Ball, K.D. Haggerty and D. Lyon (eds) *The Routledge Handbook of Surveillance Studies*, London: Routledge, pp. 1–11.

Madrigal, A.C. (2013) '#BostonBombing: The Anatomy of a Misinformation Disaster', *The Atlantic*, 19 April, <www.theatlantic.com/technology/archive/2013/04/-bostonbombing-the-anatomy-of-a-misinformation-disaster/275155>, accessed 24 July 2015.

Mann, S. (2014) 'Maktivism: Authentic Making for Technology in the Service of Humanity' in M. Ratto and M. Boler (eds) *DIY Citizenship: Critical Making and Social Media*, Cambridge: MA: MIT Press, pp. 29–51.

Manovich, L. (2001) *The Language of New Media*, Cambridge, MA: MIT Press.

Manovich, L. (2009) 'The Practice of Everyday (Media) Life: From Mass Consumption to Mass Cultural Production?', *Critical Inquiry*, no. 35, pp. 319–331.

Manovich, L. (2013) *Software Takes Command*, New York: Bloomsbury.

Marcum, J.W. (2002) 'Rethinking Information Literacy', *Library Quarterly*, vol. 72, no. 1, pp. 1–26.

Marquis-Boire, M., Greenwald, G. and Lee, M. (2015) 'XKEYSCORE: NSA's Google for the World's Private Communications', *The Intercept*, 1 July, <https://firstlook.org/theintercept/2015/07/01/nsas-google-worlds-private-communications>, accessed 24 July 2015.

Marshall, P.D. (2014) 'Persona Studies: Mapping the Proliferation of the Public Self', *Journalism: Theory, Practice, Criticism*, vol. 15, no. 2, pp. 153–170.

Marshall, T.H. (1992) [1950] 'Citizenship and Social Class' in T.H. Marshall and T. Bottomore, *Citizenship and Social Class*, London: Pluto, pp. 3–51.

Marvin, C. (2013) 'Your Smart Phones Are Hot Pockets to Us: Context Collapse in a Mobilized Age', *Mobile Media & Communication*, vol. 1, no. 1, pp. 153–159.

Marwick, A.E. (2013a) *Status Update: Celebrity, Publicity & Branding in the Social Media Age*, New Haven, CT: Yale University Press.

Marwick, A.E. (2013b) 'Memes', *Contexts*, vol. 12, no. 4, pp. 12–13.

Marwick, A.E. and boyd, d. (2011) 'I Tweet Honestly, I Tweet Passionately: Twitter Users, Context Collapse, and the Imagined Audience', *New Media & Society*, vol. 13, no. 1, pp. 114–133.

Marwick, A.E. and boyd, d. (2014) 'Networked Privacy: How Teenagers Negotiate Context in Social Media', *New Media & Society*, vol. 16, no. 7, pp. 1051–1067.

Mauss, M. (1954) *The Gift*, New York: Routledge.

Maxwell, R. and Miller, T. (2012) *Greening the Media*, Oxford: Oxford University Press.

McKay, G. (ed.) (1998) *DiY Culture: Party & Protest in Nineties Britain*, London: Verso.

McNair, B. (2006) *Cultural Chaos: Journalism, News and Power in a Globalised World*, London: Routledge.

Meikle, G. (2002) *Future Active: Media Activism and the Internet*, New York: Routledge.

Meikle, G. (2007) 'Stop Signs: An Introduction to Culture Jamming' in K. Coyer, T. Dowmunt and A. Fountain (eds) *The Alternative Media Handbook*, London: Routledge, pp. 166–179.

Meikle, G. (2008) 'Electronic Civil Disobedience and Symbolic Power' in A. Karatzogianni (ed.) *Cyber-conflict and Global Politics*, London: Routledge, pp. 177–187.

Meikle, G. (2012) 'Continuity and Transformation in Convergent News – The Case of WikiLeaks', *Media International Australia*, no. 144, pp. 52–59.

Meikle, G. and Young, S. (2012) *Media Convergence: Networked Digital Media in Everyday Life*, Basingstoke: Palgrave Macmillan.

Melucci, A. (1996) *Challenging Codes: Collective Action in the Information Age*, Cambridge: Cambridge University Press.

Meyrowitz, J. (1985) *No Sense of Place*, New York: Oxford University Press.

Meyrowitz, J. (1995) 'Mediating Communication: What Happens?' in J. Downing, A. Mohammadi and A. Sreberny-Mohammadi (eds) *Questioning the Media*, Thousand Oaks, CA: Sage, pp. 39–53.

Miller, D. (2011) *Tales from Facebook*, Cambridge: Polity.

Miller, P.D. (2004) *Rhythm Science*, Cambridge, MA: MIT Press.

Miller, P.D. (ed.) (2008) *Sound Unbound: Sampling Digital Music and Culture*, Cambridge, MA: MIT Press.

Miller, T. (2002) 'Cultural Citizenship' in E.F. Isin and B.S. Turner (eds) *Handbook of Citizenship Studies*, London: Sage, pp. 231–243.

Miller, T. (2007) *Cultural Citizenship: Cosmopolitanism, Consumerism and Television in a Neoliberal Age*, Philadelphia, PA: Temple University Press.

Miller, T. (2009) 'Cybertarians of the World Unite: You Have Nothing to Lose but Your Tubes!' in P. Snickars and P. Vonderau (eds) *The YouTube Reader*, Stockholm: National Library of Sweden, pp. 424–440.

Miller, V. (2008) 'New Media, Networking and Phatic Culture', *Convergence*, vol. 14, no. 4, pp. 387–400.

Mina, A.X. (2014) 'Batman, Pandaman and the Blind Man: A Case Study in Social Change Memes and Internet Censorship in China', *Journal of Visual Culture*, vol. 13, no. 3, pp. 359–375.

Montaigne, M. de (1993) 'On the Inconstancy of Our Actions' in M.A. Screech (ed.) *The Essays: A Selection*, London: Penguin, pp. 124–131.

Montgomery, D., Horwitz, S. and Fisher, M. (2013) 'Police, Citizens and Technology Factor into Boston Bombing Probe', *Washington Post*, 21 April, <www.washingtonpost.com/world/national-security/inside-the-investigation-of-the-boston-marathon-bombing/2013/04/20/19d8c322-a8ff-11e2-b029-8fb7e977ef71_print.html>, accessed 24 July 2015.

Moore, A. (1983) 'Behind the Painted Smile' introductory essay for the 1990 collected edition of *V for Vendetta*, New York: DC Comics, pp. 267–276.

Murthy, D. (2013) *Twitter*, Cambridge: Polity.

Nakamoto, S. (2008) 'Bitcoin: A Peer-to-Peer Electronic Cash System', Bitcoin, <https://bitcoin.org/bitcoin.pdf>, accessed 24 July 2015.

Naughton, J. (2012) *From Gutenberg to Zuckerberg: What You Really Need to Know about the Internet*, London: Quercus.

Negroponte, N. (1995) *Being Digital*, London: Hodder and Stoughton.

Newman, N. with Levy, D.A. and Nielsen, R.K. (eds) (2015) *Reuters Institute Digital News Report 2015: Tracking the Future of News*, Oxford: Reuters Institute for the Study of Journalism.

Nissenbaum, H. (2011) 'A Contextual Approach to Privacy Online', *Daedalus*, vol. 140, no. 4, pp. 32–48.

Nussbaum, E. (2010) 'Defacebook', *New York*, 26 September, <http://nymag.com/news/features/establishments/68512>, accessed 24 July 2015.

OECD (Organization for Economic Co-operation and Development) (2007) 'Participative Web and User-Created Content: Web 2.0, Wikis and Social Networking', <www.oecd.org/sti/ieconomy/participativewebanduser-createdcontentweb20wikisandsocialnetworking.htm>, accessed 24 July 2015.

Ofcom (n.d.) 'Media Literacy', <http://stakeholders.ofcom.org.uk/market-data-research/other/media-literacy>, accessed 24 July 2015.

Ofcom (2014) *The Communications Market Report 2014*, August, <http://stakeholders.ofcom.org.uk/market-data-research/market-data/communications-market-reports/cmr14>, accessed 24 July 2015.

Ofcom (2015a) *The Communications Market Report 2015*, August, <http://stakeholders.ofcom.org.uk/market-data-research/market-data/communications-market-reports/cmr15>, accessed 26 September 2015.

Ofcom (2015b) *Adults' Media Use and Attitudes*, May, <http://stakeholders.ofcom.org.uk/market-data-research/other/research-publications/adults/media-lit-10years>, accessed 24 July 2015.

O'Reilly, T. (2005) 'What Is Web 2.0? Design Patterns and Business Models for the Next Generation of Software', O'Reilly Media, 30 September, <www.oreilly.com/pub/a//web2/archive/what-is-web-20.html>, accessed 24 July 2015.

O'Reilly, T. (2006) 'Web 2.0 Compact Definition: Trying Again', O'Reilly Media, 10 December <http://radar.oreilly.com/2006/12/web-20-compact-definition-tryi.html>, accessed 24 July 2015.

O'Reilly, T. and Battelle, J. (2009) 'Web Squared: Web 2.0 Five Years On', Web 2.0 Summit, <www.web2summit.com/web2009/public/schedule/detail/10194>, accessed 24 July 2015.

Packer, R. and Jordan, K. (eds) (2001) *Multimedia: From Wagner to Virtual Reality*, New York: W.W. Norton.

Papacharissi, Z. (2002) 'The Presentation of Self in Virtual Life: Characteristics of Personal Home Pages', *Journalism and Mass Communication Quarterly*, vol. 79, no. 3, pp. 643–660.

Papacharissi, Z. (2009) 'The Virtual Geographies of Social Networks: A Comparative Analysis of Facebook, LinkedIn and ASmallWorld', *New Media & Society*, vol. 11, nos. 1 and 2, pp. 199–220.

Papacharissi, Z. (2015) 'We Have Always Been Social', *Social Media and Society*, vol. 1, no. 1, pp. 1–2.

Pariser, E. (2011) *The Filter Bubble*, London: Viking.

Park, R.E. (1967) [1940] 'News as a Form of Knowledge' in his *On Social Control and Collective Behavior* (ed. R.H. Turner), Chicago, IL: University of Chicago Press, pp. 33–52.

Peretti, J. (2001) 'My Nike Media Adventure', *The Nation*, 9 April, <www.thenation.com/article/my-nike-media-adventure>, accessed 24 July 2015.

Peretti, J. (2007) 'Notes on Contagious Media' in J. Karaganis (ed.) *Structures of Participation in Digital Culture*, New York: Social Science Research Council, pp. 158–163.

Peters, J.D. (1999) *Speaking Into the Air: A History of the Idea of Communication*, Chicago, IL: University of Chicago Press.

Pew Research Center (2015) 'The Evolving Role of News on Twitter and Facebook', Pew Research Center, 14 July, <www.journalism.org/files/2015/07/Twitter-and-News-Survey-Report-FINAL2.pdf>, accessed 24 July 2015.

Phillips, W. (2015) *This Is Why We Can't Have Nice Things: Mapping the Relationship between Online Trolling and Mainstream Culture*, Cambridge, MA: MIT Press.

Poitras, L. (director) (2014) *Citizenfour* [documentary feature film], New York: Praxis films, in association with Participant Media and HBO Documentary Films.

Poole, C. 'm00t' (2010) 'The Case for Anonymity Online', TED, June, <www.ted.com/talks/christopher_m00t_poole_the_case_for_anonymity_online>, accessed 24 July 2015.

Postman, N. (1985) *Amusing Ourselves to Death*, London: Methuen.

Potter, J.W. (1998) *Media Literacy*, Thousand Oaks, CA: Sage.

Pöttker, H. (2003) 'News and Its Communicative Quality: The Inverted Pyramid – When and Why Did It Appear?' *Journalism Studies*, vol. 4, no. 4, pp. 501–511.

Propp, V. (1999) 'Folklore and Literature' in M. Tatar (ed.) *The Classic Fairy Tales*, New York: W.W. Norton, pp. 378–381.

Qiu, J.L. (2012) 'Network Labor: Beyond the Shadow of Foxconn' in L. Hjorth, J. Burgess and I. Richardson (eds) *Studying Mobile Media: Cultural Technologies, Mobile Communication, and the iPhone*, New York: Routledge, pp. 173–189.

Rainie, L. and Wellman, B. (2012) *Networked: The New Social Operating System*, Cambridge, MA: MIT Press.

Rainie, L., Hitlin, P., Jurkowitz, M., Dimock, M. and Neidorf, S. (2012) 'The Viral Kony 2012 Video', Pew Internet & American Life Project, 15 March, <www.pewinternet.org/2012/03/15/the-viral-kony-2012-video>, accessed 24 July 2015.

Rantic (2014) 'The Day Emma Watson Forever Changed Gender Equality', Rantic, <www.rantic.com/emmayouarenext-hoax>, accessed 24 July 2015.

Ratto, M. and Boler, M. (eds) (2014) *DIY Citizenship: Critical Making and Social Media*, Cambridge: MA: MIT Press.

Rawnsley, G.D. and Rawnsley, M.T. (eds) (2015) *The Routledge Handbook of Chinese Media*, New York: Routledge.

Rettberg, J.W. (2014a) *Blogging*, second edition, Cambridge: Polity.

Rettberg, J.W. (2014b) *Seeing Ourselves through Technology: How We Use Selfies, Blogs and Wearable Devices to See and Shape Ourselves*, Basingstoke: Palgrave Macmillan.

Rheingold, H. (1993) *The Virtual Community: Homesteading on the Electronic Frontier*, Reading, MA: Addison-Wesley.

Rheingold, H. (2012) *Net Smart*, Cambridge, MA: MIT Press.

Rodriguez, C. (2001) *Fissures in the Mediascape: An International Study of Citizens' Media*, Cresskill, NJ: Hampton Press.

Rogers, S. (2011) *Facts Are Sacred: The Power of Data*, London: *The Guardian* [e-book].

Ronson, J. (2015) *So You've Been Publicly Shamed*, New York: Riverhead Books.

Rosen, J. (2006) 'The People Formerly Known as the Audience', PressThink, 27 June, <http://archive.pressthink.org/2006/06/27/ppl_frmr_p.html>, accessed 24 July 2015.

Roshco, B. (1975) *Newsmaking*, Chicago: University of Chicago Press.

Ross, A. (2013) 'In Search of the Lost Paycheck' in T. Scholz (ed.) *Digital Labor: The Internet as Playground and Factory*, New York: Routledge, pp. 13–32.

Rousseau, J.-J. (1987) *The Basic Political Writings*, Indianapolis: Hackett.

Rowan, D. (2014) 'How Buzzfeed Mastered Social Sharing to Become a Media Giant for a New Era', *Wired*, 2 January, <www.wired.co.uk/magazine/archive/2014/02/features/buzzfeed>, accessed 24 July 2015.

Rushkoff, D. (1994) *Media Virus*, New York: Ballantine Books.

Saul, J.R. (1994) *The Doubter's Companion*, New York: The Free Press.

Scannell, P. (2000) 'For-Anyone-As-Someone Structures', *Media, Culture & Society*, vol. 22, no. 1, pp. 5–24.

Scannell, P. and Cardiff, D. (1991) *A Social History of British Broadcasting: Volume 1 1922–1939 Serving the Nation*, Oxford: Basil Blackwell.

Schlesinger, P. (1987) [1978] *Putting 'Reality' Together: BBC News* (second edition), London: Methuen.

Scholz, T. (ed.) (2013) *Digital Labor: The Internet as Playground and Factory*, New York: Routledge.

Schudson, M. (1995) *The Power of News*, Cambridge, MA: Harvard University Press.

Schultz, J. (1998) *Reviving the Fourth Estate*, Cambridge: Cambridge University Press.

Seemann, M. (2015) *Digital Tailspin: Ten Rules for the Internet after Snowden*, Amsterdam: Institute of Network Cultures.

Share Lab (2015) 'Invisible Infrastructures: Mobile Permissions', 2 March, <http://labs.rs/en/invisible-infrastructures-mobile-permissions>, accessed 26 September 2015.

Shawcross, W. (1992) *Rupert Murdoch: Ringmaster of the Information Circus*, Sydney: Random House.

Shelton, M., Rainie, L. and Madden, M. (2015) 'Americans' Privacy Strategies Post-Snowden', Pew Research Center, 15 March, <www.pewinternet.org/2015/03/16/Americans-Privacy-Strategies-Post-Snowden>, accessed 24 July 2015.

Shifman, L. (2012) 'An Anatomy of a YouTube Meme', *New Media & Society*, vol. 14, no. 2, pp. 187–203.

Shifman, L. (2014) *Memes in Digital Culture*, Cambridge, MA: MIT Press.

Shirky, C. (2010) *Cognitive Surplus*, London: Allen Lane.

Shoemaker, P.J. (1991) *Gatekeeping*, Newbury Park: Sage.

Singel, R. (2010) 'Mark Zuckerberg: I Donated to Open Source, Facebook Competitor', *Wired*, 28 May, <www.wired.com/2010/05/zuckerberg-interview>, accessed 24 July 2015.

Smaill, B. (2004) 'Online Personals and Narratives of the Self: Australia's RSVP', *Convergence*, vol. 10, no. 1, pp. 93–107.

Smith, A. (2014) '6 New Facts about Facebook', Pew Research Center, 3 February, <www.pewresearch.org/fact-tank/2014/02/03/6-new-facts-about-facebook>, accessed 24 July 2015.

Smith, R.M. (2002) 'Modern Citizenship' in E.F. Isin and B.S. Turner (eds) *Handbook of Citizenship Studies*, London: Sage, pp. 105–115.

Smythe, D.W. (2006) [1981] 'On the Audience Commodity and its Work' in D. Kellner and M.G. Durham (eds) *Media and Cultural Studies: Key Works* (revised edition), Malden, MA: Blackwell, pp. 230–256.

Solove, D.J. (2007) *The Future of Reputation: Gossip, Rumor, and Privacy on the Internet*, New Haven, CT: Yale University Press.

Stallman, R. (2003) [1985] 'The GNU Manifesto' in N. Wardrip-Fruin and N. Montfort (eds) *The New Media Reader*, Cambridge, MA: MIT Press, pp. 545–550.

Stam, R. (2000) *Film Theory: An Introduction*, Oxford: Blackwell.

Stein, G. (1990) *Selected Writings of Gertrude Stein*, New York: Vintage.

Stuart, K. (2014) 'Zoe Quinn: "All Gamergate Has Done Is Ruin People's Lives"', *The Guardian*, 3 December, <www.theguardian.com/technology/2014/dec/03/zoe-quinn-gamergate-interview>, accessed 24 July 2015.

Sutton-Smith, B. (1997) *The Ambiguity of Play*, Cambridge, MA: Harvard University Press.

Swartz, A. (2008) 'Guerilla Open Access Manifesto', The Internet Archive, <https://archive.org/details/GuerillaOpenAccessManifesto>, accessed 24 July 2015.

Terranova, T. (2000) 'Free Labor: Producing Culture for the Digital Economy', *Social Text 63*, vol. 18, no. 2, pp. 33–58.

Terranova, T. and Fumagalli, A. (2015) 'Financial Capital and the Money of the Common: The Case of Commoncoin' in G. Lovink, N. Tkacz and P. de Vries (eds) *MoneyLab Reader: An Intervention in Digital Economy*, Amsterdam: Institute of Network Cultures, pp. 151–157.

Thompson, J.B. (1995) *The Media and Modernity*, Polity: Cambridge.

Thompson, J.B. (2005) 'The New Visibility', *Theory, Culture & Society*, vol. 22, no. 6, pp. 31–51.

Thorsen, E. and Allan, S. (eds) (2014) *Citizen Journalism: Global Perspectives, volume 2*, New York: Peter Lang.

Thurman, N. and Newman, N. (2014) 'The Future of Breaking News Online?', *Journalism Studies*, vol. 15, no. 5, pp. 655–667.

Thurman, N. and Walters, A. (2013) 'Live Blogging – Digital Journalism's Pivotal Platform?', *Digital Journalism*, vol. 1, no. 1, pp. 82–101.

Timberg, C. (2014) 'U.S. Threatened Massive Fine to Force Yahoo to Release Data', *Washington Post*, 11 September, <www.washingtonpost.com/business/technology/us-threatened-massive-fine-to-force-yahoo-to-release-data/2014/09/11/38a7f69e-39e8-11e4-9c9f-ebb47272e40e_story.html>, accessed 24 July 2015.

Tomlinson, J. (2007) *The Culture of Speed*, London: Sage.

Trottier, D. and Lyon, D. (2012) 'Key Features of Social Media Surveillance' in C. Fuchs, K. Boersma, A. Albrechtslund and M. Sandoval (eds) *Internet and Surveillance: The Challenges of Web 2.0 and Social Media*, London: Routledge, pp. 89–105.

Turkle, S. (2011) *Alone Together*, New York: Basic Books.

Turner, G. (2010) *Ordinary People and the Media*, London: Sage.

Urry, J. (2007) *Mobilities*, Cambridge: Polity.

van Dijck, J. (2013) *The Culture of Connectivity: A Critical History of Social Media*, New York: Oxford University Press.

van Dijck, J. (2015) 'After Connectivity: The Era of Connectication', *Social Media + Society*, vol. 1, nos. 1–2.

Vaneigem, R. (1983) [1967] *The Revolution of Everyday Life*, London: Rebel Press and Left Bank Books.

Vincent, J. and Fortunati, L. (2014) 'The Emotional Identity of the Mobile Phone' in G. Goggin and L. Hjorth (eds) *The Routledge Companion to Mobile Media*, New York: Routledge, pp. 312–319.

Wardrip-Fruin, N. and Montfort, N. (eds) (2003) *The New Media Reader*, Cambridge, MA: MIT Press.

Wark, M. (1994) *Virtual Geography*, Bloomington: Indiana University Press.

Wark, M. (1997) 'Infohype' in A. Crawford and R. Edgar (eds) *Transit Lounge*, Sydney: Craftsman House, pp. 144–149.

Wark, M. (2004) *A Hacker Manifesto*, Cambridge, MA: Harvard University Press.

Wark, M. (2012) *Telesthesia*, Cambridge: Polity.

Watson, E. (2014) 'Emma Watson: Gender Equality Is Your Issue Too', UN Women, 20 September, <www.unwomen.org/en/news/stories/2014/9/emma-watson-gender-equality-is-your-issue-too>, accessed 24 July 2015.

Wesch, M. (2009) 'YouTube and You: Experiences of Self-awareness in the Context Collapse of the Recording Webcam', *Explorations in Media Ecology*, vol. 8, no. 2, pp. 19–34.

Whitman, W. (1973) *Leaves of Grass*, New York: W.W. Norton.

Williams, R. (1983) *Keywords: A Vocabulary of Culture and Society* (revised edition), London: Fontana.

Winner, L. (1986) *The Whale and the Reactor: A Search for Limits in an Age of High Technology*, Chicago: University of Chicago Press.

Witt, S. (2015) *How Music Got Free*, New York: Viking.

Wodak, R. (2008) 'Introduction: Discourse Studies – Important Concepts and Terms' in R. Wodak and M. Krzyzanowski (eds) *Qualitative Discourse Analysis in the Social Sciences*, Basingstoke: Palgrave Macmillan, pp. 1–29.

Wolff, M. (2010) *The Man Who Owns The News*, New York: Vintage.

Wray, S. (1998) 'On Electronic Civil Disobedience', Thing.Net, <www.thing.net/~rdom/ecd/oecd.html>, accessed 24 July 2015.

Zhang, L. and Fung, A. (2014) 'Working as Playing? Consumer Labor, Guild and the Secondary Industry of Online Gaming in China', *New Media & Society*, vol. 16, no. 1, pp. 38–54.

Zittrain, J. (2008) *The Future of the Internet: And How to Stop It*, London: Allen Lane.

Zuckerman, E. (2014) 'The Internet's Original Sin', *The Atlantic*, 14 August, <www.theatlantic.com/technology/archive/2014/08/advertising-is-the-internets-original-sin/376041>, accessed 24 July 2015.

Index

Printed in the United States
by Baker & Taylor Publisher Services